International Rescue Committee for resettlement
Bob Carey (212)551 - 3000   x3074
Catherine O'neil

Catherine O'neil
E57   583-1796

Family Travels

FAMILY TRAVELS

Around the World

in Thirty (or so) Days

RICHARD REEVES

CATHERINE O'NEILL
COLIN O'NEILL
CONOR O'NEILL
FIONA O'NEILL REEVES
CYNTHIA REEVES FYFE
THOMAS FYFE

ANDREWS AND McMEEL

A UNIVERSAL PRESS SYNDICATE COMPANY

KANSAS CITY

Library of Congress Cataloging-in-Publication Data
Reeves, Richard.
Family travels: around the world in 30 (or so) days / by Richard Reeves.
p. cm.
ISBN 0-8362-2175-3 (hc)
1. Reeves family—Journeys—Diaries.
2. Voyages around the world.   I. Title.
G440.R36R44   1997   96-28516
910.4'1—dc20   CIP

Designed by Ann Gold

ATTENTION: SCHOOLS AND BUSINESSES
Andrews and McMeel books are available at quantity discounts with bulk purchase
for educational, business, or sales promotional use. For information, please write to:
Special Sales Department, Andrews and McMeel, 4520 Main Street,
Kansas City, Missouri 64111.

*To Mary Ann and Jack Garvey,
who brought the world home.*

*And to Pat and Walter Wells,
and Shireen Mazari and Farwa Zafar,
who took us into their worlds.*

CONTENTS

Chapter 1

THE PLAN

My wife's name is Catherine O'Neill. Marrying her in 1979 was like joining the Navy—I saw the world. More than once.

The first time was in 1981. I was exhausted after spending three years writing a book on the early nineteenth-century American travels of Alexis de Tocqueville to the new United States of America. I had retraced his route, talking to modern equivalents of the men and women he met before writing his great work *Democracy in America*.

I told my new wife that I had nothing left, that I was too mentally tired to grapple with the last chapter. I was surprised by her reaction then. I would not be now: If you're tired of traveling, travel.

"Let's go around the world," she said.

Her logic escaped me. I said something about having to make a living and that people like us did not do things like that, mainly because people like us do not have that kind of money.

"Fifteen hundred dollars each," she said. "Around-the-world tickets are the greatest bargain: fifteen hundred dollars with as many stops as you want, as long as you keep going in the same direction." A regular Magellan. She worked out the itinerary and tickets with Air India and Northwest Airlines. With one bag each, we flew to London, Paris, Rome, Bombay, Delhi, Calcutta, Bangkok, Hong Kong, and Guangzhou, China, Tokyo, Honolulu, and Los Angeles. In twenty-two days. It was great and I was a new man by the time I got back to my typewriter and Monsieur de Tocqueville.

Thirteen years later, in May of 1994, she said, "Let's do it again."

I gave her the same look that had no effect in '81. Then she added: "With all the kids!"

This conversation, as it happened, was on the road from Haiphong to the Bay of Tonkin in Vietnam. I figured it was the humidity or something and pretended to forget about it. Fat chance. A few days later, Catherine showed me an enormous world map she had bought for fifteen cents, its value somewhat reduced by the fact that it was in Chinese. I knew we were practically on our way. With the five kids—or six.

We each had two children when we were married in 1979. Our youngest, Fiona, was born in 1984. Our oldest, Cindie, was married. So kids meant three sons, two daughters, and a son-in-law. And then came a grandson, though we didn't know about that just then. We would make the trip in thirty days this time because that was the most time off some of us could get. "Around the World in Thirty Days"—it was actually thirty-four days—had less to do with Jules Verne than with various work and school schedules.

The "Dear Family" letter went out a month later, on June 13, 1994. Referring to a summer we spent in Pakistan and India with the three boys, then aged fourteen, sixteen, and twenty, Catherine began: "It has been eleven years since we all took our summer trip to South Asia. We and the world have changed a lot since then. . . . "

I certainly hoped so. That adventure with younger children in the early 1980s had not been a total success. Jeff, convinced he was immune to whatever lived in local water, spent three years trying to get the bugs out of his system. Conor, a surfer boy then, stood with me on the market street of a village called Chitral in the Hindu Kush, close to the hidden valleys Rudyard Kipling wrote of in *The Man Who Would Be King*. The faces on the dusty street were a living map of the world at one of its remotest crossroads; all the men were armed, many of them with Russian weapons, wearing parts of Russian uniforms taken in battle on the other side of the Kush, in Afghanistan.

"Did you ever think you'd see anything like this?" I said. And he answered: "This sucks! These people have to live this way, but I could be in Santa Monica."

"Although we are not rich . . . ." Catherine wrote to our dear family, there is a world out there we'd like to share with you. The price of admission was that each of us would have to spend fifteen minutes each night writing about what we saw and thought and felt. "We want a family activity that will stay with us for the rest of our lives . . . some fun . . . some adventure . . . learning together . . . real time to spend together understanding the different ways in which each of us might see the same thing." In other words, parent words, we wanted to give our kids something that would last longer than a car at graduation.

The first answer was an enthusiastic "Yes" from my daughter Cynthia, who was living in Florida. She and her husband, Thomas Fyfe, who are both chefs, were working in Newport, Rhode Island, for the summer. Here, Cynthia can tell that story:

The letter arrived at our summer rental and we were giddy with delight at the prospect. . . . Thomas and I had spent much of our early married life chefing on cruise ships—the family joke is that we have seen everything in the world within twenty miles of a port—but this time we could go inland at last. We had just sold Chameleon, our well-received restaurant in Fort Lauderdale, because we were doing nothing but "The Restaurant." We had decided to trade culinary success for a life—one that would allow us to go to dinner parties, have children, and go on vacation. We fully intended to do all three.

We had countless conversations of where's and why's of countless destinations. We went back and forth between keeping our lists, or certain parts, a secret and boasting about finding a perfect choice. I had to design the perfect itinerary! Since the time I was a child I had a mental file of the places I wanted to see. I had gotten to some of them, like Pompeii and Thailand. But there were still the pyramids, the Great Barrier Reef, a safari in Africa, New Zealand (I wanted to raise sheep as a child), the Great Wall of China, Istanbul, Jerusalem. The list became our summer preoccupation.

Six weeks later, on a July weekend, we were all together on the back porch of Dad and Cathy's big old summer house in Sag Harbor, a once-upon-a-time whaling village near the end of Long Island, one hundred miles east of New York City. . . . Cathy had gotten a wall-size map of the world—it was in Chinese, she said she had gotten it in Shanghai for fifteen cents—

which was hung on the screened porch. Fiona, my nine-year-old sister, and I decided the best way to mark destinations was to use color-tipped pins, one color for each person.

We had two days to "lobby" for the destinations most important to each of us. The more people interested in a particular destination, the better chance you had of actually getting there. I now had to convince as many as possible how much fun the Great Barrier Reef would be, how spectacular the Taj Mahal must be, and how beautiful Bali was. Fiona wanted to get to Papua New Guinea. "Okay," I said. "I'll put a pin there if you'll vote for Bali." We had a deal.

Come the morning of the meeting, we decided we were all willing to take an aggressive approach. This meant we were willing to take a flight every two or three days. Along with this came the decision to stay in four-star or five-star hotels. Cathy's argument was that if we were going to be traveling like maniacs we should at least have a nice place to sleep and bathe. We decided July was the best time for all of us to travel and that thirty days seemed to be about the most amount of time any one of us could manage. We had a year to clear our schedules.

Said Catherine:

The map was soon covered with pins and the trading began. Seeing wild animals in Africa was discarded when it was clear that we would have to give up two of our precious days to fly there and get back. Fiona wanted to sleep overnight on a train and see the Great Barrier Reef. Cynthia wanted to see Nepal. I wanted to see more of Indonesia. Colin wanted to spend time in China. Conor wanted to see India again, because he had been too sick to remember a lot that long ago summer. Everything seemed days and thousands of miles out of the way. So we cobbled together a route that tried to include destinations from everyone's list that seemed financially and logistically doable. That meant no St. Petersburg, because it cost too much unless we flew Aeroflot, or what was left of it after the breakup of the old Soviet Union, and I've always been afraid of that airline.

For all practical purposes, the route picked itself. Like mad dogs and Englishmen, we would spend long July days crossing and recrossing the earth's big middle, the Equator. In all probability, half the days would be close to "double hundreds"—temperatures over one hundred degrees F. and as much humidity as superheated air could hold. And some of the route decisions were going to depend on which airlines won the Catherine O'Neill Bag Lady in Manhattan sweepstakes. In January of 1995, the lady began filling shopping bags with just about every airline guide and brochure in the world. "Honing in," she called it.

She was on the phone hour after hour. Then she would come into the kitchen and tell whoever was around news like this: "Myles wants to have her tubes tied. She already has two children, but her fiancé wants to have a child with her after they get married. She's torn about what to do."

"Who's Myles?" I asked.

"The ticket agent from Garuda."

"She told you that?"

My wife is a very impatient woman, except when it comes to bargains and bargaining. Sometime in March of '95, she announced the winners to the rest of us: Singapore Airlines, Swissair, and Delta Airlines—combination around-the-world tickets for $2,628.65 each, usuable over a six-month period, with one-third off for Fiona. It would cost us another $470 each to shuttle to cities in Indonesia and Pakistan not served by our three airlines.

Then we (Catherine) decided to pay an extra $1,300 apiece to upgrade two of the tickets to Business Class, an undemocratic touch I thought might lead to family revolution. Her idea was that the upscale tickets would save us hours because it would get us on shorter check-in lines and would save us big money because we could eat a dozen or so meals in First Class lounges around the world. Besides, the two seats up front gave us a way to move kids around when they got on each other's nerves—or on ours. "We've been flying economy our whole lives, now let them," said the lady who did the heavy lifting on all logistics. "We're too old to suffer.

"If you feel guilty," she said to me, "then ride in the back."

Then she began chipping away at the overall price. In her words:

> I made all airplane reservations myself. Then I called up my regular travel agent. I told her that I had done all the work, but would list her as the travel agent, allowing her to make the 10-percent commission. However, she had to agree to give me back a portion of her fee. She did and we split the commission. The ticket prices were now 5 percent lower. That phone call saved us more than a thousand dollars. Even Richard, who would never have asked himself, was impressed this time.

Very impressed. Usually I leave the room when she starts talking about money, the same way I look away from beggars in India or New York. But I was trapped a couple of times in February and March when the subject turned from airlines to hotels. Madam was working from behind a hoarded pile of "50%-Off!" and "Two-Night Stay" coupons, saying things like: "But we're members of AAA!" Or AARP, AFTRA, PEN, SAG, the club, the Church!" "Do you give discounts for booking and paying ahead? . . . I can't believe you charge extra for a child in the room. . . . Does that include breakfast? What kind? . . . Do you give complimentary airport transit? . . . Taxes and service included? . . . It can't be that high!"

I wondered whether, when I was not around, she was capable of telling them she was Mother Teresa and had these six orphans. . . . Probably.

Frustrated by a falling dollar all over the world and the three-hundred-dollar room rate in Tokyo, she called the Japanese National Tourist Office and began "Help-p-p . . . !" Having, presumably, gotten their attention, she said: "I want to take my family to Tokyo, but we'd like to avoid bankruptcy."

A sack of "Budget Tokyo" brochures soon arrived in our house and it looked as if we might be able to average about $150 a night a room in some Tokyo hotels.

She was booking three hotel rooms a night—one for us and Fiona, one for the boys, who were really men now, and one for Cindie and Thomas, and . . .

"I'm pregnant," said Cindie, calling in October. The due date was May 1995. Wow! Grandparents. "We're still going," she said. She knew more about the world from her cruise ship days than she did about babies. But that would change. Many things might. Catherine wrote:

> We booked all stops and told them we could change the tickets up until June—after the baby was born. Cynthia's favorite stop, Nepal, was hardly an ideal destination for a newborn. There was trouble in Pakistan, demonstrations in Lahore, and killings in Karachi, some directed against Americans. The Middle East peace process looked as if it might be in trouble; we might not be able to get from Israel to Jordan. I'd just seen an article about tens of thousands of possibly rabid dogs roaming the streets of Kathmandu, Nepal. Fiona loves dogs and is impulsively friendly. Could she avoid petting strange dogs? We'll wait and see, stick to the agenda for now.

◢◢◢

TWO VACATIONS FOR
THE PRICE OF ONE

We began our travels in Los Angeles, on June 30, 1995, and returned to the United States on August 18 in New York. We used the remaining New York–to–Los Angeles leg of the around-the-world tickets—the Delta portion, which allowed five stops in the United States—for family Christmas travels to Florida and Texas. The bottom line is that we saw both the world and the U.S.A. on two separate excursions over the six-month ticket life for a little more than one hundred dollars a flight.

◤◤◤

Then there were appointments. Kings, presidents, ministers, ambassadors, writers and journalists, old friends, anybody who would have us. I would still be doing two columns a week. Catherine was sending out barrages of letters and faxes, including one to King Hussein and Queen Noor of Jordan, who had once told us, "If you're ever in the neighborhood . . . " On May 17 at 4:38 A.M.—I saw the clock when the phone rang in our bedroom—I woke to hear Catherine saying, rather sleepily: "The Prime Minister? Yes, yes, I understand, the PM. But of what country?"

It was Benazir Bhutto of Pakistan. Yes, she would love to have lunch in Islamabad. No, no children.

On June 29, the Los Angeles Reeves-O'Neills, Catherine, Fiona, and I, and Colin and Conor, met at UCLA Medical Center. "They're going to puncture my butt," said Fiona, which indeed they were, pumping in 2 cc of gamma globulin as partial protection against hepatitis. Catherine and I had asked the doctor, Claire Panosian of the Tropical Medicine Clinic, to bring up the subject of rabies and the dangers of playing with strange and stray dogs. Fiona saw through the ploy immediately and said, "Are you really a doctor?"

"Load me up, I'll take anything," said Conor. "I don't want to be sick."

And so she did. Catherine and I, who had both been abroad recently on reporting or refugee trips, needed only gamma globulin and meningitis shots. But the kids had to get doses for typhoid, tetanus, diphtheria, polio, and God knows what else.

"What are you taking with you?" asked Dr. Panosian. Catherine started a long list beginning with aspirin, Immodium, Benadryl . . . I interrupted: "We've got a backup plane for lotions and potions."

So there it was. We left Los Angeles at 3 P.M., June 30, on Singapore Airlines Flight 11 bound for Tokyo. And then it would be on to Taipei, Taiwan, on July 4 . . . Hong Kong on July 6, then a train ride north to Guangzhou, China . . . Denpasar on the island of Bali, Indonesia, on July 9 . . . Yogyakarta, Indonesia, on July 11 . . . Jakarta, Indonesia, on July 13 . . . Singapore on July 15 . . . Kathmandu, Nepal, on July 16 . . . Delhi, India, on July 19 . . . Islamabad, Pakistan, on July 22 . . . Dubai in the United Arab Emirates on July 25

Cairo, Egypt, on July 27 . . . Jerusalem on July 30 . . . Berlin on August 2 . . . and then on August 5, "home" to Paris.

We would stay in Paris, where we had lived from the beginning of 1985 to the end of 1988, for a few days seeing friends and then go out to a great old farmhouse we had rented near St. Pierre-sur-Dives in Normandy for a week of taking it very easy, seeing more friends, and getting to know our grandson or grandaughter, either way the first one.

▴▴▴

THE CAST OF CHARACTERS
(In order of appearance)

FATHER AND MOTHER, Richard, fifty-eight, and Catherine, fifty-two. He writes for a living, mainly books and a syndicated column on politics and international affairs. She writes, too, mostly political commentary, and is the cofounder of an international do-good organization, the Women's Commission for Refugee Women and Children.

COLIN O'NEILL, twenty-nine, is a television producer in Los Angeles. CONOR O'NEILL, twenty-six, has a hard-edge rock group in Los Angeles called "Your Mom." FIONA O'NEILL REEVES, ten, is in grammar school.

CYNTHIA REEVES FYFE, thirty-five, and her husband, THOMAS FYFE, thirty-eight, are both chefs. They had met in the kitchen of the Tavern on the Green in New York and were living in Florida, where they had opened their own restaurant after five years of working on cruise ships. IAN HOWARD FYFE (not part of the original plan) was born on June 15, 1995, two weeks before the trip began, delaying his parents until they had their doctor's permission to fly. You won't meet Jeffrey Reeves, thirty-two, which is too bad. He is the funniest of us all, an actor who finally decided to stay home in New York City for a couple of television gigs. "I suppose I'm going to be thrown out of the family," he told me, "but the fish are running and I've got to keep my lines in this water." We decided to let him stay a Reeves; I think the vote was 4 to 3. His humor often translates into formidable peace-making skills, which we suspected might be valuable, as you will see, particularly when Colin and Fiona were locked together for too long.

▲▲▲

THE BILL, PLEASE!

This was Catherine's preliminary budget of the basic cost of four full-fare adults and a child (our core group) going around the world in thirty days:

Airfare $14,000

Additional airfare for two Business Class seats $2,600

Hotels (two rooms averaged out to $100 per night) $6,000

Food (averaged out to $120 per day) $3,600

Admissions and entertainment (averaged out to ten dollars per person per day) $1,500.

Airport transfers and local transportation $1,400
Shopping (Trinkets and baubles) $600
Total $29,700

(Prices vary of course depending on the value of dollars in relation to local currencies and on fare and rates at any time. We also allowed for family "splurges" from time to time. Six months after we bought our tickets, economy around-the-world fares on the same airlines had dropped to $2,200 per person and 25,000 miles was listed as the absolute distance limit. There was no limit when we traveled.)

▶ ▶ ▶

Chapter 2

TOKYO

Five of us, the parents, Fiona, and the Knights of the One Bag Rule, Colin and Conor, took off from Los Angeles on June 30 on Singapore Airlines Flight 11. My guilt panged, if there is such a word, as I collapsed into a Star Trek seat in Business Class. But I got over it, playing with a personal Gameboy and a selection of twenty-two movies on my own personal television screen. Then fatigue and the release of actually being on the way took care of that. I was asleep as soon as they closed the door. You could send me as baggage. Catherine began sorting through envelopes and folders of letters, clippings, maps, and tickets she had collected during the year and over the years to make it all possible.

She does not sleep on planes, to say the least. The fearless and indefatigable arranger is among the most nervous of travelers. She must be a legend among flight attendants around the world, questioning them about the pilot's qualifications, grasping the arms of strangers, and, when she feels a bump or sees a cloud, begins by telling them, "Whatever happens, I've lived a good life. . . . "

"Today was the first day of the trip. First we took a twelve-hour plane ride and then we spent an hour and a half on a train," began Fiona. "In Japan everybody looks alike—you know, black hair, brown eyes. Except of course for us."

It was the evening of July 1 when we arrived in Tokyo, 6 P.M. local time. The bags must have mated during the flight. It was obvious as we struggled through the airport to the train platform of the Keisei Line into the city that the one-person, one-bag rule was already history. Much grumbling from our young men. Catherine and I had been to Tokyo twice before, so we knew one big thing: don't take a taxi from Narita Airport. The first time we came, in 1981, when a strong U.S. dollar was worth 300 yen, we jumped into a cab, which speeded along for twenty miles or so and pulled into a world-class traffic jam. Two hours later we were out $65. This time a dollar was worth only 85 yen and a cab ride to town would have been something like $225. The bus fare would have been $175 for the five of us. The train fare was 1,260 yen each ($16).

On the trip in, an hour and forty minutes, I took out my note-book to write that the Japanese, like everybody in the world except the Americans, treat electricity as gold. After a half-hour of rice paddies, we passed through miles and miles of suburbs. Almost all the houses were dark or showed only one lighted window. Everyone else was writing, too—we looked like a secretarial school field trip—ready to pay the price of admission to the Great Reeves-O'Neill World Tour. The laptop was on my lap, a little Packard Bell Statesman, probably made in one of these suburbs.

There were newspapers on the empty seats of the train. I opened one, a sports tabloid, as Fiona curled up next to me, ready for a nap. The page in front of me was classified advertising. I couldn't read the ads in Japanese but it was easy to get an idea of what was for sale: dozens of them had photographs of young women lifting their skirts to show they were wearing nothing under them. Some were just posing nude from top to toe.

I slammed the paper shut. Colin was laughing across the aisle, looking at the same paper. "Good journalism, huh?" he said.

We took a taxi from the Ueno station to our hotel, a Holiday Inn on the edge of the city, where we were booked for just one night—for good economic reasons known only to Catherine.

Fiona's version of the trip was short, simple, and natural: "By the time we got to the hotel I really needed to pee. That's just about all I did today; it was fun. The hotel is okay; on a scale of ten it's about a three."

It was ninety-five degrees with just about 100 percent humidity at 4:48 A.M. the next day, Sunday, July 2. I know that because Fiona appeared at my bedside at that moment to say, "I can't sleep anymore." We went downstairs and ended up at an employees' entrance with a vending machine offering everything from water to beer. The usual plastic bottle of Evian water or a can of Coca-Cola was 100 yen. On the other side of the door, in the lobby, a machine for guests charged 200 yen. The price in the mini bar in our room was 400 yen.

The two of us, father and daughter, toured the neighborhoods along the Sumida River for an hour in a steamy gray dawn. Fiona's version, written a day later, is first:

> My dad and I took a walk at five in the morning. The other people out were walking their dogs. The Japanese seem to love their pets. We went to a park and I saw a dog sitting by a lake. Well groomed, no leash. Then we saw a miniature poodle that must have had at least sixty bows on various parts of his body. . . . I have to stop writing now because we're having an earthquake. . . .

More about the temblor later. First, breakfast. Fiona and I stopped at the only store open, a 7-Eleven clone called "am/pm," and filled a bag with juice and milk, bread, and stuffed pastries for everybody. The cost was a little more than ten dollars and it turned out that I was a few yen short, like a quarter or so, and we had to unpack the bag and give back a bun. The food was lousy, sticky sweet stuff pumped full of chocolate, jellies, and curry of some kind.

"Is there something perverse in looking forward to finding out what it feels like to buy a ten-dollar cup of coffee?" said Colin as we all mapped out our first day in the big city. That led to another conversation on weak dollars and strong yen. Then Catherine and I, with Fiona in tow, moved us all across town to the Westin Grand Palace Hotel, well located between the Imperial Gardens and central Tokyo, where we had arranged to use United Airlines coupons to get rooms at half-price, for two nights only.

"The guys," as we call Colin and Conor, set off to look for Sumo tickets. It was the first day of a "Basho," two weeks of matches and pageantry. Throwing around names like Takanohana and Akebono, which meant nothing to the rest of us, Colin revealed he had become attached to the blimp-bumping wrestlers by watching the Korean lan-

Mitsukoshi wrapping.

Fiona Reeves reports on Ambassador Walter Mondale.

I HAD PICTURED SOMETHING OUT OF THE MOVIE *BLADE RUNNER*—VERY CYBER AND UNLIKE ANYTHING I HAVE EVER SEEN. BUT IT IS NOT LIKE THAT AT ALL. IT WAS MORE LIKE SOMETHING OUT OF A GODZILLA MOVIE.   —CONOR

guage channel on television in Los Angeles. Alas, they found out that Bashos are sold out weeks in advance. So they roamed the city, as described by Conor:

I had pictured something out of the movie *Blade Runner*—very cyber and unlike anything I have ever seen. But it is not like that at all. It was more like something out of a Godzilla movie. In fact, most of the city, or at least the parts that I have seen, looks to be right out of the early sixties. Something about the architecture, I don't know. . . . We stumbled across a karate tournament in a big arena, which turned out to be the Budokan, famous for "Cheap Trick Live at Budokan." My first five minutes out on the streets of Tokyo and there's a karate tournament going on. Such a stereotype. Schoolkids, boys and girls both, slapping the crap out of each other (because that's basically what it looks like to the un-trained eye) with their brothers and sisters and chums and grand-mothers (and us) cheering them on. . . . We took the subway and walked around a couple different neighborhoods and they were more what I had expected. Shin-juku—crowded with neon signs and video game parlors, pachinka parlors, and peep shows. An air of Times Square but not a lot of tour-ists, or at least not a lot of white tourists. One of the most homo-geneous places I've been, a tossup between here and Norway.

THESE BANDS ARE A STRANGE BASTARDIZA-TION OF AMERICAN ROCK—THEY HAVE ALL THE TRAPPINGS, BUT THEY LACK THE ATTI-TUDE....THEY WERE DRESSED LIKE THE BEASTIE BOYS BUT THEIR MUSIC WAS MORE LIKE JOSIE AND THE PUSSYCATS....

—CONOR

"Japanese parents must be horrified. . . ."

The place you see foreign tourists, Catherine said later, was on the seventh and eighth floors of the Mitsukoshi department store in Ginza. She found the porcelain tableware on the seventh exquisite and affordable and loved the paperwork and paintings (for as little as five dollars) on the eighth.

We all met at lunch at an ordinary noodle shop, one of the thousands in the city. This one had Muzak playing "Secret Love," Doris Day, 1954. Catherine began to order by picking a price she liked and pointing at it, willing to eat whatever came within budget. But it turned out there was an English menu, too. A little tension shows in Fiona's journal: "Every single meal, my mom chooses what we eat and never lets anyone else choose. I wouldn't mind but she always chooses gross Japanese food and I hate Japanese food."

Then we were off to Yoyogi Park in Harajuku, where Elvis imitators and other local greasers get together and play on Sundays, just for the fun of it. This is what all that looked like to Conor:

Aggressively trendy young Japanese in outfits that would fit right in on Melrose. Being the rocker of our party, I feel obliged to elaborate a little: It's not just that the rock groups are unoriginal or derivative. I wouldn't say that my band is all that original, but we rock. But these bands are a strange bastardization of American rock—they have all the trappings, but they lack the attitude. . . . They were dressed like the Beastie Boys but their music was more like Josie and the Pussycats. . . . The singers really reminded me of characters from *Speed Racer* or *Battle of the Planets*. They were all so happy and well choreographed, lacking any element of danger. Even their voices were childish. But hey, the kids seemed to like it and I bet it's a good way to pick up chicks.

His mom saw it a bit differently: "Japanese parents must be horrified at the ridiculous getups of the young rock-and-roll wanna-bes who line the approach to the park. In their leather tight pants, extreme Mohawk hairdos, and screeching voices . . . "

▲▲▲

SEX, PLEASE, WE'RE JAPANESE

The June 28 English language edition of *Asahi Shimbun* gave capsule previews of new films coming to Tokyo in the summer, all American. Each one included a short paragraph marked "Sex Level." For *Waterworld,* the Kevin Costner epic, the comment was: "Underwater? Hardly." The line on *Batman Forever* was: "With Nicole Kidman around as a sexy criminal psychologist who wants to get under Batman's cape, the chances are pretty good."

The guys' own reporting turned up this, in Conor's words:

Comparing *Penthouse* to *Penthouse*, Japanese porno mags are far less explicit than their American counterparts. I heard somewhere that Japanese men don't like to see Japanese women being extremely raunchy, but they don't mind when Western or Caucasian women are depicted that way. That probably has something to do with the popularity of Caucasian girls as "hostesses." We went to Roppongi, which has a host of

Two minutes to the earthquake.

"hostess bars." There were a lot of Western girls and they didn't seem to be tourists—if you get my drift (wink, wink, nudge, nudge). I didn't see any black girls.

▶ ▶ ▶

That evening Catherine and I went to dinner with Nick Kristoff and Sheryl WuDunn, the *New York Times* correspondents in Tokyo. There was a Domino's Pizza delivery truck at the doorway of their building—luckily not for us. We all walked to a Chinese restaurant in the neighborhood with Fiona and their two sons, Gregory, three, and Jeffrey, two. Poor Fiona promptly fell asleep at the table. Gregory was the opposite, restless and not in the mood for Chinese food. His mother produced a Ziploc plastic bag of Cheerios and soon enough he was a happy American kid who happened to be in Tokyo. We had been talking about China, where they had shared the Pulitzer Prize for international reporting the year before, but we switched to parenting, laughing about another husband-wife *Times* team, Phil Taubman and Felicity Barringer, who had in the bad old days of communism and food shortages lined an entire wall of their Moscow apartment with Corn Flakes, Cheerios, and most every other breakfast cereal for their two young sons.

Back at the Grand Palace, Catherine and I steppped off the elevator on the twelfth floor, looked at each other, and said in a tiny chorus, "Where's Fiona?"

Panicked, I went back downstairs to a totally empty lobby. Hurrying over to the desk, I passed a cluster of armchairs. Curled into one of them, sound asleep, was our little girl. She had dropped out and off to sleep as we walked from the door to the elevators. Jet lag.

The next morning, as told (and felt) by Catherine:

The earthquake struck at 8:53 A.M. our second morning here. We were all in our hotel room. Conor was writing at the computer and announced, "There's an earthquake." Slowly, each of us began to feel the shaking. We were on the twelfth floor of the hotel. We ran out in the hall. No one else on our floor did. And the shaking stopped. We guessed it had been a four or a five on the Richter Scale. Like all Los Angeles people, we know Richter Scale details.

Said Colin:

I've lived through some of the big L.A. quakes—'71 and '94 and countless aftershocks. This was no puny temblor and was no doubt amplified by our twelfth-floor perch. . . . Mom called the front desk and asked whether there had just been an earthquake and whether it was big or small. "Madam," said the concierge, "sometimes in Tokyo we have earthquakes. Check your television." Everyone but us did seem incredibly blasé. A quick check out the window revealed unfazed salarymen smoking butts on the balconies above us.

The phone rang. "Madam," said the concierge, "it was medium." The next day's paper said the Richter reading was 5.6 and the epicenter was in a bay fifty miles from Tokyo. It was big enough to stop rush- hour train traffic. (For those who have never had the pleasure, you do not feel quakes in cars; the tires absorb the shaking.)

Catherine and I had a morning appointment with the United States Ambassador, former Vice President Walter Mondale. "Can I come?" said Fiona. The guys declined and saw some more Japanese beating each other up. Kendo, this time.

Wrote Colin:

> It's samurai stick-fighting. We didn't go inside but we saw the participants warming up outside and they were even more vicious than the karate kids. This is a very combative culture. Maybe it's part of the national psychology of an island nation that has staved off invasion.

Conor was less philosophical: "I get the feeling that everyone around here could kick your ass."

Ambassador Mondale did seem a touch surprised when Fiona marched in with a notebook and pen, but he recovered and was soon showing around pictures of his grandchildren. We all talked for forty minutes or so, mostly about trade.

"It's always so slow and grudging. They like to sell and they don't

Fiona, surrounded by "adultists."

like to buy—it's as simple as that," said Mondale. His job, he said, is to deliver a message they still don't want to hear: "We can't continue to live with this trade imbalance. . . . If they don't produce [the opening of markets] here, there's going to an explosion back home in the United States. They said to me once, 'you have to understand the sociology of our country. Trade issues in Japan mean jobs for our people.' I told them, 'If you think our sociology likes unemployment, you've got to start thinking again.' Power here is disaggregated. . . . Ministries are linked to their constituencies. Bureaucrats have more power than politicians [and when changes are proposed] they ask the people affected—farmers or telecommunications companies—and of course they say no. . . . If we did that, we'd be the most protectionist country in the world."

Fiona, it turned out, was writing this:

> Really boring. Politics are stupid. Watching the news is the stupidest—I personally don't find it interesting to watch a bunch of people arguing. . . . The only good thing about being here is the big comfortable chairs we get to sit in. Then a waiter came in. . . .

"What'd you think?" I asked Fiona as we left the office.

"I think you're all adultists," she said. "The waiter came in and brought you all coffee or water but just ignored me. How rude!"

In the hallway we bumped into Emi Lynn Yamaguchi, a Japanese-American Foreign Service officer who had been an assistant in the embassy's press office when we had last been there in 1985. This was her first week back after almost ten years; now she was in charge of the office. I asked: "What's changed?"

"Divorce," she said. "It was almost unknown when I left. Now it's all over, in books and films—and in life. The Japanese are becoming more like everybody else."

"I THINK YOU'RE ALL ADULTISTS," FIONA SAID. "THE WAITER CAME IN AND BROUGHT YOU ALL COFFEE OR WATER BUT JUST IGNORED ME. HOW RUDE!"

We walked across the street to the Okura Hotel, where Catherine and I had stayed in the old days, when a dollar was worth three hundred yen. Now it was too expensive for us, but Catherine had told Colin and Conor to meet us there for a splurge lunch.

"So," asked Colin, "how was Mondale?"

"Great," I said. "I wish he were President."

"Excuse me," said Catherine. "I stood next to this man on the platform in San Francisco when Mondale was nominated in 1984. He said and he wrote that they should give Mondale a gold watch and give the nomination to Gary Hart."

"Whoa!" Colin said. "How do you explain that, Reeves?"

"I've grown."

Fiona liked the Okura, offering the opinion that it was probably an eight on her ten-scale. I'm sure. It is also five hundred dollars a night. The guys loved it, too. The first time I saw it years ago, when someone else was paying the bills, the great lobby was filled with squads of American businessmen trying to out-bow Japanese customers and suppliers. It can't be done. "The hotel is beautiful," Conor said. "It reinforces my affinity for two things from the Japanese culture that I already knew I liked: food and design."

Our young men were fascinated watching the collision and collusion of Japanese and American culture, like magnets attracting or repelling, depending on how they approached each other.

Conor continued:

I've heard a lot about the Japanese being a bunch of racists. But I haven't experienced anything personally. But then again I might be too much of an outsider to pick up on the nuances. I do think it is ironic that even if they do think of us as a bunch of savages, they can't help but want to be like us, and our culture is infesting and destroying theirs. Ha! Ha!

His sightings included: Harrison Ford on a billboard hawking Kirin Beer, next to one with Charlie Sheen smoking Parliament cigarettes. Face to Face, a California punk band, blasting out on the streets. *Batman Forever. Little Women. Legends of the Fall.* Michael Jackson's "HIStory" was being showcased on major billboards by his corporate sponsor, Sony. McDonald's. KFCs. Dunkin' Donuts.

Their mom added:

> This is my third time in Tokyo. The first time was in 1981. Then I remember thinking that everyone was very traditionally dressed. Now there are many young people who are aggressively following fads, young women wearing very high-heeled uncomfortable shoes, some with dancer's wool leggings as part of their costume on this sweltering July day. Fashion victims.

And then there was Nomo. Hideo Nomo, the former Japanese major leaguer having a great rookie year with the Los Angeles Dodgers, was getting more coverage than trade negotiations and other wars. The *Asahi Evening News* of July 2 had a front-page story under the headline THE SECRETS OF NOMO'S SUCCESS, quoting the Japanese consul in Los Angeles as saying: "He does not feel the same sense of isolation as American players often feel in Japan because the U.S. West Coast has people from many different cultural backgrounds—including Asians."

In more than a dozen locations around the city, giant television screens on the sides of buildings drew enthusiastic crowds each time Nomo pitched. The Prime Minister sent him a fax congratulating him in the nation's name when he was chosen for the National League All-Star team. One television station featured a half-hour pregame show with prominent Japanese, from politicians to actors and singers, calling on Nomo to do his best against the Americans. The United States Senior Open golf tournament was on television, with only one player being shown, Isai Aoki, the only Japanese in the tournament.

▴ ▴ ▴

IS JAPAN REALLY IN TROUBLE?
Catherine handles the economics, both macro and micro, in our crowd. During the late 1980s, she worked for the International Monetary Fund in Washington and can talk as if she still does. "There's Mommy's favorite brand," says Fiona, pointing at signs marked "Discount."

This is part of what the discount lady saw and thought in Tokyo:

It's amazing to be in Japan with a crippled American dollar and read every day in the papers about the terrible economic straits Japan feels it is in. The Tokyo stock market hit a nine-year low the day after we arrived. The government is unpopular. The banks have 40 trillion yen in outstanding bad loans on their books, ten times the debt load of American savings and loan companies when the U.S. government stepped in with a rescue package. Real estate is said to be overvalued by 6 trillion yen. Bankruptcies are up 48 percent during the past year.

Things simply cost more than they should. One talk show here featured a woman who saves money by ordering things from overseas catalogs because the prices are so much lower than in Tokyo.

JOB HUNTING OFFICIALLY BEGINS was a headline in the *Asahi Shimbun* on July 2. In the story students graduating in 1996 called this year "the employment super ice age." The Japan Travel Bureau, popular among female graduates, was hiring one hundred university graduates. It received fifty thousand job inquiries.

▰▰▰

We all went down into the subway with Colin trying to figure the route back to the Grand Palace, tracing the train lines on a wall map and muttering. Fiona, treading an old male-female fault line, walked up to a man and said: "Excuse me, do you speak English?" He didn't, but the second one she asked did, and showed us the way. I'm not sure Colin was amused by his little sister's precociousness.

On the train back, a group of very young Japanese schoolgirls . . . Well, let Fiona tell it:

When we were on the subway a bunch of Japanese girls about six years old, in school uniforms, kept walking back and forth through our car just to stare at me.

THERE ARE MORE BOOK RETAILERS THAN IN THE UNITED STATES. IT WAS INTERESTING THOUGH THAT THE MOST CROWDED FLOOR IN THE STORE WAS THE THIRD, THE FOREIGN BOOK FLOOR. AND THE MOST CROWDED AISLE ON THAT FLOOR WAS THE MAGAZINE AISLE, FEATURING HUNDREDS OF AMERICAN PUBLICATIONS INCLUDING *DIRT BIKE, ARCHITECTURAL DIGEST, ROLLING STONE, NATIONAL GEOGRAPHIC, SURFING,* ETC....—COLIN

So they did, giggling and huddling, checking out her hair, her shoes, and her best little black-and-white dress. One of them, nudged by the others, veered off toward us during one circuit and came close enough to say "Hi!" and run off after her friends.

Fiona's brothers were amazed, too—that the little girls, looking like little Madelines, could safely ride subways by themselves. It did seem odd only weeks after the country had been paralyzed by the poison gas released in packed cars by religious terrorists. There was also a piece in the day's *Japan Times* headlined, PERVERTS HIDING IN PLAIN SIGHT IN PACKED COMMUTER TRAINS. The paper reported that 75 percent of female students at two high schools in Osaka said they had been the victim of men rubbing up against them or stroking them on rush-hour trains. City officials had designated two all-female cars for students. But that was as far as they were willing to go, according to an Osaka Transport Bureau spokesman who said: "Since we have male passengers, too much emphasis on molestation would hurt their feelings."

Later that day, Colin and I decided to check out a bookstore in the Ginza and he saw it this way:

If Japan were melted down into an ingot of land and remolded, it could fit into Wisconsin. But in Japan there are more book retailers than in the United States. It was interesting though that the most crowded floor in the store was the third, the foreign book floor. And the most crowded aisle on that floor was the magazine aisle, featuring hundreds of American publications including *Dirt Bike, Architectural Digest,*

Rolling Stone, National Geographic, Surfing, etc. . . . God Bless America, but don't send us any of your crappy cars.

That night, with Fiona doing the planning, we went to Johnny Rocket, a far-from-home fifties-style American hamburger joint. Colin got to know what it feels like to drink a six-dollar Coke.

▲▲▲

LOSERS WRITE HISTORY, TOO

BOMBS FELL TO JUSTIFY OUTLAYS read a front-page headline in the *Japan Times* five weeks before the fiftieth anniversaries of the United States' use of atomic bombs over Hiroshima and Nagasaki at the end of World War II. The story under the headline argued that the dropping of the atomic bomb had little to do with the war—it was done for domestic political reasons, to prevent postwar congressional investigations of the $2-billion Manhattan Project to develop the bomb before Germany or Japan.

The story was based on a sixty-seven-page paper by an American historian named Stanley Goldberg, a document that was printed in full by at least one of Japan's national magazines. Interpreting (or misinterpreting) National Archives data in Washington, Goldberg wrote: "The use of the atomic bomb against Japan had at least as much to do with politics internal to the United States and with politics internal to the American military bureaucracy as it did with the beginnings of our international competition with the Soviet Union or with the war against Japan."

The history of that event was big news because of Japanese anger at President Clinton, who had just said he had no intention of apologizing for President Truman's use of the bomb. In fact, Clinton said he thought Truman made the right decision given the information he had that historic summer fifty years ago.

Winners write history, it is said. But smart losers try to rewrite it, and the Japanese are very smart. Their more or less official line now is that the American use of the bomb was so horrible that it balances, even excuses, the history of atrocities that began with the Japanese invasion of China in 1937 and their attack on Pearl Harbor on December 7, 1941.

▶▶▶

Chapter 3

TAIPEI

Day four of our adventure also happened to be the Fourth of July. Colin picked up the story:

Up at the crack of dawn in Tokyo, spent a couple of painless hours in the air with Singapore girls. The landing strip in Taipei is lined with golf courses and antiaircraft guns. Tropical jungle with pleasantly unbearable heat and humidity. Our hotel, the Grand Palace, is perched high on a hill and of truly monumental scale. It had starred on CNN and in all the international newspapers three days ago because the top several floors were in photogenic flames. The staff, noticeably looser and more jovial than their Nipponese counterparts, greeted us warmly. . . .

Conor added:

I'm not too good with physical descriptions, but I can say that if you saw a shot of this place in a movie there would be a big Chinese gong sound accompanying the image. It seems like a throwback to some colonial time, and because it was empty and the staff was so jovial it reminded me of a Chinese version of the *Hotel New Hampshire*. I instantly loved it.

The warm greeting was understandable. After seeing the fire footage, we talked about whether or not to change our plans. The vote was unanimous: No way! It turned out that we were five of only nineteen guests being served by a large staff. Everyone else had canceled after seeing pictures of the fire, which destroyed the top couple of floors of the "new building" of one of the world's most striking hotels, visible for many miles in the style of a giant pagoda over the city.

I was told later by a magazine editor in Hong Kong that the Palace was having problems before the fire. Some traveling businessmen were avoiding the place because it does not allow

I'M NOT TOO GOOD WITH PHYSICAL DESCRIPTIONS, BUT I CAN SAY THAT IF YOU SAW A SHOT OF THIS PLACE IN A MOVIE THERE WOULD BE A BIG CHINESE GONG SOUND ACCOMPANYING THE IMAGE.   —CONOR

unattached working girls upstairs. Taipei's sex tourism, they say, is second only to Bangkok's—you can buy most everything, except a haircut, at the places marked by neon barber poles.

▶ ▶ ▶

SEX, PLEASE, WE'RE CHINESE

Catherine was surprised by the openness of the sex trade in Taipei, writing:

> The incredible spread of a red-light district right in central Taipei was a surprise to me. The barbershop poles became almost comical in their ubiquitous presence were it not for the sad sight of so many young girls sitting in modern hotel lobbies, with short, tight skirts, waiting for customers. I did not expect such a relatively rich country with a sense of traditions to be such a major center for prostitution.

Actually, prostitution is part of the tradition. While we were in the country, a new law was passed out of a parliamentary committee for debate that would levy fines of more than three quarters of a million dollars for clients of child prostitutes. Newspapers reported that the government seemed ready to try to rid the country of tens of thousands of child prostitutes.

▶ ▶ ▶

After the Grand Palace fire: four of the nineteen guests.

Our rooms were immense in the old style, before air conditioning and before the universal sleekness of first-class hotels, with high ceilings, polished wood floors, and great balconies overlooking the city. There had apparently been stories in the Taipei papers speculating that the fire was arson, presumably to collect insurance money. When the manager spoke to us about the fire he kept referring to it as a "fire from natural causes," all in one breath. If electricity is natural, he had a case. The wiring, with copper showing through, looked as if it had been put in by the local equivalent of Thomas Edison.

The other big story in the *China Post* was about a shoot-out at the airport: "Gangster Shih Chih-chin had passed the customs inspection without his five hidden handguns being detected. He was discovered by an alert policeman to be carrying guns under his clothes. He shot himself to death after being wounded by police fire."

The pool down the hill was about the largest I've ever seen and Fiona and I headed for it. This was double-hundred country: the temperature was over a hundred degrees (Fahrenheit) and the air was heavy with humidity. Then we all stuffed ourselves into a taxi and headed for town. Catherine liked the fare. Four dollars.

Taipei itself was not impressive. On the walking-bicycle-motorbike-automobile progression that defines the cities of "developing" countries, Taipei is in transition from mopeds to cars. The new prosperity of the country shows in the bustle of the streets, a new central railroad station, and new subway construction everywhere, but the housing, stalls, and open storefronts are still as they were when the country was poorer. Food is still being cooked in many places outdoors on the streets. The only new and tall downtown building—excepting world-class hotels built by those old Taiwanese families, Sheraton, Hilton, and Hyatt—is a twelve-story Japanese department store, a Mitsukoshi. "Lot of mangy mutts," was Conor's observation. "Ramshackle sprawl," added Colin.

WE STOPPED IN A DIM SUM RESTAURANT FOR LUNCH. I WENT INTO THE BATHROOM AND BY THE TIME I CAME OUT, EVERY-ONE HAD ORDERED. I AM PRETTY GOOD WITH CHOPSTICKS AND LIFTED A SMALL PINK THING FROM A BOWL OF CLEAR LIQUID, SAYING: "AH, WHAT'S THIS?"

"IT'S A NAPKIN, DAD," SAID FIONA. "I SPILLED SOME WATER AND USED IT TO CLEAN UP."

—RICHARD

Fiona did not like the way dogs looked or were treated. But she liked palm trees, put-ons, and people. "I used to think there were palm trees only in California, Florida, and Hawaii. What did I know, I'm only ten years old," she wrote.

And she ended her report of the first day with:

There were a lot of people selling things on the sidewalk. I didn't like any of the toys, but I did like the calligraphy a man was doing in a shop and I asked him how much it cost and he gave it to me. He was really nice.

(Back home in Pacific Palisades, we took the calligraphy to our local experts at the Rickshaw Chinese Laundry, who after consultation

Dim sum: "It's a napkin, Dad."

Catherine. Trinkets. Baubles.

with parents and grandparents, said the message of the sheet was something like an oriental version of "The truth shall make you free"—and good men would find that truth in the temple.)

In the end you can gauge countries and the whole world on whether or not you like the people you meet. Conor gave the city his highest rating, "Gnarly," and said something I thought was interesting: "You compare a place not always to home, but to what came immediately before." And he liked Taipei better than Tokyo.

Not shy about his opinions, he wrote:

Compared to Japan, it is third-worldy and less like America in that way. But it also seemed more real or more open. The people seemed a lot more laid back and content. I think the Japanese are the Brits of Asia—an uptight, imperialistic island with people who find it hard to let it all hang out. If that's true, this place is more like Italy, right down to the hordes of teenage couples out at night on dates on their Vespas. In Taipei there's a good healthy anarchy in the way people cross the street, ride escalators, and wait in line for tokens. In Japan it was rigid, rigid, rigid.

Colin and Fiona agreed. "Seductive," Colin said. Fiona went back to her first impression of Japan, the convenience store that made us unpack because we were a few yen short. "In Taiwan," she concluded, "they would just say, 'Forget it, have a nice day.'"

(For the record: The Taiwanese are not crazy about the Japanese. From 1895 until the end of World War II in 1945, Japanese troops occupied the island of Formosa, as it was then called.)

We liked the people we met. It was as simple as that. Not that they much cared. Said Conor:

I wrote earlier about Japan that I didn't experience any discrimination while I was there and that's true. But I have noticed that things feel different here in Asia. In America, I'm not used to being the minority. But there are hardly any white people here at all. I feel kind of like Ralph Ellison's Invisible Man. Instead of standing out for being unique, it's as though I don't exist at all. When nothing relates to you, your difference is negated. Except for the occasional curious child, people seem to not even notice you.

We stopped in a dim sum restaurant for lunch. I went into the bathroom and by the time I came out, everyone had ordered. I am pretty good with chopsticks and lifted a small pink thing from a bowl of clear liquid, saying: "Ah, what's this?"

"It's a napkin, Dad," said Fiona. "I spilled some water and used it to clean up."

We walked over to the Mitsukoshi. "Just like America," said Conor, "except that the people are all Chinese." We followed the noise of video games to the twelfth floor, which was called "Cyberspace." It was dominated by a "Batcave," a promotion for the movie *Batman Forever*—American, of course—and clips were being shown everywhere on television screens, with Mandarin subtitles.

Coming out of the Batcave, thinking deep thoughts about what the Marxists called the "cultural imperialism" of the good ol' U.S.A., I came upon a scene which will be described and repeated forever, told around campfires wherever men named Reeves or O'Neill congregate.

This is Colin's telling of the tale:

Mom hopped onto a model road bike and threw Fiona onto the back of the seat. In front of her there was a video simulator where you actually have to ride and lean into the turns and everything. She was tearing up the track, laying the bike low through corners and showing no mercy for the throttle—and proceeded to set the second highest score ever posted on this machine. Who knew?

"That's when I knew we were really on vacation," added Conor. "It was a lot of fun."

American bridesmaid. Taiwan soap opera.

Now this is Catherine describing the same thing in a style that might be called Mother Modern:

The place was filled with what appeared to be a cross section of Taipei's more well-off teenagers and preteens, who were busy spending their parents' hard-earned money on elaborate virtual reality games. I know because I played one, driving a fast motorcycle against a screen. I didn't do too badly, but it is the closest I will ever come to motorcycle racing. . . . The boys and Richard were all excited.

It's funny what impresses your adult children and husband.

THE YOUNG MAN, QUITE HANDSOME, WAS WEARING A WHITE TUXEDO WITH SEQUINS PATTERNED ACROSS THE SHOULDERS AND BACK.... THE YOUNG WOMAN WAS VERY PRETTY AND HER GOWN WAS SO ELABORATE THAT A BRIDESMAID WAS ARRANGING THE LONG TRAIN.... FIONA WENT UP TO SEE THE BRIDE AND WHEN WE ALL GOT CLOSER WE SAW VIDEO CAMERAS AND MICRO-PHONES. THEY WERE SHOOTING A SOAP OPERA.   —RICHARD

You do, dear.

From Mitsukoshi, we walked to the railroad station over a pedestrian bridge spanning a main street and subway construction. At the far end, just at the top of the stairs leading down into the station, stood a bride and groom. The young man, quite handsome, was wearing a white tuxedo with sequins patterned across the shoulders and back. Just a little something left over from Elvis in Las Vegas. The young woman was very pretty and her gown was so elaborate that a bridesmaid was arranging the long train, fanning it out over shallow and grimy pools of rainwater. Rush-hour people were swarming around this odd little grouping. Fiona went up to see the bride and when we all got closer we saw video cameras and microphones. They were filming a local soap opera.

We watched for a couple of minutes, backing away from the crush, while the director tried to get clean shots of his stars. Local folks ignored the show, rushing for trains or over to the Batcave. Born in the U.S.A.

The ties between Taiwan and the United States are more like an overplotted novel than plausible history. Or maybe a children's book: this is the little country that could.

▲ ▲ ▲

ASIAN VALUES

In general, Asian countries, or at least their leaders, have a certain contempt for what they see as the permissiveness of the United States. Two examples of why East is East and West is West are these in Taiwan:

- Exactly half of Taiwanese students in national surveys report that they have been hit by their teachers. There is, however, a new and small movement to end physical punishment in the schools.
- If a child is born to a male citizen of Taiwan married to a foreigner, the child has all rights of citizenship. But if a child is born to a female citizen married to a foreigner, the child has to apply for an Alien Resident Certificate in order to live in Taiwan.

▶ ▶ ▶

For the twenty-five years after the Communists of Mao Tse-tung won the civil war against the Nationalists of Chiang Kai-shek—and Chiang and one hundred thousand men fled to Formosa—this island was practically an American colony. It was protected by the United States Navy patrolling the hundred-mile-wide Straits of Formosa separating the island from the mainland. Beginning in 1949, United States taxpayers bankrolled a corrupt and inefficient police state that called itself the Republic of China, with a population now of 21 million, claiming to be the true government of hundreds of millions of Chinese who had never seen or never even heard of Formosa or Taiwan by any name.

Then in the 1970s, we walked out on them. At the beginning of that decade, President Nixon decided to end American opposition to the People's Republic of China's (the mainland Communists) claim to China's seat in the United Nations. Then, in 1979, with Jimmy Carter in the White House, the United States formally recognized the Communists as the one true government of one true China. The United States closed its embassy and Taiwan was noncountried, a poor dictatorship.

On their own, in less than twenty years, the Taiwanese built one of the world's most formidable little trading nations and then a young democracy. Of course you have to come here to see that—this was my first visit—because, officially, the country does not exist. The U.S. official presence here is something called the American Institute, which calls Taiwan not a state but "An Economy."

Well, it has become quite "an economy," grown from making umbrellas and cheap toys under American guidance to the world's largest manufacturer of notebook computers on its own. The per-capita income of the Taiwanese has passed ten thousand dollars (higher than South Korea's, higher even than that of New Zealand or Spain). Taiwan's democratic politics showed some free-wheeling energy on the day we arrived. A debate on financial disclosure for legislators and high appointed officials ended up in a fistfight on the floor of the National Assembly. Fisticuffs aside, Taiwan politics is now early American-style, which you might expect since President Lee Teng-hui and fourteen of the twenty members of his cabinet were educated in the United States. And while we were in Taipei, it was announced in Washington that members of the U.S. Congress were planning a tribute to Madam Chiang Kai-shek, now ninety-eight years old—the former first lady of China and then Taiwan was alive and well, living in New York City. Who knew that?

So much for politics. Thirty-one thousand Taiwanese hold American passports and there must be more McDonald's restaurants per square mile here than anyplace on the planet. "An indicator of disposable income," wrote Catherine. Movie billboards and television listings included *Casper, the Friendly Ghost . . . Braveheart . . . Batman Forever . . . Pocahontas . . . French Kiss . . .* "Hard Copy" . . . "Entertainment Tonight" . . . "Larry King Live," and on and on. A van we rented was nowhere to be seen at the appointed hour and the owner of the rental company, John Song, tried to reassure us by saying: "No problem. My brother teaches at UCLA. He has tenure."

They take education very seriously. A headline on the front page of the July 4 *China Post* read PRAYING FOR GOOD RESULTS. Under it were photographs of parents at a Buddhist temple clutching the test admission cards of their sons and daughters as they prayed and burned incense for spiritual help in getting their children into a good university. More than 125,000 high school students were taking the Joint College Entrance Examination, competing for 53,000 places in Taiwan's universities. Another photo showed a mother standing in the rain with an umbrella and chair for her daughter to use during breaks.

Above all those pictures, though, there was a headline across the top of the page: HAPPY BIRTHDAY AMERICA! Inside there were advertisements from Cadillac, Chevrolet, Saturn, Buick, Aetna, Northwest, Ford, Delta, Dale Carnegie, Johnson and Johnson, Citibank, Metropolitan Life, Continental Air, Sprint, AT&T, and 3M. Stories included a guide to Abraham Lincoln's house in Springfield, Illinois, and an explanation of the GI Bill of Rights.

That night we went to the Regent Hotel, a world-class marble and chrome tower. It was American Classics night and Conor recorded it this way:

> This could be in the San Fernando Valley, one of the nicer parts . . . A country/western band—Pollo Loco from Montana—set up on a stage with a silver-gray 1957 Cadillac Coupe De Ville, and posters of James Dean and Marilyn Monroe, Madonna, and Michael Jackson. Living in L.A., I forget just how famous famous people are. You see them around town and it's not that big of a deal. But when you see huge movie posters of Mel Gibson and Jim Carrey on the main square in Taipei, or see kids in Tokyo wearing Snoop Doggy Dogg T-shirts, you are reminded of how pervasive it is.

The rest of the crowd in the restaurant was local, cheering Pollo Loco's versions of "Amazing Grace" and "Ghost Riders in the Sky." I missed most of it because I had managed to lose my wallet. I went back to the hotel, retracing steps in the hope . . . Miraculously, it was no problem. A citywide radio alert sent by the Grand Palace revealed that only one taxi had taken a young, brown-haired white girl, Fiona, to the Regent. The wallet was found on the floor of the backseat, where four of us had crammed in—finally I acted on a lesson I had long ago learned, putting the wallet where it should have been all along, in my sock above the ankle.

Conor continued:

> After dinner Mom and I took a walk from the Regent. It was as though we were taking a walk from a hotel at Times Square; two or three random turns and we were on prostitute row. Every door had a neon swirling barber pole out in front of it. But we both felt as though we were safer there than we would have been in an equivalent American neighborhood. . . . Huge four-story, gold, chrome-plated, or mirrored buildings with lobbies filled with lounging sexy young women. . . . There was no pretending about what was going on.

The next morning, after Fiona and I took an early swim—with a dozen or so young men swimming laps, in training for future Asian Games and Olympics—we piled into one of John Song's vans for a visit to the National Palace Museum. "Awesome" was our consensus description. The collection of six hundred thousand items representing four thousand years of Chinese art and achievement can be compared only with the Louvre in Paris or the Metropolitan Museum in New York. Perhaps I exaggerate, but I don't think so. The treasures here, "looted" or "liberated" from the mainland in the late 1940s by the defeated Nationalists, gave us a great deal of insight into why the Chinese have always considered Europeans barbaric interlopers in their own Middle Kingdom.

Somehow I got separated from everyone else when we arrived and was by myself walking up the five great stairways leading to the entrance on the top level with a small Chinese woman trailing several

IT IS ALMOST IMPOS-
SIBLE TO DESCRIBE THE
CARVINGS, THE PORCE-
LAINS, THE PAINTINGS,
THE MINIATURES, THE
JADE, THE TAPESTRIES,
AND THE LACQUER-
WARE. THEY LEFT ME
BREATHLESS.

—CATHERINE

steps behind me. At the doorway, a guard waved me back down to get tickets on the first level. The same thing happened to the woman, who padded along behind me down the great stairways. She said to no one in particular in perfect California English: "Goddamn oriental logic. They make you crazy, these people."

She was from Oakland.

I can't speak for the logic, but the art was spectacular. "It is almost impossible to describe the carvings, the porcelains, the paintings, the miniatures, the jade, the tapestries, and the lacquerware," wrote Catherine. "They left me breathless." Added Conor: "Mind-blowing." Said Colin, who has a degree from Swarthmore in art history:

The American approach to culture at the National Museum.

The foremost collection of porcelain in the world, thousand-year-old poison gas catapults and acupuncture training models, miniatures carved out of peach pits whose mind-boggling detail can be seen only with magnifying glasses, highly accurate water-drip clocks from the eighth century B.C. The oldest thing that I noted was a water vessel from 2300 B.C. It was very much like an ancient Greek amphora—similar shape, same red and black colors, except the design was a swastika motif. There was use of abstraction in fourteenth-century landscape paintings. The paintings are all narrative; they tell stories or are representative of lore (and the stories are great) but they are also very abstract and compelling on a purely visual level. Calligraphy that looked like Franz Klein or Robert Motherwell. . . . Conor summed up my speechless state: "These Chinese, man . . . I'm not gonna mess with 'em.'"

The guys and I were absorbed in the "Oracle bones"—turtle shells burned and carved with holes and lines. Once upon a time wise men (or total frauds) used them to answer such questions as, "Who will be the next emperor?"

Fiona, however, saw it differently: "There were crowds of people looking at old turtle shells that I found extremely boring."

We were on a roll now, heading downtown to Chiang Kai-shek Memorial Hall, which we called "The Adoration," a mix of history and propaganda presenting the man as the legitimate ruler of all China, the country he never saw again after being driven off the mainland by Mao and the Communists. Photos, memorabilia, and slogans link Chiang and Dr. Sun Yat-sen, the founding father of modern China. The main hall is dominated by a giant painting, done from a 1923 photograph that showed Sun Yat-sen and Chiang, his military commander, sitting together

WE WERE ON A ROLL NOW, HEADING DOWNTOWN TO CHIANG KAI-SHEK MEMORIAL HALL, WHICH WE CALLED "THE ADORATION," A MIX OF HISTORY AND PROPAGANDA PRESENTING THE MAN AS THE LEGITIMATE RULER OF ALL CHINA.... —RICHARD

Hey, Mom, catch the Nose-Dropping Divine Progenitor.

in a railroad passenger car. The banner under them read: "One Heart, One Soul, the Joining of Titans."

One of the most recent photos on exhibit showed Chiang in 1970, then the unelected President-for-Life of the Republic of China, shaking hands with a great American supporter, the governor of California, Ronald Reagan. It was only a year later though that President

Nixon began the shift of United States support to the People's Republic of China, the Communist government of the mainland.

As I was scribbling down captions and slogans, Colin was approached by a young man with a more limited vision of history. "Hello, American," said the kid. "I'm Bruce Lee."

"And I'm Chuck Norris," answered Colin, trading the name of another karate movie icon.

"Want to score some 'poulet'?" said the Bruce.

Not sure what kind of chicken he was turning down, Colin said, "No, thanks. Maybe next time, Bruce."

We split up for a time, then, with Catherine and the guys temple-hopping while Fiona opted to go with her father to talk to people at the U.S.'s pseudo-embassy, the American Institute. I got a good fill on changes in Taiwan, but Fiona did a philosophic riff on disconnects between power and fashion, writing:

> A certain man, who is probably extremely powerful, has pants on that go up to right below his knees and make him look horrible when he sits down. But I didn't say anything about that because I decided it was best to stay on his good side.

The gents and their mom were quite taken with the working temples of Taipei, filled with worshipers, young and old, in modern and traditional dress, lighting incense sticks. Their favorite icon and the subject of much family speculation and debate was, in English, "The Nose-Dropping Divine Progenitor."

Colin described their rambles this way:

THE GENTS AND THEIR MOM WERE QUITE TAKEN WITH THE WORKING TEMPLES OF TAIPEI, FILLED WITH WORSHIPERS, YOUNG AND OLD IN MODERN AND TRADITIONAL DRESS, LIGHTING INCENSE STICKS. THEIR FAVORITE ICON AND THE SUBJECT OF MUCH FAMILY SPECULATION AND DEBATE WAS, IN ENGLISH, "THE NOSE-DROPPING DIVINE PROGENITOR."—RICHARD

Conor, Mom, and I walked among giant iron cauldrons coughing clouds of incense smoke, bags of groceries laid as offerings—fruit, flowers, cookies, cakes, candy, Chee-tos, tea, and even Wesson Oil—towering racks of candles, children riding bicycles among ancient, hunched worshipers, black-and-white televisions crackling in dark corners, and I knew that even with a lifetime of sleepless nights and a bottomless pocket of cash, I would never be able to penetrate or begin to really understand this heart of lightness.

Fiona and I had to settle for statistics at the State Department's lonely outpost ten blocks from the Chiang Memorial. Literacy, 92 percent; $100 billion in gold reserves, second in the world to Japan; per capita income $12,000, compared with $443 in 1971; one telephone for every two persons and one television for every three.

"It's a middle-class place now," said an American official. He offered Fiona a copy of the State Department briefing book, but she declined.

"Why didn't you take a briefing book?" I asked outside.

And she answered: "I'm not interested in reading about underwear."

Taiwan, according to that book, is the largest foreign investor in Vietnam, second in Malaysia, fourth in Thailand, and fifth in Indonesia. Foreign investment and the massive gold reserves are the reason Taiwan's new wealth does not show in the glittering way of Hong Kong. About a quarter of Taiwan's exports go to mainland China through Hong Kong. There are believed to be about twenty-five thousand mainland manufacturers which are secretly owned by Taiwanese—with an estimated total investment of between $6 billion and $20 billion, compared with $42 billion for the United States.

There is money here, but also a commitment to a kind of Spartan thrift. A local magazine offered "remanufactured" laser printer cartridges for twenty-five American dollars, but the same journal also had six pages of advertising for new yachts. The day's *China News* reported that Microsoft's Bill Gates was still the world's richest person, at least according to *Forbes* magazine back in the United States, but Tsai Wan-lin of Taiwan had moved up to sixth place. The owner of construction and insurance companies around Asia was worth $8.5 billion, according to his local paper, which also said Tsai was a recluse living behind twenty sets of guarded gates and ate only congee and pickles "for health and thrift."

There could also be a war here. For decades, the Communist government in Beijing has threatened to invade Taiwan, classifying it as nothing more than an illegal province—viewing Taiwan the way Abraham Lincoln viewed South Carolina in 1861. Remember 1960: one of the issues debated by John F. Kennedy and Richard Nixon in that presidential campaign was what the United States should do if the Communists invaded Quemoy and Matsu, two small islands between the two Chinas. In the end, there was no invasion because the People's Republic did not have the military capacity, particularly with American warships patrolling the Strait of Formosa.

But now the People's Republic does have the capacity to destroy Taiwan—with missiles, nuclear or conventional. And, ironically and dangerously, younger Taiwanese are calling for declaring their little country's independence from China, an action Beijing says will bring "rivers of blood."

The irony is that the old man, Chiang Kai-shek, and his Kuomintang Party accepted the same view of Taiwan as that of Mao and his successors. The old guards of both Taipei and Beijing saw, or see, the island as part of China—to Chiang it was the legitimate China and to the mainlanders it was an outlaw child.

But Chiang's men and their descendants represent at most only 15 percent of the people of Taiwan. Before democracy, the numbers did not matter so much because Chiang's guys had the guns. But that has all changed with time. President Lee Teng-hui, who triggered a Beijing-Washington crisis by visiting the United States to receive an honorary degree from his alma mater, Cornell, is from a family that has lived on Taiwan for generations. He is, after all, democratically elected, and in a democracy, numbers are all—and greater and greater numbers of Taiwanese want to see their country become independent. In fact, independence is part of the platform of the Democratic Progressive Party, the principal opposition to Lee's Nationalist Party, the inheritors of Chiang's Kuomintang.

The Taiwanese, more and more it seems, want respect. They want to be part of the world—and have the odd notion that they have earned the right of self-government.

As we left the island, Chinese missiles were plopping into the sea near us—without warheads, just an exercise, according to Beijing. Lee responded by vowing to develop weapons that would "terrify and stop" any attack from the mainland.

◢◢◢

THE FUTURE IS EAST

After spending time in each country, all of us filled out a questionnaire that Catherine prepared. One question was: "Will This Country Be Important in Your Lifetime?"

These were the answers she got as we flew from Taipei to Singapore:

"Yes, very soon. Maybe next week in light of China's military exercises in nearby waters. Taiwan may be the straw man for an escalating conflict between the United States and China."—Colin

"Yes. I think China is going to take it back."—Conor

"Yes. It has limited control over its own destiny, which depends on what happens in Beijing."—Richard

"Yes. They are on their own. Others won't help. With China opening up to business, foreign investors will be more solicitous of China's wishes. Could hurt investment in Taiwan. Yet, Taiwan is one of the largest investors in China. You figure."—Cathy

◣◣◣

Chapter 4

HONG KONG

No matter how many times you have done it, flying into Hong Kong is an experience never to be forgotten. Over the years, Catherine and I, together or alone, had each done it a dozen or so times. But it was the first time for Colin and this is how he saw it:

> The plane splits right through a jungle of apartment buildings with what seems like just a couple of feet between each wingtip and a thousand living room windows as it descends into a rare clearing in this most densely populated area in the world. The runways are surrounded by high-rises, and you feel like you're on the floor of Madison Square Garden.

Once again we stayed at two hotels. The first night at the Sheraton in Kowloon, the part of the old British colony which is part of the mainland of China, looking toward the fabulous island city on Hong Kong itself. Then we moved across Salisbury Road for one night, to the more expensive Regent. Colin described it:

> The Regent, which they say is the best hotel in the world, deserves its reputation. It serves up one of the most spectacular views I've ever seen, facing the steel and glass bluffs of Hong Kong. Skyscrapers starting at the waterfront and climbing back into the distance up the hill create the illusion of impossible heights.

This was another Catherine O'Neill production. We had United Airlines 50 percent–off certificates for the Sheraton, which saved us

THE VIEW OF HONG KONG WAS COMPLETELY SPELLBINDING, EVEN MORE SO AT NIGHT: THE WORLD'S LARGEST NEON SIGN IS AMONG THE MANY THAT GLARE ACROSS THE HARBOR AND IT DOESN'T EVEN STAND OUT AS BEING EXCEPTIONAL. —COLIN

enough money that we could kid ourselves that we could afford to spend a last night at the Regent itself. Which we did, loading our proliferating bags into a taxi at the Sheraton, then after everything and everybody was buttoned up in the taxi, Catherine smiled, glanced across Salisbury Road at our destination, and said, "The Regent, please."

The driver looked as if a relative had died. But there was no other way we were going to make it across the ten lanes of traffic zooming along Salisbury Road. Luckily none of us understand Chinese, so the driver's angry wails were lost on us. When Catherine looked away, I gave him a sizable tip, thinking I might be preventing a tong war—against us.

As soon as we arrived, we took the Star Ferry across the harbor from Kowloon to Hong Kong Island, one of the world's most exciting rides, for just forty cents. This was Conor's initial response:

> I'm not sure I like it. It's really corporate. It's also really futuristic in a sort of unreal utopian way. It almost seems like some city planner said, "Okay, let's build the most futuristic city we can. We certainly have the money!" It's like a giant Century City on the water—big corporate plazas connected by elevated covered walkways, the world's greatest escalator to Victoria Peak. You never have to walk on the ground level. I'm not even sure if they have sidewalks down there. It's all marble and granite and shiny metal. It looks kind of like "Logan's Run." As Colin said, "This town is very James Bond." When you take one of the pedestrian offramps into a building, it is in its own totally self-sufficient, self-contained world. There's a shopping mall, banks, grocery stores, Laundromats, parking garages, offices, and condos all in one high-rise.

Colin took up the narrative when we got off the ferry:

After a well-concealed memory lapse, Richard located his favorite restaurant in town—a dim sum lunch room in some
municipal building near the ferry terminal. The fare was
sometimes frightening and always delicious: sesame-crusted
bean paste, unnamed vegetable matter in clear wrappings,
gelatinous substances with tastes I know no words for, as well
as the authentic template for the more familiar dumplings
known to patrons of places like the Hard Rock Café or Wok
Fast. . . . Awesome.

We went to the Regent that night for dinner, marveling at the
light behind us; there is so much neon on the shopping streets of
Kowloon that night can be brighter than day in gray winter weather.
The main restaurant is also considered by some to be the best in the
world. Our friend Patricia Wells in Paris, rating the restaurants of the
world for the *International Herald Tribune,* rated it second best. A big
splurge, tempered by significant FHB, family-hold-back.
    Colin continued:

The view of Hong Kong was completely spellbinding, even
more so at night: the world's largest neon sign is among the
many that glare from across the harbor and it doesn't even
stand out as being exceptional. Beautiful dining room, jade
place settings, ivory and silver chopsticks, flower petals in center arrangements carefully folded over by hand. There seemed
to be three staff for each guest. Great. But I got a little tense
when the conversation turned to my professional future. I recently quit what seemed to many to be a great job—a globe-
trotting producer for Channel One, the school television news
service headquartered in Los Angeles—and I have nothing
planned for when I get back. It wasn't a grilling or lecture by
any means, just some words of encouragement and advice,
but I slept fitfully as a result.

So did we. That's what parents do when their children reach a certain age—light grilling, heavy encouragement, and heavier anxiety.

"The lap of luxury," said Fiona approvingly when we settled into the Regent, a "Summer Special," just $279 for the one night we dared. She and her brothers immediately headed for the pool, which happened to be right outside the window of our room, 419. Said Colin:

> We padded through the hallways in deep pile terry robes and slippers, arriving poolside where we were handed chilled tumblers of ice water. . . . As Richard said as we arrived, "The colonies are a lot of fun—if you run them." Conor and I had an informal contest, tossing Fiona for both height and distance. . . . We each have our strengths—mine being the vertical and Conor's the horizontal. In Australia, midgets are tossed as serious pubsport, like darts. I think Conor's distance technique would score more points, but my big beautiful rainbow arcs would wow the crowds.

I watched them from the window, the boys grunting and laughing, Fiona squealing in flying delight. My heart sang; it was one of the happiest moments of my life. That night as Catherine and I were dressing for dinner with friends on the Hong Kong side, Fiona said, "Do I have to go?"

The flying kid had discovered the joys of Room Service. She said she wanted to do "Lady things." In elegant privacy she washed her hair, bundled up in the world's thickest terry-cloth robe, and ordered dinner. We set a limit on how much she could spend and she ordered Brie and grapes. "I spread the cheese very slowly on a cracker and then I take a puny little bite and put it down again and take a sip of water," she reported later. "It took me an hour to eat like a lady."

▲▲▲

ON LUXURY

You can now get the same "things" almost anywhere on the planet if you can afford them. So luxury has come to mean more and better service. Is there a Service Central think tank somewhere around here to think up new ones? If so, the Regent Hotel in Hong Kong is a favored client.

On the evening Fiona was "being a lady," two men came in wearing gloves and slippers. They brought in new towels and bathroom supplies, just to make sure perfection reigned while we slept. Their slippers were designed to minimize indentations in the carpets and ensure no stray dirt entered our room.

In the lobby the next day, I asked a man with a hotel nameplate on his dark blue suit where I might find a men's room. "Allow me to show you, sir," said he. "May I accompany you?"

▶ ▶ ▶

We had a rather sobering evening with our friends and their friends, all representatives of big American and British firms, all planning on leaving Hong Kong before the ninety-nine-year lease held by Great Britain since 1898 expires and control of the island reverts to mainland China on July 1, 1997. They just don't believe the frequent assurances from Beijing that nothing will change in this Mecca of commerce—6 million people with per capita annual income of $11,000, almost half as much as the United States but more than thirty times as much as mainland China's $361 per capita.

It was a great life, they said, still is. But our friends, these young Western capitalists, prefer discretion to valor. The "Get Out!" symbols are all around. Beijing has announced that it will create a Court of Final Appeal to "assist" in transitional matters—and that "acts of state" would be exempt from any court action. Then the day we arrived, Beijing announced that the twenty-seven-thousand-member Hong Kong constabulary would be replaced by twenty-seven thousand men of the People's Liberation Army on July 1, 1997.

That seemed to be just one more signal that whether or not the old Communist leaders keep their word—and whether or not they are capable of running the most capitalist city in the world—Hong Kong's future will be Asian not Western. Our time is up. Catherine wrote:

On the ferry between Kowloon and Hong Kong.

Our friends said Beijing's representatives and local allies no longer even bother to meet with the British governor-general, Christopher Patten, who has been pushing for a "democratic" Hong Kong, something the British never supported during their century and more of power here. Richard mentioned that he was surprised at how many people, including Patten, are going around talking about elections and such as if there were actually some sort of political process here. It's all pretend. Pretend and wait. At the local swimming club Patten uses, we were told, it's embarrassing how few members even talk to him anymore—at least in public.

In the morning, as Fiona excitedly told us about her night of luxury, she glanced out the window and said, "My God, she's naked!"

So she was. A beautiful young woman was leaping out of the shallow water every minute—part of a television commercial being filmed at the hotel. Two assistants were splashing the lady a bit as she leaped up and down. Fiona was on the phone with her brothers, saying: "Colin, Conor, get in here, there's a naked lady in the pool."

They filmed the same shot over and over again. For five hours. There can be, we learned, too much of a good thing.

We were all long gone by then. Colin and Conor decided they wanted to see Macau, the old colony that the government of Portugal will turn back to China in the year 1999, two years after the British vacate Hong Kong and Kowloon. Colin had this to say:

Over six-dollar cups of coffee, Conor and I discussed our transit options for Macau. We agreed on the Turbocat, a jet-propelled catamaran with a seating capacity of two hundred. When we arrived at the pier, we learned that the fare was eight dollars, double what the guidebook had prepared us for, but the cheaper option, a high-speed ferry, didn't seem as exciting and didn't leave for several hours.

The ride to Macau took us through an archipelago populated mainly by James Bond's arch-foes, who reside in semi-subterranean labyrinths and plot the ransoming of the Free

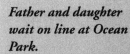

Father and daughter wait on line at Ocean Park.

Hong Kong at night.

AS I LOOKED AT THE YOUNG PEOPLE ON LINE FOR RAGING RIVER, I THOUGHT THAT IN MANY WAYS THE FUTURE OF CHINA DEPENDS ON THEM. THEY SPEAK TWO LANGUAGES, ONE OF THE EAST AND ONE OF THE WEST; THEY ARE LITERATE IN ALL MODERN TECHNOLOGIES. THEY UNDERSTAND SOPHISTI-CATED WAYS OF BUSINESS...AND THEY WILL SOON BE PART OF A COUNTRY WHICH WILL DESPERATELY NEED THEIR SKILLS. NOW THEY ARE VERY TRENDY TEENAGERS WEARING DENIMS, CAMP SHIRTS, DOC MARTEN SHOES, AND CARRYING SMALL BACKPACKS....WILL THEY BE REFUGEES LEAVING IN BOATS OR WILL THEY STAY AND BECOME PART OF NEW CHINA'S ELITE?

—CATHERINE

World. The Turbocat itself was also right out of a James Bond picture, except for the Elvis Presley medley on the karaoke screen, with lyrics rolling over melodramatic tableaux of Japanese actors playing out sappy romantic scenes completely unrelated to the words of the songs. . . . On land, Conor dropped a coin into a cauldron of lucky turtles. Maybe it worked, maybe not. Are you supposed to land on the shell? Do you conk them on the head? . . . Took a bus to a jai-alai casino, where they don't actually play jai-alai. . . . People couldn't stop staring at my beet-red, soaking head and wondering when I would crumple to the floor. The heat is incredible. I have been known to pass out from this kind of heat. It is so overwhelming and debilitating that it's almost funny and enjoyable. And it has only just begun. . . . it promises to be a major, outspoken character on this expedition.

Then Conor added:

The tour books describe Macau as the Las Vegas of the region. Let me set you straight on that: Vegas it ain't. It ain't even Reno, which is surprising given how much the Chinese love to gamble. . . . There are a lot of tall buildings and more being built, but it has a real sleepy feel about it. As we walked around in the afternoon it was so dead in some parts of town I wondered if they were observing siesta. . . . In this part of the world they like to crank the air conditioning. Sometimes it's good, like on a crowded city bus or when it pours out from stores onto the hundred-degree street as you're walking by. And sometimes it works against you, like when you're stuck on a three-hour train ride wearing short pants and short sleeves and didn't think to bring a sweatshirt.

THEN WE WENT ON THE CRAZY GALLEON. I WAS SURPRISED WHEN MY MOM GOT ON, TOO. EVEN THOUGH SHE CLOSED HER EYES THE WHOLE TIME, SHE WAS STILL THERE. THEN MY DAD AND I WENT ON THE OCTOPUS. THE WHOLE TIME I WAS SAYING "CHOCOLATE" OVER AND OVER AGAIN, BECAUSE I WANTED IT TO BE MY LAST WORD.
—FIONA

Meanwhile, the folks and Fiona were off on the far side of Hong Kong, to Ocean Park, the city's amusement park and aquarium. The setting was amazing; the place was kind of chiseled into the mountainsides over the China Sea with gondolas taking us from one area to another. "The gondola rides," I wrote, "are high, high above the sea and, listening, I realized that the views were spectacular—if your eyes were open. Mine were—sometimes."

"It's the biggest amusement park in Asia," wrote Fiona, whose eyes were wide open. "It's built into three mountains, which is why you have to use cable cars. First we went on the Raging River ride and while we were on it, there was a monsoon rain and everybody got soaked." Twice, because the monsoon was real.

Then we went on the Crazy Galleon. I was surprised when my mom got on, too. Even though she closed her eyes the whole time, she was still there. Then my dad and I went on the Octopus. The whole time I was saying "Chocolate" over and over again, because I wanted it to be my last word.

Catherine wrote:

The views of Hong Kong's harbors from the cable car alone are worth the price of admission. The park covers 215 acres and includes an enormous aquarium, a multilevel indoor atoll reef, with the greatest variety of fish I have ever seen—incredible colors, shapes, and designs. There is also a selection of rides, including a flume ride called Raging River, a roller coaster, a ferris wheel, lots of shows and performances with dolphins and other sea creatures and—you get the picture. Fun! Adult admission is about sixteen dollars—children eight dollars.

The place was filled with graduating classes from local schools on class outings. The personalities of people at the park were much softer and more patient than those you see in the frenzy of downtown. People waiting on line for rides were hit with a couple of downpours, but everyone just laughed and kept on waiting their turn.

She is a very serious woman, my wife, who has done refugee work all over the world, and she added this:

As I looked at the young people on line for Raging River, I thought that in many ways the future of China depends on them. They speak two languages, one of the East and one of the West, Chinese and English; they are literate in all modern technologies. They understand sophisticated ways of business . . . and they will soon be part of a country which will desperately need their skills. Now they are very trendy teenagers wearing denims, camp shirts, Doc Marten shoes, and carrying small backpacks. The latest. Soon it will be cell phones and briefcases. But they are the ones who will be most affected by

1997 and who may affect 1997 in turn. Will they be refugees leaving in boats or will they stay and become part of new China's elite?

Next, Catherine headed for one of her Hong Kongs, taking along Fiona for a shopping tour, beginning, she reported, at the China Arts and Crafts Store right off the Star Ferry stop on the Kowloon side:

> It is big, and loaded with beautiful things made in China. Each time I've been here I've bought heavy cotton damask tablecloths and napkins, enormous dinner napkins. They are my standard wedding present for those I cherish. They are heavy in the baggage, though. We also bought lovely Chinese porcelain soup bowls and porcelain soup spoons in Hong Kong, at a shop selling Chinese goods on the very top of Victoria Peak. Then we went out again to buy gifts for friends in Pakistan, knowing we were never going to quite match them in a generosity contest.

More weight. More bags. More memories, too. But Conor did not see it exactly that way:

> A travel day—a day for stress, a day for everyone's character defects to shine brightly. My dreams were interrupted around 6 A.M. by the combination of a wake-up call and Richard knocking on our door. . . . Mom and Fiona were still in the room waiting for the bellman. Mom was washing her face or putting on makeup or something in the bathroom, Fiona was lying face down on her bed refusing to put her second shoe on. The bellman was running late. I could see what direction things were going. In retrospect I'm reminded of one of Reeves's famous lines: it was the summer we traveled through Italy and Mom was having a full-blown stress attack. Colin and I were a little freaked out by it so Colin took Richard aside and said, "Rich, I think Mom's having a nervous break-

down." "No," Rich coolly responded, "She's just a carrier." But I digress. . . .

What ended up happening is that Fiona walked out of the room after angrily putting her shoe on and disappeared into the stairwell. I got downstairs and relayed this to Richard but he just sent Colin and me off in a cab to the airport with half of the luggage. By now we are at least a two-cab group and on this morning we turned out to be a three-cab group. . . . Anyway everyone was stressed out and freaking out and I'm sure it wasn't the last time, but we made our plane and we all got bumped up to business class so I guess it was all for the best. We were moving on to our fourth country.

▰ ▰ ▰

HONG KONG, ACCORDING TO RICHARD
Baroness Lydia Dunn was very big in Hong Kong. Of Chinese ancestry, she was born in the city and grew up to be the senior member of the British governor's policy-making Executive Council and a senior executive of Swires, one of the great old trading hongs that made the island a player in global commerce. Since the day in 1987 that Great Britain made an agreement to turn her crown colony over to the People's Republic of China, the baroness (titled by Queen Elizabeth) insisted that she was staying on.

While we were in her city, she announced that she was moving to London with her British husband and would become executive director of the Swire Group. "Family factors" prompted her decision, she said, trying to play down the political and economic impact of what she was doing.

Her denials had been part of the nothing-will-change wishful thinking (or propaganda) of the previous ten years. A lot of the talk about China not killing the golden goose was a way to keep the merry-go-round going and to coax a last few million bucks out of a money machine that depended on cheap labor in China connected to a sophisticated distribution and export network in the colony.

"Family factors . . . the children's schooling . . . my parents' health," are the euphemisms that the four hundred thousand Hong Kong residents holding foreign passports use rather than say they are ready to get out while they still have a chance. Among others leaving are prominent journalists, even those with ties to Beijing. A leading member of pro-democracy movements, Emily Lau, announced she, too, is going to England, saying: "I have no wish to be jailed. It would be no good for me or my family."

Accommodation to the inevitable had become the order of the day. The Royal Hong Kong Jockey Club and the Royal Hong Kong Yacht Club are dropping the first word of their names. There is obvious self-censorship in the press. Rupert Murdoch, that giant of laissez-faire, dropped the BBC News from his Star Channel cable selections because Beijing hates real news and Murdoch loves the potential of giant profits in China's billion-person market. Textbooks are being revised to eliminate references to the Republic of China (Taiwan) or to events in Tiananmen Square in 1989. TVB, the island's premier television operation, ignored police estimates earlier this year that there were twenty-seven thousand people at a rally commemorating the killing of students in the square by the PLA—reporting instead that the protesters numbered only twenty-five hundred.

The system China's tie-wearing new Communists made or inherited is profoundly corrupt. In Hong Kong, it is said that the cost of doing business with China is 5 to 10 percent higher than it should be—because of bribes. Whichever number is more correct, the price is increasing. There was a time when you could open a factory with docile cheap labor by giving air conditioners to the head men of villages, local Communist Party officials. Now functionaries of the People's Republic want cash up front, equity, and pieces of the take forever. That does not make them so different from anyone else selling political power—zoning permits and all that. What makes them different is that many old Communists simply do not understand that investment comes first and profits take a little longer. And as more bribe-takers enter the business chain from resources to manufacturing to delivery, there comes a point where there could be too little profit for anyone.

These Chinese, old Communist bully-boys, are perfectly capable of killing the golden goose or anything else. There are ignorant thugs in high places in what we used to call "Red China." I love Hong Kong, but I think that thought will soon be in the past tense. If I lived there and had the options of Baroness Dunn, I'd do what she is doing—getting out while the getting is good.

▶ ▶ ▶

"**U**p at dawn again, this time for a train ride into China," wrote Colin, quickly warming to his subject:

Red China. Commie China. Home of the original Yellow Peril. The country that Newt Gingrich wants to "hurt". . . . Sat next to Mom for the ride: Look at that, a building! . . . Do you see this!? . . . It's a commuter train stop! . . . Look! Construction!"

So it went. I know she means well, but she had taken this same ride fifteen years ago and the contrast meant something to her. I was seeing it for the first time and could plainly see that there were buildings and commuter train stations and all the rest. . . . One piece of her narration did prove very interesting and useful: after a trip to the head, she described the facility as being just a hole through the floor of the train. I took several more leaks on that ride than I needed to . . . wind felt great.

Tough, kid. But part of our idea of the trip was to give them a baseline view of the world of their times, so they could provoke their own children one day—tell them what southern China looked like back in '95.

Back in 1981, there was a small settlement on the Chinese side of the border with Hong Kong, a village surrounded by miles and miles of rice paddies. Now stands Shenzen, a new city (and industrial zone) of a million people, producing much of the world's toys and compact discs. Where water buffalo roamed, Mercedes and BMWs now pushed through crowds.

All things Chinese have to be prefaced with population numbers, beginning with the fact that the overall population is more than a billion. For Catherine and me, this was our fifth trip during those fourteen years. The last one was just a year before, to Beijing, Shanghai, and Nanjing, where we saw for the first time some of the consequences of the country's shift from the totalitarian order of communism to the energetic chaos of capitalism. The lifting of travel and residence restrictions, to give one example, made it possible for rural folk to go to the big towns. Now tens of millions of them in bulky peasant jackets are huddled around railroad stations, immigrants to the cities in desperate search of the prosperity they have seen and heard about on television. Many of them are without money or work or salable skills to survive in this new kind of world. In Shanghai, there were more cranes and construction than we had ever seen. A new city of high-rise housing was being built on the outskirts of old Shanghai—new homes for the Chinese being moved out of downtown and the riverfront to make room for Hyatt hotels, shopping centers, office buildings, and luxury housing, most of it for foreigners bearing gifts of investment.

The same thing is happening in Guangzhou and smaller cities in Guangdong Province, which is being called "The Wild West of the Far East." The area is as much a part of its capitalist neighbor to the south, Hong Kong, as it is of Communist Beijing to the north. There are few rules here and most of them have been broken beyond repair in the province's rise from dusty paths and bicycles to the world's fastest-growing economic region.

Getting rich may be glorious, as the Communist Party now preaches, but it also became a very dangerous business in many places. In many ways, parts of China are reverting to something like the warlordism that dominated much of the country's history. Murder, mayhem, kidnapping, gang wars, and payoffs are the local substitute for "infrastructure," the developed world's word for commercial necessities ranging from state-of-the-art telephones to laws and courts to resolve business disputes and other unpleasantries.

Back to the numbers of China. When we travel for work or pleasure, we like to take a train early one morning and go as far as we can for lunch and a walkabout before taking the last train back. In Beijing the year before we had asked someone for the name of a smaller town we could get to. "Oh, go to Tianjen," we were told. "Great food and a little antiques market." So we did just that and did have a great time. I found a seventy-five-year-old copy of Adam Smith's *Wealth of Nations,* which should be a best-seller in China these days. But . . . the population of that charming little town with a great food market is more than 7 million. It is about the size of New York.

This day we got off the Hong Kong train in Guangzhou, the city we used to call Canton. Back in 1981, after long and grumpy checking of papers, you were discharged into a great dusty field where a guide waited to take you to the Dong Fang Hotel, a bed with mosquito netting all around and a telephone connected no farther than the front desk or hall porter. The enormous dining room was lined with young women who stood against the wall, wearing dark slacks and white tops, a workers' cadre assigned to the hotel. It was a bicycle city then, with everyone we saw wearing a uniform or the plainest of peasant jackets and pants, almost all of them blue. Now that square is choked with foreign cars watched over by the painted and smiling faces of happy consumers on gigantic billboards advertising most everything from Sony to Salem cigarettes.

Inside the station, there was a sign I remembered from the old days, warning in English: "Inflammable, explosive, and dangerous goods are prohibited from bringing into the station or railway cars just for the safety of yourself and others."

But it all looked different to Conor's younger eyes:

The first thing I noticed was how crowded it was. Lots and lots of Chinese. I also noticed that it was kind of run-down and seemed to be very disorganized. Chaotic, actually. Especially the way people drive. We drove through town on what I assumed was one of the main roads—an elevated two-lane job kind of like the old West Side Highway in New York. The one that was condemned. On the average there was about ten feet between the guardrails and the buildings that fronted on the highway.

This was the beginning of Fiona's account of visiting the Qin Ping Market, the central market of Guangzhou. You can buy anything that moves, snakes for instance, and anything that used to:

We went to a market where they had every tail you could ever think of . . . where they peel the skin off dead flies and eat them. Pretty gross. But I had fun and bought some nice things. . . .

▲▲▲

THE LEGEND OF ROMPS, ACCORDING TO CONOR

When we made our now historic voyage to Pakistan in 1983, Mom brought with her a very large, very shapeless, very heavy garment/duffel bag we called the Romps. Romps was either the brand name or the name of the model but in any case it said Romps on it. The Romps was the bane of our existence that summer. Well, the Romps and amoebic dysentery. It started off as a container for film, medicine, peanut butter, Lipton's Cup O' Soup, and God knows what else, and ended up being the vessel for all kinds of lacquerware, silver, leather goods, plates, jewelry, linens, picture frames, and assorted shalwar kameez. The Romps, I think, is the main reason that Colin and I were so adamant about insisting that everyone travel light and be responsible for his/her own baggage when planning this trip.

We had to carry that damn Romps everywhere, and by the end of that summer it literally took two people to lift it. Every

> WE WENT TO A MARKET WHERE THEY HAD EVERY TAIL YOU COULD EVER THINK OF...WHERE THEY PEEL THE SKIN OFF DEAD FLIES AND EAT THEM. PRETTY GROSS. BUT I HAD FUN AND BOUGHT SOME NICE THINGS....   —FIONA

The "pharmacy" at Qin Ping Market, the central market of Guangzhou.

"What language is that?"

time we crossed a border we had to unpack and then repack the Romps. There was no way that any customs official was gonna let that beast pass through unmolested. It got to a point where we would just open it up and dump out the contents without even being asked.

The whole excess baggage thing is really a problem for me. I don't really mind helping people carry their stuff, but it goes against my entire travel philosophy. I believe everyone should be responsible for their own luggage. I bought a shirt today and to accommodate it I threw one of my old shirts away. . . . Mom on the other hand just keeps acquiring more and more stuff, like someone out of *A Passage to India*. In a couple of weeks I know there will be a new Romps and we're going to need a family of Sherpas.

In Guangzhou we happened to buy each other gifts. I bought Mom a painting done on a piece of silk that weighs a few ounces and could easily fold up to fit in your back pocket. She bought me (and Colin) a clunky, cumbersome walking stick that has to be carried separately as a carry-on item for the next month. And I feel bad saying it. I know it's the thought that counts, and it was sweet of her to think of us, but . . .

▶ ▶ ▶

So she did, in transactions described by Colin:

Mom and Fiona went off to secure copious amounts of huge, heavy, cumbersome things that we don't have enough bags or hands to carry. . . . Big baskets of snakeskins, dried bugs, stretched lizard skins . . . this first section we walked through seemed like the pharmacy aisle, no doubt chock full of remedies for Conor's current, er, work stoppage. Lots of great smells; aromas I can't really describe because I've never smelled anything like them before and therefore have no useful frame of descriptive reference. . . . I could say musky, pungent, bitter, or whatever, but that hardly gets the job done. . . .

On Trinket Street, Mom got down to some serious haggling, with Fiona watching the way a bear cub would watch Mama Bear swat a salmon out of the river. I expressed my amazement

LOTS OF GREAT SMELLS; AROMAS I CAN'T REALLY DESCRIBE BECAUSE I'VE NEVER SMELLED ANYTHING LIKE THEM BEFORE AND THEREFORE HAVE NO USEFUL FRAME OF DESCRIPTIVE REFERENCE....I COULD SAY MUSKY, PUNGENT, BITTER, OR WHATEVER, BUT THAT HARDLY GETS THE JOB DONE....

—COLIN

"Gross!"

"Like a bear cub being trained by its mother."

I TRIED TO MAKE A VISUAL JOKE BY TRYING TO WRITE SOME CHINESE IN THE BOOK. I DON'T KNOW HOW FUNNY THEY THOUGHT IT WAS. MAYBE THEY DIDN'T GET IT. MAYBE I WAS UNINTENTIONALLY SAYING SOMETHING ABOUT HIS MAMA.   —CONOR

at Mom's stamina for this sort of thing. Richard, though, put it into perspective with a sweeping wave of his arm back toward the bazaar full of yelling, carting, weighing, and sampling: "Colin, she is one of them."

For Conor, though, it was no fun at all:

Stall after stall of people selling weird roots, dead snakes, seahorses, starfish, dragonflies, and lots of other things that I couldn't begin to identify. People pulling on your shirt, trying to get you to buy their stuff. And haggling. I hate haggling so much that I'll allow myself to get ripped off. . . . I was waiting for the rest of the group, jotting down some notes in my notebook, and I started to draw a crowd of poor, sort of toughlooking young Chinese guys. They were looking over my shoulder to see what I was writing. One guy, the toughestlooking one of the bunch, wanted to get a better look so I let him flip through the pages to "read" the rest of my notes. It's not like he could read it. I had to tell them what language it was. I said, "English" and pointed at the pages. I swear I could see the hostility light up his eyes. It kind of freaked me out. To lighten the situation, I tried to make a visual joke by trying to write some Chinese in the book. I don't know how funny they thought it was. Maybe they didn't get it. Maybe I was unintentionally saying something about his mama.

▲ ▲ ▲

BEYOND TIANANMEN SQUARE

The 1989 massacre of students demanding democracy in Tiananmen Square may be seen one day as a prologue to greater Chinese disasters.

The dissenters who gathered there guessed wrong about the timing of the political modernization of the world's largest nation.

Communism is dead in China, at least as ideology or discipline. But the Communists still have the offices and the might to keep the peace and collect bribes. But the old masters are learning that enforcing laws and collecting taxes in a freer country is more difficult than breaking and bending people to totalitarianism. People laugh at party dogma and do their best to avoid party apparatus. The problem for the now and future leaders of China is to find a new ideology to bind the billion together—give them something to believe in beyond dollars.

At the moment, the rulers are looking back to the good old days—five centuries before the birth of Christ. From President Jiang Zemin down, the Communists have begun chanting the classic doctrine of Confucius, a man and legend they once scorned. Xinhua, the government's news agency, now calls Confucianism "good medicine for a crisis of morality."

It's a good fit, at least on paper. Confucianism teaches obedience. It is a discipline that grants, respects, and accepts the authority of fathers and rulers.

China looks great. Relatively. By that I mean the parts seen regularly by outsiders, or at least the parts of it people like me get to see regularly. There are prosperous cities and smiling people on land where men and women worked like animals to grow rice only ten or fifteen years ago. But all the news of economic growth and confident trade negotiations with American and European companies obscure the fact that an old order is collapsing and will do anything within its power to survive as long as possible.

We all got together for lunch at the White Swan Hotel, a fifteen-year-old, world-class hotel that was an early symbol of China's rejoining the world after the brutal and insane excesses of the Cultural Revolution at the end of the 1960s. I remembered sitting in the gigantic lobby on a misty afternoon not long after the hotel opened feeling like an alien, of the flying saucer kind, as I watched junks and battered cargo ships move slowly up and down the Pearl River.

Colin wrote:

A pretty swank hotel. A big indoor waterfall, huge jade sculptures that must have weighed a thousand pounds, ornate, gilded cages of birds.

One after another, Chinese families came in, posing for photos in front of the waterfall, this rare example of luxury in their country. An example of how far they'd come, according to Richard, who said there used to be photographers everywhere because families were too poor to afford their own cameras.

It was here, in the dim sum restaurant, that Mom first reintroduced her Chinese translation of mineral water: "Sohdah." (For maximum effect, utter at full volume.) The word was used in all languages. . . .

At lunch I inadvertently ate chicken feet, but to my credit, I didn't like them. After every dish was emptied except the one with the gristly meat, Richard asked if anybody had tried it. I said that I had and he asked what I thought. I asked him what it was. He laughed. I told him I thought it was a little bony. .

After lunch, the men, Colin, Conor, and I, deserted the ladies to walk around Shamian Island, the old quarter of the city reserved for foreign "concessions" in the nineteenth century. That's when British, French, Americans, and Germans won their wars to bring Christianity and opium to the natives. Now we're selling Boeing and Salems. The island was crumbling when I last saw it, but the grand European-style homes and old churches, used then as mass housing and small factories, are being restored now. There are neat bicycle parking lots for construction workers with a drawing of a bike over the English words: "Take Care of Stations."

This was Conor's description:

Mellow, low stress level. It was a really cool area, unique as far as what I've seen in Asia—old colonial buildings on wide avenues. Huge old trees with Spanish moss hanging from the limbs, an oasis in this hectic city. It had the feel of a place from a different age, like somewhere out of a Gabriel García Márquez story (except everyone was Chinese, not South American). . . . It was also about ninety degrees and humid, which tends to bring out the quiet side of folks. People were basically just sitting quietly in the shade, speaking in hushed tones.

A young Chinese guy, about twenty, came up to me and asked (in a British accent): "Excuse me, are you from the United States? Because I heard you speaking American English. . . . " We chatted a little and he told me that he was in art school. I asked him if he was a painter and he gave the universal answer: "I try to be." After that I had no choice but to buy

"Excuse me, are you from the United States?"

one of his paintings, for Mom. It was a traditional Chinese painting—a vertical flower arrangement on green silk. It's weird to see a young guy like that doing traditional (in my view sterile) paintings like that. Anyway, I decided not to tell him that I had just seen the finest works of traditional Chinese art in the world and that he would probably never get to see them because they're locked up in a museum across the way in Taiwan.

Meanwhile, Catherine wrote:

Fiona and I set off to go to the busy commercial part of town on Liuersan Lu. We stopped in the Post Office, where she bought a stamp album and several magnificent stamps for about $1.20 to add to a collection that swelled as we went from country to country. We also checked out the main department store, the Nan Fang, right on the river. We bought a small tapestry of pandas woven into fabric for a friend of

Fiona's—and picked up some walking canes as presents. And we had fun. The store is not even close to world standards, but every floor was crowded with people buying things like household appliances.

"THEY WORE CLOTHES LIKE US, ONLY TIGHTER," ADDED FIONA.

"Buying" products, all made in China, was the story as far as I was concerned because I remembered walking empty aisles in this store fourteen years ago. The closest anyone came to buying then was standing in the streets looking into dusty windows at black-and-white televisions no one could afford. The window shoppers of yore were all dressed in the same peasant costume. Now they have televisions of their own and the old-style pajamas are gone in the city. Women dress in modest, but modern fashion. . . . Little girls' dresses in stores were very fancy with lace and ruffles."They wore clothes like us, only tighter," added Fiona.

We all got together again at a street market. Catherine and Fiona emerged carrying stunning old door and window panels from the houses in this city being torn down, as in Shanghai, to make room for new foreign businessmen and the new towers of modernizing China.

Colin sensed a growing revolt:

Richard has begun insisting that we ship things home if we continue to aquire baubles at this rate. But his insistence means nothing in the face of Mom's will. She has decided that all will be carried. For the duration. If we ship it back, the cost of doing so negates any bargains gotten on the road. She also seems to think that she has happened upon an infinitely stuffable piece of luggage with magical properties. We call it "Romps," in memory of a bag with that name on its side that we once dragged through South Asia years ago, saying it carried our dead uncle.

Finally, this time we all had the same answer to Catherine's question of whether this country will be important in our lifetimes. "Yes!" each of us said.

Why? We all had the same answer again, for better or worse: "One billion reasons."

Chapter 6

DENPASAR

I did not want to go to Bali, expecting it would be something like Miami Beach in costume. "Ruined!" I was sure. By "Them!" Of course, "we" are "them"—the "them" liberated or launched as world travelers by the miracle vehicle, the magic carpet: the jet plane.

Catherine's heavy suitcase of travel files included a 1969 *National Geographic* article talking about efforts to preserve Balinese culture because, by then, forty travelers or tourists were coming every day. Well, ruin is in the eye of the beholder. A very rich man able to see the world before the jets, Averell Harriman, once told me, quite unself-consciously, that it was too bad that ordinary people could now go to the wonderful places once reserved for people like him. The South of France was one example he used. Ruined by "them"—or "us."

As for Bali, before we came in great numbers, it had become a place of picturesque poverty—and of neighbor killing neighbor. In 1965, called "the Year of Living Dangerously" by Indonesians, forty thousand people were killed in Bali during the planned slaughter of Communists and "sympathizers" that escalated beyond that horror into a national bloodbath of ethnic and religious revenge and personal pillage—a settling of scores beyond the imagination of outsiders. In all of Indonesia, the more than thirteen thousand islands once called the Dutch East Indies, the death toll was estimated to be at least a hundred thousand.

"What happened here?" asked Colin. "Tell me about that year." You are always flattered when your kids think you actually know something they don't, but there is so much to tell about Indonesia. It is the fourth-largest country in the world (with almost 200 million people, it ranks just behind the United States) and this was the first of four stops we planned in the great archipelago stretching more than three thousand miles across southern seas from Malaysia to Australia.

Now Bali is indeed often crowded with "them," unloaded from jet planes and cruise ships. It is also irresistible, this Hindu island in the world's largest Muslim country, with miles of shops for T-shirts, for crafts, for most anything the tourists want. The narrow roads were jammed from airport to beach, jammed with Toyota and Suzuki four-wheel drive, big air-conditioned vehicles. Somebody is making money here. We were exhausted, reeling, by the time we reached our hotel at eight o'clock at night after two plane rides, a three-hour stopover at Singapore, and an hour in an Indonesian Customs line, only to be turned away to fill out two more forms. And then there was the half-hour in the van sent by the hotel, the Bali Padma.

But the temperature was only 84 degrees, cool compared to Japan and three Chinas. A few skewers of pork and a bottle of local beer and I was ready for bed. The younger gentlemen headed straight for town, such as it is. And this was Colin's report:

> Australians everywhere, the locals address you as "mate." The Balinese are extremely physical, putting their arms around you and patting you on the back all the time . . . at first I thought it was a pickpocket decoy, but it turned out to be just the Balinese way, and it's a good way, and I'm a suspicious, small-minded bastard.
>
> Conor and I went looking for some festivities and cheap hats, both of which we found in abundance. I picked up an assortment of wide-brimmed lids for my precancerous condition, and a sharp pair of shorts for two bucks before we hit the main drag. We ducked into an open-air bar—again no walls—and were cordially greeted by a barman who was obsessed with Richie Sambora. The place was plastered with photos of previous wild nights—lampshade-wearing revelers and the like. As we spent the next few hours chatting with various partyers who passed through, Indonesian and foreign vacationers, it became clear that the bar-strewn road that rings Bali is the Bourbon Street of Asia: open-air bars luring people

in with gimmicky touches (Australian rules football on the tube; cover bands doing Guns n' Roses and Nirvana; Fuzzy Navels, etc.), the day of the week never being an issue because none of the customers ever have to work the next day—just lay on the beach until their annual two weeks expires. The house band kicked out the Jimmy Cliff covers with gusto that night, as I'm sure they do every night. It was seventy-five degrees that night, as I'm sure it is every night. . . . Conor and I got our asses kicked at billiards before calling it a night and walking back to the hotel.

His brother saw it this way:

This was the first place on this trip that I was able to easily talk to people. The people are great. Really friendly. Really mellow . . . A guy named Sandy, from Jakarta, was a drummer in a rock band. He was on vacation. He was broke. I bought him a beer, he showed me pictures of his family. The other guy, whose name I didn't catch, was a real metal head—Metallica, Deep Purple, Ozzy Osbourne, Sepultura, and especially (strangely) Richie Sambora, the guitarist from Bon Jovi. He was really into the fact that Richie had ended up marrying Tommy Lee's (the drummer from Mötley Crüe) ex-wife Heather Locklear. "The old Mötley Crüe . . . [he gave the thumbs-up sign]. Now . . . [thumbs down]." I had to agree with him. Colin and I hung out for a while, talking with some Aussies, getting schooled by the local pool sharks, and watching the Balinese cover band. When we left they were playing Nirvana's "Smells Like Teen Spirit." I thought that was funny.

Reading that, I thought . . . Nothing.

I did not have the vaguest idea what these guys were talking about, that part of my brain being filled with tunes and lyrics now called "Golden Oldies." If we fade with age, it may be because we can hear two beats of a song from 1958, three minutes of nonsense we have not heard in more than thirty years, and remember every word, every note, every affectation and pathetic vocal trick of a teenager from Philadelphia in an echo chamber. How can this be?

◂▴▴

WHAT IS INDONESIA?

Indonesia may be the most interesting country in the world as the twenty-first century begins. The country's thirteen thousand islands span thousands of miles and several centuries, with citizens ranging from world-class businessmen with private pilots in Bali to "former" cannibals and headhunters (there is some dispute about whether old habits are really dead) living in treehouses in Irian Jaya on the island of New Guinea.

The population is growing at almost 2 percent a year. Most of the islands of the archipelago are uninhabited, but one of them, Java, has a population as large as any country in Europe. The per capita income is up to seven hundred dollars or so a year. The literacy rate is said to be 82 percent, but that figure is probably made up. Life expectancy is sixty-three years. There is one telephone for every eighty-five people and one television for every sixteen.

It was called the Dutch East Indies for 350 years of colonial rule by Holland until the Dutch army was driven out and independence won in 1949. Officially, Indonesia is a democracy—"guided democracy" is the phrase its leaders use—but it has been under military rule for almost its entire history. President Suharto came to power in a military coup in 1966. Emergency laws still require government permission for any meetings of more than five people, including concerts or theatrical performances.

▸▸▸

Conor was the first one up the next morning and reported:

I accidentally woke up early and couldn't get back to sleep so I went down to check the surf. First time in the Indian Ocean.

It was just beach break in front of the hotel but it looked pretty good—solidly overhead and early enough and the right tide for it to be clean and peaky. I rented a little tri-fin from some guy on the beach (seven bucks American for two hours) and paddled out. I was really stoked to be surfing in Bali. It's one of those things that I always sort of dreamed about in the back of my mind. I caught a few waves, nothing really too outstanding, I wasn't really used to the board or to the break. But it was definitely fun. Then the conditions started to change and I got continually pounded by eight- and nine-foot closeouts. I somehow managed to get caught inside for every set. It was pretty sloppy by the time my two hours were up. So it wasn't the session of my lifetime but it was cool. I never made it to Uluwatu, one of the premier lefts in the world, and I'm sure I'll be chastised by a lot of my surfer buddies, but what the hell. This is not a surfing trip, and to tell you the truth, with the rigorous pace we're keeping I just felt like I could do without another excursion to see something that I wouldn't be able to fully appreciate, what with having to leave for the hills later in the afternoon . . . You know?

No, not exactly. While Conor was surfing, Catherine and I appeared with our books and Colin came out to record this all for posterity with a beautiful old Bolex 16-millimeter movie camera he loves. Fiona began her day out on the beach, bargaining with a local kite-maker. She wrote:

> Then I went over to this giant pool. One section has soccer goals for in-pool games, one has basketball hoops for games, and there are two empty sections for swimming. And there's an in-pool bar for the Australians—drink, drink, drink.

That last line was from a taxi driver the night before, who said: "Oh, we love the Australians. Disco and drink, drink, drink." Sure enough, most of the guests were Australians and they took about every seat in the water bar in the shallow end of the pool, but they weren't drinking water. Fiona settled for banana juice. So did her father, but he thought it was the worst!

Catherine saw these things a little differently than I did, particularly when it came to my "reading":

It was the first visit for all of us. I booked through a Los Angeles tour broker which specializes in Indonesia. We stayed in the Kuta-Legian Beach area so Conor could surf. Our hotel was affordable, enormous, and beautiful, with grounds right on the ocean, with high wooden-ceilinged public rooms and restaurants open to the air. . . . I loved sitting under a palm tree in a chaise-lounge looking out at the rolling surf. Richard snoozed.

Fiona negotiated for a lovely silk kite—shaped like a bird. She got the price she wanted, 10,000 rupiahs, about $4.50. . . . Around me, people took advantage of the masseuses who went from chaise to chaise offering what looked like their very pleasurable services. . . . Conor suddenly appeared with dreadlocks all over his head, looking quite horrifying. He said that three young women had braided his hair for about ten dollars. He must have had about eighty braids. . . . It had been too long since I fully enjoyed a plunge in the ocean, but the warm waters and the rolling surf lured me in. It was great. The waves had broken and rolled toward the shore with so much power that one grabbed me and tossed me about. I lost my glasses, which I had foolishly brought into the surf. Kuta Beach is a little tacky and touristy—but it's also fun. One of the most perfect family vacation destinations I can remember. The other guests were from New Zealand, Japan, Australia, and countries throughout Europe. Not too many Americans. They must stay over on Nusa Dua.

Out of the waves, Conor picked up his story:

Hanging around the hotel, Colin and I saw lots of Australian kids with really stupid-looking corn-row hairstyles with beads in the braids that Balinese girls do. I decided I had to have it done. So after lunch I walked out down the street and stopped at the first girl who said, "I blade yoh haih?" She told me her name was Susanna. After agreeing on a price (I'm sure I was getting ripped off) I sat down on her mat and she and two of her friends, Lisa and Mona Lisa, went to work.

Now, I had only cut a deal with Susanna, so the whole time they were tugging at my hair, Lisa and Mona Lisa kept saying things like, "Connah, you give me good tip, honey? I helping, do good job," and "Come on, Spunky. Three girls working, one girl take three hour. You give tip, okay? You remember my name, Connah? Lisa and Mona Lisa. You no forget us, okay?" (They were really good about remembering names. Every tourist who walked by they called out to by name— "Hi Carol! How are you? Good! You come back later, okay?") One of the girls, Lisa, I think, even started singing. First, she began humming some traditional Balinese melody, and then adding words: "Connah, you give good tip, okay? Three girls do such good job. You give ten thousand each." It was really very funny and everyone had a good laugh over it. When I say everyone I must explain that there was a crowd around me— other braid girls and masseuses, guys trying relentlessly to sell me rings and watches and perfume, friends just sitting in the shade eating lunch, curious little kids. They really liked it

> ...AFTER LUNCH I WALKED OUT DOWN THE STREET AND STOPPED AT THE FIRST GIRL WHO SAID "I BLADE YOH HAIH?" SHE TOLD ME HER NAME WAS SUSANNA. AFTER AGREEING ON A PRICE (I'M SURE I WAS GETTING RIPPED OFF) I SAT DOWN ON HER MAT AND SHE AND TWO OF HER FRIENDS, LISA AND MONA LISA, WENT TO WORK. —CONOR

"Quite horrifying" to a mother.

Fiona gets her kite.

when I started singing back to her in the same melody: "Hurry, are we almost finished? It is taking so long. I look in the mirror and maybe give you tip."

Their explanation was flattery: "Why you have thick haih? You haih so thick, take long time. Very handsome. You have girlfriend in America? Susanna, she love you." (They all laughed.) "You come live Bali, Susanna be you girlfriend." More laughs, with Susanna playing the part of the silent blushing schoolgirl. These are young, pretty girls. It was great. When they finished I paid up. Lisa and Mona Lisa pretended to be unhappy with their tips. I explained to them that they should get a cut from Susanna, and I'm sure they did. After all, how much can I allow myself to get ripped off? I went back to the hotel room to look at my new 'do in the mirror. I looked at least as stupid as any of those Aussies. I figured it was a success.

Back at the hotel it was a total St. Tropez-in-the-tropics scene. International tourists (German, French, English, Australian, Japanese, American) just lounging in the sun doing nothing or next to nothing. Letting it all hang out. Kids horsing around in the pool, beautiful topless women getting tan, fruffi tropical cocktails, the whole bit. Very relaxing.

The tanners stayed on the beach and Catherine, Fiona, and I headed into the hills of Bali, to a village called Ubud. Hours later, they followed. Wrote Colin:

Around sunset, Conor and I got our own taxi to follow the others up to the hills. Our driver briefed us on the various handicraft specialties of the towns we drove through, especially quick to point out the "reputable" places where his friends and relatives worked. At one point our momentum dragged to a near standstill as we came upon some celebratory procession that spanned from one side of the road to the other.

It was a volleyball team and its followers dancing and chanting and looking like they were all gonna have a big night; they had just won an important game and there were friendly salutes as our car inched by.

Chapter 7

UBUD

D awn comes so suddenly to Bali that it has been called "the morning of the world." On one of those mornings, Conor wrote:

Ubud is maybe the most beautiful place I've ever been. It made me think of the character in *Apocalypse Now* who instead of killing Colonel Kurtz decides to join him, writing a postcard to his family back in America that reads, "Sell the house, sell the car, sell the kids, I'm never coming home." The view from our room down a jungle canyon with women walking single-file up winding, narrow trails in colorful outfits with baskets balanced on their heads and the sea off on the horizon was fab. I only wish Mom and Richard didn't feel compelled to wake me up at dawn to appreciate it.

In the Hindu legends that are at the soul of Balinese life, the evil spirits are in the sea. Few of the people swim or even walk the beach. The ocean is to be feared. The gods who protect the Balinese and their island are in the mountains. So perhaps the gods are protecting them now against

> UBUD IS MAYBE THE MOST BEAUTIFUL PLACE I'VE EVER BEEN. IT MADE ME THINK OF THE CHARACTER IN *APOCALYPSE NOW* WHO INSTEAD OF KILLING COLONEL KURTZ DECIDES TO JOIN HIM, WRITING A POSTCARD TO HIS FAMILY BACK IN AMERICA THAT READS, "SELL THE HOUSE, SELL THE CAR, SELL THE KIDS, I'M NEVER COMING HOME." —CONOR

us, the prosperous foreigners who congregate at the water's edge. Ubud is strung out along a gorge and a river valley in the Gianyar hills twenty miles above the beach. It is not undiscovered but neither is it overrun. The Villa Bukit, where we stayed in two seventy-five-dollar-a-night "huts," is a collection of thatched-roof cottages laid out along the rim of the canyon that Conor saw as he woke up. In our hut, Fiona woke, looked over the warm palmy jungle, and said: "This is the way I was meant to live. Do they serve breakfast in bed?"

No, they didn't. We had to walk all of fifty yards or so down the hill to the Villa's restaurant. That was one of the world's simplest and most beautiful buildings, a thatched-roof, open-sided platform

Fiona on the Villa Bukit: "This is the way I was meant to live."

A Barong dance in Batubala.

hanging out over "our" canyon. Breakfast, for us, was a wonderful flying saucer attack of banana pancakes and mounds of melon and papaya. An Indonesian family next to us, from Jakarta, had heaping plates of *nasi goreng,* a rice and curry dish. They were pumping such impressive amounts of chili sauce that Colin murmured, "Wow!"

Catherine and I had been to Indonesia once before, in 1987, both doing some work in Jakarta, which is on the island of Java. We took a train to Bandung, a small city that was once a hill station for the Dutch rulers of the Indies. The route up crossed over dozens of breathtaking (literally) bridges that jumped from mountain to mountain. The gorges below us were terraced to use as rice paddies and most

of those squares of water were the vibrating green color of young rice shoots. My reaction that day eight years earlier was exactly the same as Conor's when he woke up in Ubud. It was the most beautiful of sights, perfect for me because I am more attracted to the works of man than the works of nature—the mountains, the bridges, and the paddies being worked by men and women who often looked up to wave brought all the beauties together for me. There are many levels of life in Indonesia, good and bad, some of them denied or carefully hidden from outsiders, but, God! it's a stunning place.

The hills of Bali, not as steep as those in Java, are terraced, too. The old wooden and thatch architecture suits the surroundings and the newer building style might be called red brick templar, a visual echo of the Hindu temples everywhere in the mountains. The villages along the ridges are devoted to different crafts or ornate galleries of Balinese arts—painting, furniture, jewelry, masks, small home temples, the spiritual good-and-evil dances from the Mahābhārata, the holy book of Hinduism, in the amphitheaters of temples from centuries long past—all a celebration of artistic expression. The diversity of the wood carving or wood and stone sculpture shows in the prices, ranging from a dollar or two to fifty thousand dollars.

We were talking about Balinese cremation ceremonies, described in the thirty-year-old *National Geographic* article, when our car was stopped by a parade across the road. Men and women in traditional dress, the women wearing colorful sarong skirts with black lace tops, and the men with black shirts and sarongs, were on their way to a cremation, following a white-covered bier carried by ten men, all crossing the road toward a sign that read: KAPALI GROUP'S CREMATORIUM.

That night, in what was once the pavilion of a palace in the town, we all went to a performance of a local Legong dance troupe, one of the many variations of dance and puppet shows that make Indonesia quite different from most of the world. The performances, based on both the Mahābhārata and local lore, seem to be the ongoing literature of the islands set to the music of ancient percussion instruments, particularly the *gamelan*. Exaggerating a bit, it is, in Western cultural terms, something like nightly Shakespeare and (or on) television. I say that because once, in Bandung, we went to a *wayang golek* performance—the same tales, using puppets instead of dancers and actors—in a theater that might be a modern equivalent of the Globe in seventeenth-century London. Food shops ringed the auditorium, the play went on all through the night, and spectators were free to roam, sit, and chat anywhere they wanted to, including on the stage with the musicians and the play's director, who was the chief puppeteer.

During the wars against both the Japanese and the Dutch in the 1940s, the dances and plays were used to transmit news and messages through changes in action and dialogue that were incomprehensible to enemies. In fact, while we were in Indonesia this time, Mohammad, who uses only one name like many Indonesians, a reporter and former editor of *Tempo,* a news magazine shut down by government order the year before, presented an eight-hour shadow play, a form of *wayang* with two-dimensional puppets behind a back-lit screen. The subject, in his words, was: "The mania of control, the intolerance to people with different opinions."

The politics I get better than the dance; most all of that is as incomprehensible to me as to the more ignorant of government censors. But Catherine appreciated the Bali versions more than I did and she wrote:

> The performances are graceful, but difficult to describe. In the *Legong* dance three girls in lovely, colorful costumes dance to entertain the king. They have extraordinary control over their eyes and their neck and head muscles, which all move in coordination with their arms, hands, fingers, feet, and toes. . . . The next day we watched the *Barong* dance in an open-air temple in Batubala, the stone carving village. Even in simple settings, the costumes are colorful and the movements are controlled in a way not familiar to the dances of the West. The *Barong* was a

struggle between good and evil. Witches take possession of people and, with overtones of the Bible and the story of Abraham and Isaac, one of the characters is willing to sacrifice her son. . . . Ultimately there is a fight between the spirits representing good and evil. Onstage, as in life, it is not easy for good to triumph without the help of other spirits and characters.

Conor added that night:

I was glad to have seen it, but the pacing was a little slow for my American commercialized MTV quick-cut attention span. Colin and I also walked through the main open-air market in town. Like the one in Guanzghou it seemed as if it were from another century. (Even more so actually because of the provincial dress and the fact that it was in a small village as opposed to a city of 9 million.) Lots of fruits and vegetables and dried spices that I have never seen before.

▴ ▴ ▴

TO SHOP OR NOT TO SHOP

There are at least two sides to any story—or any family. Here is a tale of three O'Neills and a Reeves. The subject is shopping.

Said Catherine in Ubud and back home in Los Angeles:

A word must be said about the lovely things which now decorate the rooms of our house. I regretted, after previous trips, that I had not been open enough to the beauty around me. So I had decided that I wanted to return with visual expressions of the aesthetic sensibility of Indonesia. I brought along bubble wrap and an extra bag.

The men just could not have cared less about shopping, but Fiona and I found each other; we were "soul mates." She loved looking at the items in the bazaar. (We had given her fifteen dollars per country to spend on things she wanted.) Her

Okay? On its way to our living room wall. Conor can carry it.

Who is that masked girl?

first purchase was a silk-screened kite which she bought on Kuta Beach. She and I consulted on colored wood carvings of people in procession (now in the living room), paintings with intricate designs of Balinese dancers (now in the bathroom), a painting which we gave Richard of Balinese field workers (now in our entry hall), *wayang golek* puppets (displayed by the fireplace), a Buddha head, a Chinese ceramic pillow and celadon jars—all in the living room now. These last two were bought in the antique bazaar of Jakarta. . . . We even have a beautiful new batik suitcase, which I bought for fifteen dollars to carry our new "treasures."

"Did you see it? Did you see it?" was the word passing from one to another of our party. "The Batik" was the new Romps.

Commented Colin:

Billed as an "artists' colony," but more accurately described as a "trinket-peddlers' colony," which is not to say that it isn't completely soothing and enjoyable. And the trinkets are inexpensive and beautiful: lots of shirts made of printed and woven Balinese cloth; wood and stone carvings that aren't spit out by machines; high-quality bags and hats . . . all to be had for a song. Thus far in the trip, I have been self-righteous in my criticizing of Mom for her obsession with baubles, but in Ubud I was seduced by the local crafts . . . and stocked up accordingly.

Mom. She's acquired a second bauble bag now—hereafter described as "The Batik bag." At the Denpasar airport, we needed three porters. And we still had five bags waiting in the Singapore airport, where we had checked them while changing planes between Hong Kong and Bali.

▶ ▶ ▶

Some of this, to be sure, is a come-on for tourists. The best restaurant in the hills, Murni's Warung, another set of thatched platforms cantilevered down a river gorge along the main road, displays a small reprint of a favorable newspaper review—from the travel section of the *New York Times*. The same *Times* piece included the standard interview with the standard old-timer expatriate, a Spanish artist in this case. He had come to Ubud thirty years before when it was, to him, an unspoiled paradise and then "they" came and ruined it. Please. Other old-timers we spent time with remembered a poor and dispirited place where dancers in tatty costumes and artisans without inspiration went through the motions of their culture for the loose change of foreigners. Times change and so do foreigners. The money the tourists bring may demean the culture of Bali, but they are also subsidizing and preserving it.

The Balinese, after all, were doing these things for and to themselves for a very long time before the Reeveses and O'Neills and others like us came by. Many of the craft villages have statues or other works by the roadside or on the little traffic circles that divert traffic their way. One of them touched my own vein of romanticism: a statue of a small boy on a water buffalo looking down at a book in his hands as the animal plodded along. A version of the young Abe Lincoln reading by firelight.

The next day Catherine wrote:

I worry about a lot of things. One of them is rabies, or anything else carried by animals. That particular worry peaked when we all visited the Monkey Forest in the hills, a small national park that was a must-see once Fiona heard about it. . . . One hundred and sixty sacred and very aggressive monkeys were walking around and trying to grab things from tourists. Fiona is so animal-friendly that both her father and I were in a quiet panic. We did not want to ruin her enthusiasm for animals . . . but we definitely *did not* want her bitten. We encouraged distance; still one of the animals bared his teeth when Fiona wasn't fast enough with a peanut. And then we saw an adult man, one of a group of Germans, with a bunch of small bananas in his hand. A monkey spotted it, too, leaping onto the man's head to try and grab the bananas. He and his friends had all they could do to get the angry monkey literally off his back. We did not stay too much longer in the famous and revered Monkey Forest.

Colin picked up:

After we'd had our fill of the monkeys, Richard, Fiona, and Mom headed off to a neighboring village, presumably to buy stuff, and Conor and I decided to spend the day on our own, exploring the area on foot. We started walking in the direction of the hotel, stepping over mad dogs and feeling quite like Englishmen. ["By American standards they are pretty mangy and they all seem to be the same strain of mutt," said Conor. "Medium build, pointy ears, medium length, and invariably filthy coat with varied markings."]

It was a long, memorable walk. The best way to really check out this town. After a few detours—checking out the local open-air market, grabbing a drink and some cold soup— we arrived back at our hotel a few hours later. I had always heard that Bali was amazing, but treated those reviews cautiously, thinking they were just the ravings of hard-core surfers and people who like to sit in the sun no matter where it is. But by the time we started packing to leave, I understood that I would soon be spreading that same word. . . .

By the time we left for the airport for the flight to Yogyakarta, we and the bags had expanded to a caravan of two cars. Colin reported from car one:

Very mellow and calm ride to the airport. Beautiful scenery, radio playing . . . It was a clear, sunny day with a strong breeze, and as we got down to sea level, the kites started appearing. The Balinese are serious about kites and this was a great day for flying. The kites they fly are huge—we passed a group of eight guys carrying a single kite along the road—and

you could see them miles off in the distance. . . . I will definitely return to Bali.

"This was A-plus," said Catherine as we followed in the second
car. I thought so, too. The landscape was beautiful. People were laughing wherever we went—and that's wonderfully contagious.

Looking out the window as we drove down past the shops on
Ubud's main street, Fiona said: "They sweep and sweep, whether it's
dirty or clean." Then she turned to me and offered a ten-year-old's
highest praise: "This is fun! I like going around the world," she said.

So do I.

Chapter 8

YOGYAKARTA

"This will be my first wonder of the world," said Fiona on the short flight from Bali to Yogyakarta, the capital city of the sultans of Java. But before there were sultans there was the wonder of Borobudur. The great Buddhist temple twenty-five miles outside the city was built over one hundred years in the eighth and ninth centuries, with thousands of individual carvings and bas-reliefs in a Hindu manner. Hidden for centuries under layers of volcanic ash, it can be compared only with the pyramids and Angkor Wat in Cambodia.

Colin's commentary began:

> Landed at a little airport with a comical baggage system. Richard had a bit of a fit, which he thought was because of something Conor and I did, but was actually because of the ridiculous amount of luggage we have. . . . Mom and Richard went off to have a quiet dinner alone, while Conor and I dined on a scrumptious buffet of Indonesian food at a floating restaurant, sitting shoeless on the floor, with geckos crawling on the ceiling and the occasional bat swooping through the wall-less room. . . .
>
> We stayed at the Ambarrukmo Palace Hotel. Serviceable at ninety dollars-a-night—a 1950s-modern hotel built on the grounds of an old palace in what is now a city of 3 mil-

"THIS WILL BE MY FIRST WONDER OF THE WORLD," SAID FIONA ON THE SHORT FLIGHT FROM BALI TO YOGYAKARTA, THE CAPITAL CITY OF THE SULTANS OF JAVA.

98

lion people. We, the parents, slipped out to see a production of the Hindu epic *Ramayana* under the stars. Catherine wrote:

> I had always wanted to come to Yogyakarta for another glimpse of Javanese culture and history. Again, I was not disappointed. . . . We knew the basic story from Peter Brook's twelve-hour production of the Mahābhārata, which we saw when we lived in Paris during the 1980s. But now I understood more about where Brook discovered some of the sweeping movements and stylized posing of the actors. . . . Prince Rama's true love Sinta is stolen from him and great adventures ensue. When Rama finally sees her again, he doubts her purity—and asks her to take a "holy bathing" by jumping into a burning fire. I guess it's always been tough being a woman.

Colin moved on with his adventures, writing: "The next morning we hired a van to take us to Borobudur. Mom helpfully pointed things out: 'Look at all the stones! . . . Look, we're on a bridge! . . . Look, a motorcycle parking shed! . . . ' "

He was probably exaggerating. I don't remember any shed—or having a fit, either. And I did not know where Conor got the hat he was using to protect his Irish head from the sun. It looked like a doily and I began saying, "Who's the guy in the girl's hat?"—a bit of around-the-world humor I do not think he appreciated.

Said Conor:

> The blistering pace of this trip was starting to catch up with me, not just the travel but the number of events crammed into each day and the responsibility of coherently taking it all in and then writing about it. Colin was feeling the same way, so on the drive out to Borobudur we were reduced to wisecracking imbeciles in the back of the minivan.

Actually it was great fun. The guys reverted, the years falling away, with great good humor, beginning to punch each other—these guys filled the spare moments of childhood beating the hell out of each other—and calling, "Mom! Did you see what he did? . . . He did it first . . . Mom! Fiona's making fun of me." I don't know about them, but I loved it. Giddy time.

▲ ▲ ▲

FIONA'S LIFELINE

One of the specialties of the Ambarruko Palace in Yogyakarta was the fortune-teller in the corner of the lobby next to the bellman's desk, where there would be a shoeshine stand in an American hotel. He was very old, or looked that way, and appropriately wizened. He wore a turban and his name was Gunesaputro.

Fiona was intrigued. After questions about numerology and searches across her young palms—with a bellman translating—Fiona received a piece of tissue-thin paper with a handwritten future.

Her lucky number is thirteen. Her prophet is Adam. She will be married and have two children. She will work for a company or for a government. Her dim star will last between the ages of twenty and thirty. After that her bright star will emerge.

▶ ▶ ▶

Fiona's fortune: "A bright star emerging . . ."

This was Catherine's description of Borobudur:

It is colossal and it is amazing to realize that it was built two centuries before Angkor Wat. Giants built this place, but for more than ten centuries it lay under blankets of volcanic ash, ignored and feared by the local people, who had converted to Hinduism . . . and later to Islam. It is an enormous stupa built on several terraces. Each terrace has stone relief carvings depicting different scenes from the life journey of Buddha. If you walk in a clockwise circle on each level, you will follow a story through. There are fourteen hundred narratives carved on the terrace. The highest terrace opens up to reveal seventy-one bell-shaped carvings, many with statues of Buddha inside. Legend says that if you can touch a particular part of the body of one of these Buddhas your wish will come true. Lines of Japanese tourists were straining to reach a Buddha 150 feet above the base of a high hill. Fiona and I were, too. We twisted and turned ourselves reaching inside the bell where, it is said, if you touch Buddha's toe you will be blessed.

THE HIGHEST TERRACE OPENS UP TO REVEAL SEVENTY-ONE BELL-SHAPED CARVINGS, MANY WITH STATUES OF BUDDHA INSIDE. LEGEND SAYS THAT IF YOU TOUCH A PARTICULAR PART OF THE BODY OF ONE OF THESE BUDDHAS YOUR WISH WILL COME TRUE.... FIONA AND I...TWISTED AND TURNED REACHING INSIDE THE BELL WHERE, IT IS SAID, IF YOU TOUCH BUDDHA'S TOE YOU WILL BE BLESSED.

—CATHERINE

Conor was enthusiastic, too, writing:

Eddie, our extremely informative, friendly, and laid-back tour guide, not only enthusiastically related stories from the life of Buddha depicted in the stone carvings, but he also taught me my second word of Indonesian: *thida.* It means "no" and I like

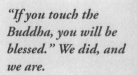

"If you touch the Buddha, you will be blessed." We did, and we are.

Eddie and the Hats . . .

to use it on the hordes of peddlers who try to push their wares on people like me in this part of the world. Mom has no use for this word. At Borobudur when we met up back at the van, Mom and Fiona seemed to have one of every trinket that I had so emphatically refused. My other Indonesian word was taught to me by the Braid Babes of Bali: *Gilah.* It means "Crazy" or "Psycho." Anyway, after the tour it didn't take much for me to convince Mom to give Eddie a good tip, so you know he must have been good.

We touched the famous Buddha in the stupa and made wishes that are then supposed to come true, kind of like the Indonesian equivalent of kissing the Blarney Stone. Some of the Indonesians wanted to have their photos taken with the far-out Americans.

Fiona wrote:

I was walking along the top reading the stories, and an Indonesian lady started pretending she had a camera in her hands and clicking it. I thought she wanted me to take a picture of her family, so I stopped. She pulled out a disposable camera and when I held out my hand, her daughter grabbed it and her mom took a picture of the two us. Then she took a picture of two people I didn't know hugging me. That was that.

Conor wrote:

Fiona posed with a young Muslim girl, and Colin and I posed with a guy in a Nirvana T-shirt.

I WAS WALKING ALONG THE TOP READING THE STORIES, AND AN INDONESIAN LADY STARTED PRETENDING SHE HAD A CAMERA IN HER HANDS AND CLICKING IT. I THOUGHT SHE WANTED ME TO TAKE A PICTURE OF HER FAMILY, SO I STOPPED. SHE PULLED OUT A DISPOSABLE CAMERA AND WHEN I HELD OUT MY HAND, HER DAUGHTER GRABBED IT. THEN SHE TOOK A PICTURE OF TWO PEOPLE I DIDN'T KNOW HUGGING ME. THAT WAS THAT.

—FIONA

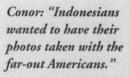

Conor: *"Indonesians wanted to have their photos taken with the far-out Americans."*

Tourist-ready at Borobudur.

And that was all we could say to each other: "Nirvana." The back of his shirt read, "crack smokin', fudge packin', ass kicking motherfucker," so I hope he wasn't wearing it for its religious connotations.

I guess such elevated messages mean we are finally civilizing the ancestors of the peoples who built this massive and magnificent work of art and human imagination. Eddie, our guide, already was. Said Colin:

He told me he had grown up somewhere nearby and had been coming to the temple and practicing his English on tourists since he was six years old. He was only moonlighting, or as he called it "moonlightening," as a guide. His regular job was some civil service gig. Eddie described with great passion the meanings of the legends depicted, as well as the history of the actual temple itself, and I got the feeling that while the money didn't hurt, this was a labor of love for him. . . . There were food stalls and souvenir stands and an elephant ride below the great temple. Conor and Fiona jumped on the back of the elephant . . . and headed out for a stroll.

Eddie made a final point to us all: "They say the Englishman, Thomas Raffles, discovered this in 1812. But I think local people knew about it all along."

Colin concluded:

After we had finished our tour of Borobudur, and Mom secured a few baubles for herself, we got into the minivan and set off for another temple. Upon arrival, Mom and Fiona quickly and efficiently jumped out of the van, everything synchronized like a team of Navy SEALS, and got straight down to the task at hand: trinketry. When everyone was back in the van, taking stock of recent aquisitions, and we were headed to our next point of interest, I asked Mom what she thought of the last temple and she answered with a hearty laugh that indicated a certain level of self-awareness.

Catherine on the next stop:

On the way back, we also stopped at Keraton, the Sultan's Palace, built in the eighteenth century. It is a series of covered pavilions and outdoor areas. It is in the center of town and has some interest because the Sultan, whose powers are now only symbolic, still lives in the interior pavilion.

Colin, no respecter of emperors, unclothed or otherwise, saw it his way:

The place was surrounded by a throng of food vendors, trinket hawkers, rickshaw peddlers, and numerous other people who would make a ground assault on the palace incredibly difficult. A very clever first line of defense—the human moat. . . . I hope the postcard sales are going well because the place could use a fresh coat of paint for starters.

Now this is the story of the midnight ride of all of us here—on BEMA, the state railroad.

Catherine first:

As I write this I hold in my hand a fax requesting "Beds for five people in air conditioned compartments on the overnight train from Yogyakarta to Jakarta." I also hold a fax confirming the reservations, "Executive Class," for thirty-two dollars a person.

The confirmation, however, failed to mention one thing: sleeper service had been discontinued four years ago. I just found that out from a railroad agent, who then warned me to be careful on arrival at the Jakarta station in the dark. I promptly had him call the Hilton in Jakarta and request two taxis to meet us. Perhaps to cheer me up, he said, "Your seats, of course, will be fully reclining. . . . The guys, who have been muttering about wanting to see Bali the "real way," reacted with indignant disgust when I told them of our overnight plans. . . .

This was Colin:

In the planning stages of this trip, we each supplied a few places we'd like to see, or things we'd like to do. Fiona's list was headed by an overnight train ride. Seemed like a lot of fun to everyone, and the itinerary was created to accommodate one. The overnight ride was planned for the Yogyakarta-Jakarta leg. At the time, everyone assumed it would be your classic overnight train: compartments, bunks, dining car, a good way to see the countryside . . . and any trepidation was quelled with the understanding that in Indonesia we would certainly be traveling first class.

Well, for what it's worth, we were in first class on the 6 P.M. Jakarta Express. And, we were told, every seat was taken. At the station, watching a world-class sunset, we loaded up with Cokes, the local beer, spring rolls, and the wares of ubiquitous Dunkin' Donuts. The company seems to own Indonesia, shops are everywhere—the nod in the direction of local custom is imitation *satóy,* round little holeless doughnuts served on a stick like chicken or pork. Catherine came out of the station, excited to have found a copy of *Newsweek International,* saying the guy told her, "It just arrived today." Maybe it did, but it was fifteen weeks old. The issue was dated March 30.

The sun dropped like a stone. By 5:45 it was dark, a fact that became increasingly relevant as we realized that there was going to be no electricity on the train until it began moving in the direction of Jakarta, three hundred miles away. And that meant we, and everybody else, were going to have to find our seats, 10-A, B, and C and 11-C and D, in absolute and total pitch-black tropical darkness. The scramble most reminded me of tag-team wrestling, with blind wrestlers carrying

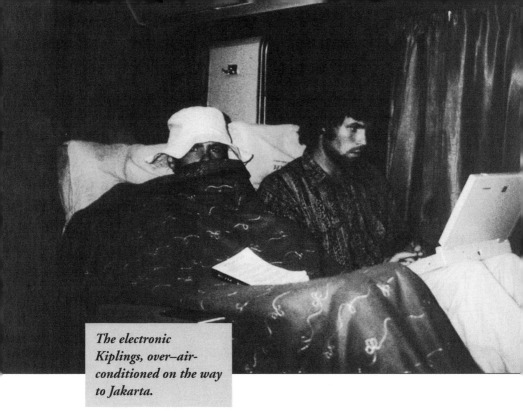

The electronic Kiplings, over–air-conditioned on the way to Jakarta.

heavy and bulky bags. Colin, bless-him-forever-and-I'll-never-say-a-bad-word-about-him-again, had a little flashlight. . . . He learned something traveling the world searching out hidden Soviet nuclear warheads for Channel One.

Said Catherine:

> It was like a scene out of a madhouse. Everyone scrambled on board into the pitch-black of the cars, stifling in unbearable heat and humidity. We successfully fought for space for our six bags plus wood-carved panels and hats. For a moment I feared that the air conditioning or power would be out for all eleven hours.

Hot, hot, hot, there was complaining about the heat in three or four languages. Then the air conditioning came on and the temperature descended to something that felt like forty, maybe thirty-two degrees—everyone was standing on seats rooting around for sweaters and coats. Men began coming through the cars, dragging giant bags of blankets. Other men came at the same time, passing out circular silver trays stacked fifteen high. That was followed by other men offering rice with some meat and glasses of hot tea and bananas. A movie came on—*The Shadow*—and Conor announced that he was in it, as an extra.

As a man pouring tea moved around, Colin announced, "You guys just missed Conor." The movie star himself had just announced that, statistically, "Train travel is not as safe as flying."

The star's mother was writing:

THIS RIDE WAS LIKE A HELLISH ALL-NIGHTER ON THE IRT. IT BEGAN WITH THE BATTLE FOR SEATS IN THE TOTAL DARKNESS, WHICH BECAME BLINDING FLUORESCENT WHITE LIGHT AFTER THE TRAIN BEGAN MOVING—AND THE TEMPERATURE INSIDE PLUMMETED...IT WAS LIKE TRYING TO SLEEP IN THE REFRIGERATED ICE-CREAM TROUGH OF A SUPERMARKET, DURING AN EARTHQUAKE. ELEVEN HOURS...THIS IS HOW THEY GET PEOPLE TO CONFESS DURING WARTIME. —COLIN

I have a scarf wrapped around my throat. As I write this we are all putting on warmer clothes. . . . Colin is saying, "This sucks. But it's only ten more hours." . . . Conor just took off his shorts, then sitting in his underwear, pulled on long pants. . . . Now Fiona has just returned from the bathroom to announce, "It is so gross, Mom. They had a bucket of water on the floor and it tipped over while I was on the toilet." . . . We are all at a critical underwear and sock point. We have been sweating and on the move for four days . . . and even when we washed, the humidity in the rooms was too much, nothing dried.

Colin elaborated later:

This ride was like a hellish all-nighter on the IRT. It began with the battle for seats in the total darkness, which became blinding fluorescent white light after the train began moving—

and the temperature inside plummeted . . . It was like trying to sleep in the refrigerated ice-cream trough of a supermarket, sitting upright on a stack of Breyer's, during an earthquake. Eleven hours . . . This is how they get people to confess during wartime.

The heavy floor plates between the cars, over the giant hooks that link the cars, were bouncing, flying up, clanging all night—flying inches from a fellow crouched down wiping the dinner trays. You could hear metal straining. The train itself began to bounce. Train men came back with a bag of pillows, then they returned and collected 750 rupiah for each one. Conor tried to sleep with a Singapore Airlines mask, personalized with the words "Piss Off."

Colin wrote:

On the plus side, I don't think we had to pay all that much extra for the walking pneumonia we developed, or maybe it was Legionnaires' disease. And at some point, attendants did come through the car with refreshment—more bananas.

I reached my breaking point about six hours in. I couldn't sleep, despite my best efforts, because the car was rattling violently from side to side and up and down; my nose had started running and breathing was difficult; the fluorescent lights were unwavering, nothing could be seen out in the black night. . . . I used all my powers of meditation to numb myself to the conditions, with some degree of success. . . . But there is a good reason for the legal time limits imposed on sensory-deprivation tank operators. I began yelling, "This sucks! My God! This sucks!" with a maniacal half-giggle that must have wigged out anybody nearby who spoke English, or anybody who didn't speak English for that matter. . . . Based on the cracks Richard has been making since that night, I think I must have really annoyed him. Oh, well . . . hopefully it won't be the last time that happens.

Considering such thoughts, Conor wrote:

One thing about traveling with your family—you can't take anything anyone says or does personally. Everyone is going to act like a jerk at one time or another. Now you hate 'em, now you don't. It's no big thing.

We made it to Jakarta in time to join a 5 A.M. taxi scrum for the few vehicles around Jakarta station. There were supposed to be a couple of cars from the Hilton but they were nowhere in sight, so we fought our way (and baggage) into two cabs. As we closed the door, somebody standing outside put a sign on the windshield in front of me: "Richard Reeves Family."

We unpacked those cabs and packed the Hilton cars. I paid off the two abandoned drivers, using my back to shield the transaction from Catherine. I rode in with Colin and Conor, talking about the last time I saw the city, in 1987.

"What were you doing?" asked Conor.

"Carrying your mother's bags," I said.

That was literally true. She was then public affairs director of the *International Herald Tribune,* traveling the world making plans for the paper's hundredth-anniversary celebrations. We went around the world on that gig, too.

"Yeah," said Conor. "That was when you left me in Paris holding the fort with Kelly Fincham."

They both laughed, remembering Kelly, who lived with us in Paris, baby-sitting wee Fiona, and who is now an editor of the *Irish Times* in Dublin. They were getting conspiratorial. Colin said: "Yeah, like the time they left me on Sixty-second Street with that crazy . . ."

I didn't like the way this conversation was going. But I was rescued when we reached the Hilton and conversation turned again to the number of bags we were unloading.

Still having the time of his life, Colin concluded:

Eventually arrived at the Hilton in Jakarta in a daze, dropped the bags on the floor of room, turned off the A/C, and decided to take advantage of the ungodly hour by calling the office where I used to work in Los Angeles to check if all my back pay had been deposited into my account yet. Big mistake . . . I reached the assistant business manager, a good guy. When I learned that the figure they had paid was substantially less than what I was actually owed, my exhausted delirium got the better of me. "Whaddya mean you're not gonna pay on that expense report! . . . Receipts?! . . . I gave you the goddamn receipts, you chiseling bastard! . . . I just hope that no tires get slashed around there! . . ."

Conor rolled over and said, "You're insane" before we both passed out. I love train travel.

Chapter 9
JAKARTA

atherine and I had last been in Jakarta in 1987. In fact, her passport was issued there on March 6 of that year. At the airport. We had flown in that day and then were confined in a customs office because Indonesia had this rule that no one would be allowed in the country if their passport expired in less than six months. They have a lot of rules in Indonesia.

It took a couple of hours to get her out of there, even with help from the American embassy and from local agents of the *International Herald Tribune*. While she was detained, though, she saw a good deal of Indonesia's shaky relationship with the wonderful world of faster and faster communications. The country's censorship laws at the time extended to all foreign publications. Young army officers at the airport were supposed to go through the *Trib* and other newspapers and magazines and black out any unfavorable mentions of Indonesia and its president, General Suharto. Of course, most of these young officers understood almost no English or any other foreign language. So, they often just let journals pile up, rather than risk making mistakes their superiors might discover.

It was a big problem for the *Trib*, but it was solved by the paper's local representative, a very sharp woman named Setiawati. She trained a small cadre of her employees to recognize "Indonesia" and "Suharto" in Western languages—and then take rollers dipped in black tar and cover entire pages or stories. Good or bad stories, all gone—the idea was to take no chances and get the papers on the street.

Once in the streets ourselves, Catherine and I loved the city, not very Westernized or modernized in those days. It was and is one of the

IN THE OLD PORT, WE
SAW THERE WERE STILL
DOZENS OF HIGH-MASTED
OLD WOODEN SHIPS,
SIDE BY SIDE ON A LONG
WOODEN WHARF—A
SCENE FROM THE SEVEN-
TEENTH CENTURY.
HUNDREDS OF MEN,
BAREFOOT, WITH DIRTY
RAGS WRAPPED AROUND
THEIR NECKS AND FACES
AGAINST THE BURNING
TROPICAL SUN, RAN UP
AND DOWN NARROW
GANGPLANKS—CARRYING
DOWN LUMBER FROM
THE OUTER ISLANDS....
—RICHARD

noisiest and most energized places in Asia—or perhaps that is a euphemism for being not very well run. On our last day there, we met with the Foreign Minister at the Hilton, where he liked to swim in what was more like a calm and quiet city within the city. The grounds were immense. "I love this hotel," Catherine said then. "If we ever get back here"—which we were determined to do—"we'll stay here."

Which, of course, we did this time, using the last of our United 50-percent-off hotel discount coupons to bring the room rate down to ninety dollars a night. And they had the rooms ready for us when we appeared at the gates at 5:30 A.M., straight from the Jakarta Express.

▲▲▲

HAPPY BIRTHDAY

There were Christmas tree lights strung along every block and almost every house when we arrived in Jakarta, the capital of Indonesia. What the country was celebrating was the fiftieth anniversary of its Declaration of Independence on August 17, 1945, during a national conference called "Fifty Years of National Revolution. Examination, Remembrance and Reflection."

The reason for that conference and others and for books and speeches is that there is still argument about what happened in Indonesia and in a few other Asian countries during the 1940s. The declaration by Indonesian patriots was written and distributed between

The sailing ships of the Indies docked in Jakarta.

the time of the Japanese surrender ending World War II and the return to power of the Dutch colonialists and their army. Japanese revisionists insist now that the war in Asia (which included the occupation of Indonesia) was an exercise in anticolonialism. They try to make the same argument that the invasion of British Malaya and Singapore and French Indochina (now Vietnam, Laos, and Cambodia) was to liberate their Asian brothers from the oppression of the European colonial powers.

There is a certain plausibility, though little truth, in that argument. One of the unintended consequences of Japanese aggression was, in fact, the collapse of Asian colonialism. No matter how they were brutalized by the Japanese, other Asians saw something most never believed possible: men who looked something like them were crushing the giant Europeans. President Suharto, who seized power as a general, was trained as a soldier by the Japanese occupying his country.

▶ ▶ ▶

We were dazzled before dawn by lights along every block, celebrating the fiftieth anniversary of the country's revolution against its Dutch rulers. Then in the daylight after a couple of hours of sleep we were stunned by the explosion of silvery towers that now rose above what colonial masters called the Dutch East Indies. New money showed in many places. Jakarta seemed as exciting as ever, but now in the modern way: new Asian prosperity towering over the slums and floating garbage along the canals the Dutch had built to make the place look like Amsterdam on the Equator—breeding mosquitoes that made it one of the world's unhealthier cities.

In the old port, we saw there were still dozens of high-masted old wooden ships, side by side on a long wharf—a scene from the seventeeth century. Hundreds of small, dark men, barefoot, with dirty rags wrapped around their necks and faces against the burning tropical sun, ran up and down narrow gangplanks—carrying down lumber from outer islands, then running up with great bags of rice on their heads to feed the crews and the other small men back in disappearing forests. Environmental rape with economic motives, the same thing Americans did in the 1850s with the pine forests of Michigan.

The family, not surprisingly, seemed to be in different time zones that first morning. Fiona said she wanted to come out with us, but the guys would not be moved. We decided to go first to Mini-Indonesia, a sort of world's fair of the archipelago. The center of the park is an artificial lake in which principal islands—Java, Sumatra, Bali, Lombok, Irian Jaya, and others—are represented by grassy scale models. You fly over this miniature of the country on cable cars that go from one "island" to another, twenty-seven in all, in the style of Disney World. You land and sample the food and products, architecture, and dances of, say, Java. Only samples, of course, because you are reminded again that Java has as many people as any country in Europe.

It was melting hot and there were not many other people out that morning, but we had a great time. The best of it, for us, was the park's giant aviary. All the birds I had never really believed existed outside encyclopedias turned out to be real, alive, and well in Indonesia. They were inside a cage about the size of the Houston Astrodome. Giant mynah birds, hornbills, storks, and pelicans of all kinds. Fiona seemed to be taking pictures of every one. So was her father. Amazing stuff. Meanwhile, back at the Hilton, Colin and Conor took their time taking their measure of Jakarta. "We laid low," wrote Conor. "Colin and I needed a break from our traveling companions and from our hectic schedule."

"Watching the great James Garner portraying a lovable capitalist on HBO Asia," was Colin's description of the morning. Then he went on:

> Around midday, Conor and I took a walk to the Senaya stadium, where the Indonesian Open Badminton Tournament was being held. I played a lot of badminton in college, and the two of us had been watching bits of a telecast of the previous day's action. But the images just weren't doing any justice to the game, or changing Conor's impressions of it: a courtly game played in suburban backyards by flailing geeks who can't handle giving or taking a forearm shiver. I was eager to dispel

this misconception, and was talking up the rigors of the sport quite a bit during our approach to the stadium. We got into the grounds through a gap in the perimeter fence, which seemed strangely underguarded. And we soon learned why. The day's play hadn't yet started and the only people around were setting up souvenir and food stands. We wandered around for a while, even getting inside the stadium, where we both tried out the latest Arnold Palmer model putter at the pro shop. Nobody questioned our right to be there, no doubt because of our utter disregard for authority.

Agreeing that our outing had been a bust, we decided to head back to the hotel. As we were approaching the breech in the perimeter fence, we saw three Indonesian kids walk by. As we got to our exit gap, a bunch of cops pulled up. A couple of uniformed officers on motorcycles and several men in plain-clothes, who piled out of a windowless van. As Conor and I hung back at a safe distance, the cops started smacking the kids around. It wasn't a huge shock, but compelling nonetheless.

Conor described the incident this way:

When we reached the stadium, Colin started me off by saying: "Do you know how many people were killed in there? Thousands. They used to just round 'em up off the streets, take 'em in there, and shoot 'em." He was making it up, but visions of killing fields flashed before my eyes. Richard had described to me what had happened in the sixties in this country, how thousands and thousands of people had been slaughtered in the name of God or democracy or whatever, so I had that on my mind. Minutes later . . . I watched a bunch of policemen swoop up out of nowhere on some seemingly in-nocent kids and slap the shit out of them. I was fascinated but I didn't stare out of fear for my own freedom. Now, cops slap the shit out of kids in every country in the world (God knows I've taken my lumps in the good ole U.S.A.) and these kids could have been guilty of some serious crimes, but nevertheless it gave me the creeps. It gave me the feeling that there was something lurking just beneath the surface and that violence could erupt out of nowhere at any time.

I thought of a line from Robert Sam Anson's book *War News,* where Prince Sihanouk of Cambodia is quoted as describing his people as his "nation of Buddhas." Anson saw that beautiful quality in the Cambodian people and I thought I saw it in the Indonesians. But Anson also saw the flip side of the Cambodian personality—how they were given to intense brutality and even genocide.

Back to Colin:

After we left the stadium area and went on our merry way, stopping at a car show at the convention center, we passed through a surly group of locals. They were all checking us out, elbowing one another and saying things in tones that were not friendly. Luckily, the local constabulary was flexing its muscle not more than a hundred yards down the road. So, we shot these guys a brief flash of our self-confident sense of diplomatic immunity, plowed straight through the center of their ranks, meeting any eye contact they cared to offer, and headed back to our air-conditioned, HBO-wired chamber. . . .

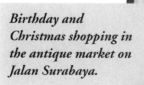

Birthday and Christmas shopping in the antique market on Jalan Surabaya.

Fiona in the canal slums of Jakarta.

▲▲▲

WHAT'S ON THE TUBE?

"Allowing too much freedom in modern electronic broadcasting will do us much harm," editorialized one Jakarta newspaper, *Republika*. Colin and Conor decided to take their chances, surfing local television, or the more liberal hotel variety, which was complete with pay channels.

Wrote Colin:

> The room was equipped with HBO Asia, which, although it edits the films to suit "Asian Sensibilities," offered the following movies, programs, or portions thereof *sans* f-words and exposed breasts:
>
> *Barbarians at the Gate, Continental Divide, King Ralph,* "The Larry Sanders Show," *Mambo Kings, Meatballs, Me, Myself and I* (with George Segal and JoBeth Williams), *Men of Respect* (John Turturro and Peter Boyle), *Mortal Thoughts, Motorama,* and John Carpenter's *The Thing.* We also watched a lot of CNN International, Star Sports, and "V" channel, which is an Indian music video channel. One of the public service announcements on "V" decreed, "Pirated cassettes are bad Karma." Star Sports was televising the Indonesian Open Badminton Tournament.

Moving right along, the *Jakarta Post* carried these two headlines on July 15: TV COMMERCIALS DEMORALIZE YOUTH and INTERNET USERS WARNED OVER IMMORALITY.

▶▶▶

Indonesia is not a free country. "Guided democracy" was the phrase created by President Sukarno, the man who announced the Declaration of Independence and twenty-one years later was overthrown by General Suharto in a military coup. Now Suharto uses the phrase to justify laws and actions against freedom of assembly, freedom of speech, and freedom of religion.

There are block captains in Jakarata whose job it is to spy on their neighbors. On the day we arrived, the chief of the National Police reminded new graduates of the Police Academy that 1997 would be an election year—"guided" elections in which one hundred of five hundred legislative seats were set aside for military officers— telling his men: "If it is possible every officer must be equipped with a video minicam to record every detail of every demonstration and public gathering to collect evidence of crimes with political nuances." A couple of days later, newspapers were reporting on the trial of a "soothsayer" arrested for allegedly calling the prophet Mohammed a "dictator." At the same time, police dispersed an "unlicensed seminar"on Islam. The organizers, local professors, were facing four years in prison for holding a "public gathering without an official permit." Permits are required if five or more people gather—that was an old Dutch colonial measure that now serves the purposes of new rulers.

To a Western skeptic the whole thing comes across as a justification for men on white horses and presidents-for-life. But the powers that be, led by Suharto, see such restrictions of freedom as the only way to hold together a country that may be inherently unstable because it is so large and is trying to embrace multitudes of different cultures and religions. Another take on that was offered in an editorial in the Indonesia *Business Weekly* on the stands that week welcoming a new United States Ambassador, Stapleton Roy: "He has a distinguished record . . . now if the United States could just chill a bit with their fascination on human rights."

[Such beauties as freedom are often in the eyes of beholders. "It's a free country" is a line that's true in few places in this complicated world—at least in the eye of a skeptical American. But, to be fair, this skeptic does remember that many of the elements of guided democracy were part of the beginnings of the United States of America at the end of the eighteenth century—limited franchise (only white males could vote), elite legislatures (United States senators were appointed rather than elected), and indirect selection of presidents (the Electoral College).]

As we were getting ready to leave Jakarta, a professor named George Aditjondro asked for political asylum in Australia after police called him in for fifteen hours of interrogation for "insulting a government body." The insult was saying that the country's democratization was threatened by the wealth and greed of the families of government officials.

You need a guide to understand newspaper reports like that. Decoded, that story meant Professor Aditjondro was questioning the new wealth of relatives of President Suharto, particularly his children, who have an uncanny knack for becoming the local partner of Western companies winning contracts for privatized toll roads and other profitable totems of modernizing Indonesia—all that without putting up any money of their own. One Suharto son, Bambang, is associated with Hughes Aircraft, Sumitomo, Ford, Union Carbide, Nestlé, and a German telephone company. Just lucky, I guess.

NO BARS ON OFFICIALS' CHILDREN was a front-page headline in the day's *Jakarta Post.* Said that story:

> "There is no regulation banning the children of government officials from running businesses," State Minister of Administrative Reform T. B. Silalahir issued this statement after meeting with President Suharto. "These children are Indonesians with rights similar to other citizens," he told reporters yesterday. "Once they are no longer dependent on their parents, once they have their own families, they are free."
>
> "You'll find corruption, collusion and nepotism everywhere in this world," said the minister.

So you can. The story went on with quotes from the President's son Tommy, saying it was "pretty legitimate" and his sister, Tutut, adding that the children of officials had to make a living like anyone else.

And some Indonesians believe it could be worse. In Bali a merchant had told us, "So they steal. At least the Suhartos understand business and its problems."

In fact, the old man himself was beginning a campaign to encourage entrepreneurship in a society more comfortable with government-driven economic decision-making. Whether or not he knew what he was talking about, President Suharto said:

> Entrepreneurs thrive on creating new things. They take risks and like to relate to people. To the ordinary "businessman," making big money as quickly as possible is the end. That is why, once they make money they tend to show off, living a materialistic lifestyle. In countries where entrepreneurship is well advanced, such as the United States, Japan, Taiwan and South Korea, thousands of businesses fail each month, but the same number start up, partly because the publics in those countries do not look down on people who suffer bankruptcies. There is a license to try again and again. We think this is the kind of public perception that should be promoted to enhance the spirit of entrepreneurship.

Speaking of entrepreneurship, there were also newspaper stories of schoolteachers asking parents for bribes of up to a hundred dollars to guarantee higher marks and admission to prestigious secondary schools. Terrible, but not our country, not our problem. That afternoon we roamed the city with Fiona, counting the McDonald's, Pizza Hut, and KFC (Kentucky Fried Chicken) outlets in shiny new shopping malls until we ran out of fingers and toes. There were none the last time we saw the city, but now the franchise uniforms give employees the look of private armies. At McDonald's, where we had lunch, they wear purple for some reason and wear baseball caps, marked with their job. "Toilet keeper" was on one girl's cap.

▲▲▲

ASIAN VALUES, WESTERN PRESS

There were hearings on freedom of the press in Indonesia's House of Representatives while we were in the country and one of the speakers for the government was a retired general named Moetjib, who is governor of the National Resilience Institute. He was asked a rather basic question: "Should journalists report fact or fiction?"

"Sure we have to tell the truth," he answered. "But as a responsible person, truths that could lead to excessive chaos in society would be best left unsaid. In this case, a little lie wouldn't hurt."

Three Indonesian magazines were closed down last year for raising questions about the astounding financial success of the family of President Suharto, the most powerful of the country's "retired" generals. Since then, the government has formed a closed-shop journalists union of sorts so that it can prevent reporters from reporting by kicking them out of the union.

That is the way the game is played by the "Tigers," as Asian nations like to describe themselves and their economic successes. In Singapore foreign publications are banned for real and imagined slights to that city-state or its founding president, Lee Kuan Yew. Malaysia banned business dealings with British companies after the *Sunday Times* of London reported on bribery in the government. But they are pussy cats compared to the People's Republic of China, where Xi Yang, a reporter for a Hong Kong journal, was sentenced to twelve years in jail for publishing a "state secret"—the secret being a change in interest rates paid by the national bank. In Cambodia, where there are no laws to deal with the press, two editors and a reporter were assassinated during the year.

Despite that, practitioners of journalism in Asia-Pacific think they are making progress in opening their markets to a product called information—some might even say truth. One journalist in Jakarta saw the hearings in the House of Representatives and the debate over the three closed magazines as a significant step forward. "In the past when they closed a paper everyone just forgot it," he said. "Now, almost a year later, people are still talking about the magazines."

Amnesty International offered a different opinion. Reflecting on some of those events and attitudes, the London organization issued a report on press freedom around the world, which concluded: "Throughout much of Asia, the exchange of ideas and information continued to take a backseat to the exchange of goods."

That says it. The same attitude was reflected by an American official, quoted anonymously in the *Washington Post* during Secretary of State Warren Christopher's visit to Vietnam, which took place while we were in Indonesia: "In the old days we wanted to make Asia safe for democracy. These days we want to make it safe for American exports."

▶ ▶ ▶

There is still a yawning culture gap between them and us. But, like most of the peoples of the planet, they are becoming more like us—for better or worse. An American diplomat moving on to a new posting told me: "You do what you can. The freight train is on track. Ninety percent of the people here are getting some education and there is now a lower birth rate. They worked things out with Islamic leaders. The middle class is growing. And"—he leaned forward—"there is not a cabinet minister or general anymore with two wives."

Looking around stores, Catherine wrote:

Little girls wear dresses, as did American little girls of forty years ago, and the families we saw often included three generations. The grandmas often wore long skirts and head scarves, while the moms were more likely to be dressed in modest Western fashions.

Outside, in another new Jakarta phenomenon, traffic jams, magazine hawkers walked from car to car offering reading material to a captive market of sweating drivers—including old issues of *Vogue, Cosmopolitan,* and *Maisons et Jardins.* The taxis are Fords, but most of the private cars are Japanese, particularly Kijangs, which are stripped-down Toyotas assembled locally. The jams are new in a place that had little motorized traffic only a decade ago and so are the toll roads and "diamond lanes" for vehicles carrying more than three people. While we were there, police pulled a raid on "three-in-one children," arresting hundreds of kids who rent themselves out to sit in the cars of commuters in the diamond lanes.

ON THE *JALAN*
(STREET), I SPOTTED A
HEART-SHAPED SILVER
BOX FOR JEWELRY. "THIS
LOOKS GOOD FOR MOM'S
BIRTHDAY," I SAID TO
FIONA.
  "DAD," SHE SAID, "YOU
GAVE HER A JEWELRY
BOX LAST YEAR AND TWO
YEARS BEFORE THAT."
               —RICHARD

We stopped at the Antique Market on Jalan Surabaya. It was unchanged from years past and Fiona liked the stalls as much as we had years ago. One seemed to specialize in old Decca 78-rpm records, the next in blowguns from the out-islands, and another in old twin-lens reflex cameras. Fiona picked one of the old cameras, a 1950s Yashica 635, as a gift for Colin's upcoming birthday, which we would be celebrating in Berlin.

Her report included:

They have nice little shops where I bought a coin that had been made into a bottle opener and a medicine bottle made of bone.

My mom's birthday is even closer, in three days, so my dad and I went shopping. . . .

Right. On the *jalan* (street), I spotted a heart-shaped silver box for jewelry. "This looks good for Mom's birthday," I said to Fiona.

"Dad," she said, "you gave her a jewelry box last year and two years before that."

Oh. The lady herself wrote:

I found a Chinese ceramic pillow, in a lovely floral design, which I bought here, and two small celadon vases. I was also delighted with having a soul companion who quickly picked up the tactics of bargaining, and deciding what something was intrinsically worth to you—and knowing that this was the basis on which to make a purchase. Her firm "no" disappointed many a vendor.

The next day Fiona took in a history lesson with us in old Batavia, once the capital and center of Dutch Jakarta, a classic crumbling colonial city, with building fronts last seen in Amsterdam. It is a charming place in the middle of this rising Asian city, at least to look at. The Dutch City Hall is the oldest building in Jakarta, first built in 1624 and filled with old oil paintings and furniture of the stolid-looking burgomaisters who ran the Dutch East Indies. Attacked and burned by a Sultan's army from Yogyakarta in 1629, it was rebuilt in 1707— and more than 80 percent of the building dates from that time, including dungeons used for political prisoners.

Our little American girl, listening to an Indonesian history student who volunteered to take us around the building, was shaken but fascinated by the cells built into the foundation like caves. "Oh, my God," she said when she tried to, and could not, stand up straight inside. The height was less than four feet and the Dutch jammed twenty or thirty native political prisoners in a cell, chaining each man to cannonballs or hundred-pound blocks of concrete.

Outside the cells, the young man showed Fiona the old well, where common criminals were sometimes kept up to their necks in water, standing on a wrought-iron grill which could be pulled out from under them. Recent excavations have revealed tunnels leading from such wells, leading to speculation that the gentle Dutch flushed prisoners into the ocean. Certainly our guide believed they did. For some reason, he was not impressed by the descendants of those Dutchmen issuing high-minded critiques of the human rights practices of Asian governments.

Our next stop, in a hired car, was along the city's waterfront, where the new malls and Charles Jourdan shops merged into the festering canals and shacks of Asian poverty near Sunda Kelapa Harbor. The "homes" were made of scrap, scrap anything—flotsam and jetsam, wood, cloth, tin, cardboard. Some things never change, or they change very slowly; the last time I was along these banks, children in the shacks were dying of dengue fever. This time it was diarrhea. The papers reported four childen dead and two hundred hospitalized just outside the city.

The central dock at Sunda Kelapa is almost a half-mile long. It was lined with the world's largest collection of working sailing ships— as it has been for a very long time. Ignoring "Keep Out" signs in three languages, I walked along counting the wooden ships with high masts and sails, stopping when I reached sixty. Men, most barefoot, were running everywhere with their back-bending loads of timber and rice. Some even wore ski masks against the sun in the killing heat. Scurrying. Trucks weaved through them, loaded with the lumber, which was stacked ten feet high in mud along the docks. When I lifted a camera to take pictures, men in suits, bosses of some kind, yelled at me to get off the dock. It could have been to protect the new wordly image of Jakarta, but I suspect the men were shouting at me because it was really just too dangerous out there. Dropping a load of swinging lumber on a fool American might mean wasted time answering questions or filling out forms.

Fantasy Land, the city's amusement park, was on the Indian Ocean, too, not far away, and we headed that way with our driver, Ajep. There was a big sign near the gateway for the Duracell Bunny, the one that taps a drum and keeps going and going. . . . I know it's

Richard and Fiona: a new attraction at Fantasy Land, Jakarta's amusement park.

supposed to be the Energizer Bunny, but someone stole it here—that's what copyright protection and intellectual property rights are all about. We had a great time, riding, yelling, staring and being stared at by everyone else. We were, or seemed to be, the only foreigners around. Roller coasters, the Log Flume, merry-go-round, a rock 'n' roll show, Skee-Ball, and cotton candy—an international language. We took the Raging River ride next to a veiled young Indonesian woman and her family. After we all climbed out soaking wet, she asked Fiona if she could take a picture with her. We were the exotic ones.

WE TOOK THE RAGING RIVER RIDE NEXT TO A VEILED YOUNG INDONESIAN WOMAN AND HER FAMILY. AFTER WE ALL CLIMBED OUT SOAKING WET, SHE ASKED FIONA IF SHE COULD TAKE A PICTURE WITH HER. WE WERE THE EXOTIC ONES.

—RICHARD

And we were the rich ones, too. Admission was five U. S. dollars and four dollars more covered all the rides.

"Great park, " I said to Ajep, our driver.

"Yes. I hear it's wonderful," he said. "I would like to take my six-year-old, but it's too expensive for us."

Chapter 10

SINGAPORE

C olin began:

Another travel day. Woke up absurdly early for a flight to Singapore. . . . Plodding through the Singapore airport with sixteen pieces of luggage to pick up the four others we had left in storage, we were walking straight into the jaws of a potential disaster. It seemed there was a manhunt on for the culprit who had scrawled "Led Zep Rules" in the mezzanine men's room. That culprit was Conor, who went a little bonkers with a Sharpie indelible marker when we passed through the airport a week earlier. Somehow, he managed to elude the dragnet, pass the handwriting check at customs, and keep his cool until we were safely en route to our hotel, the Mandarin on Orchard Road, the main drag.

With parents knowing nothing of such things, luckily, considering the local penalties for such behavior—flogging in a celebrated recent case involving an American teenager—we all arrived in Singapore, the shiny island city-state linked by a causeway to the southern tip of the Malaysian peninsula. It happened to be the day of the one hundred and fiftieth anniversary of the the *Straits Times,* the country's English language newspaper. Prime Minister Goh Chok Tong spoke to the staff and his remarks were the lead story the next day. The paper reported:

The Singapore press should develop its own model of journalism which would help perpetuate the country's virtuous cycle of prosperity, the Prime Minister said. It should not ape the

Western press, which held itself up as an adversarial watchdog of government. . . . The press should help forge consensus, aid nation-building, and create a climate in which the country could progress.

The country has progressed spectacularly since breaking away from the Malaysian Federation in 1965. Goh is the second prime minister, succeeding Lee Kuan Yew, a brilliant and chauvinistic politician who as much as any man or woman in history created a nation in his own image—and is still around to watch over Goh and to espouse and implement his theories on race, genetics, and "Asian values." Those ideas were the reason Lee pulled away the island, mainly Chinese in population, from Malaysia, which is a Muslim republic of primarily Malay ethnic heritage.

The politics of ethnicity are clear and open in both countries. In Malaysia, only Muslim Malays are allowed to hold political office, leaving a Chinese minority in control of most commerce. In Singapore, Malay and South Asian citizens of the country are not allowed to become military officers or learn to fly combat aircraft. The laws of Singapore offer money and premium housing to highly educated citizens (a euphemism for ethnic Chinese) for having more than one or two children, while trying to discourage any increase in the size and number of large Malay families.

▲▲▲

EAST IS EAST AND . . .

American news coverage of Singapore in recent years involved a single story: the flogging of a high school student from Ohio named Michael Fay, who was living with his father in the island city and was sentenced to flogging across the buttocks, a traditional punishment in this part of the world, for spray-painting graffiti and scratching some cars with a knife or screwdriver. The case blew up to such proportions that President Bill Clinton personally asked the Singaporean authorities to overturn the sentence. They did not, though they reduced the number of strokes from six to four.

▶▶▶

Singapore is among the most modern, efficient, safest, cleanest, and healthiest places on the planet. There are new skyscrapers everywhere on the three-hundred-square-mile island. The per capita gross national product is more than fifteen thousand dollars a year, up from a couple of hundred dollars at the country's founding thirty years ago. Among Lee's achievements has been the elimination of the Chinese tradition of spitting in public. Heavy fines, even prison sentences, have eliminated that unsanitary nuisance along with jaywalking and other habits the founder considered antisocial. A kind of mind control is so pervasive that in 1987, at a forum on Asian prospects—organized by Catherine for the *International Herald Tribune*—then Prime Minister Lee Kuan Yew and Lee's son, who was then commander of the Air Force, both spoke on the same day—but the *Straits Times,* eager not to offend either man, pretended that the speeches were on different days so they could give both men top-of-page-one play.

A year before that we happened to be in the city when they banned the use of chopsticks in street food markets. Disposable plastic spoons and forks presented in sealed cellophane fitted in with the "Singapore way." What did that mean? "More sanitary," said someone in power.

I hate the place. Visually it strikes me as the world's biggest hotel lobby. Politically it is a velvet police state. But they do have a great airline.

Now the rest of the family will tee off on Singapore, beginning with Conor:

Basically lame. Driving in from the airport I thought I might like it. It was so modern. But I really didn't. There was no color. Everyone basically looked the same, decked out in fancy Western outfits. It's a big climate-controlled shopping mall. I knew it was illegal to spit on the sidewalk, so I did. . . .

Colin wondered:

Do you think the kids here just have sex like mad because they can't do drugs? I hope so, but maybe they just jaywalk.

In fact, the whole place was strangely clean. There is a complex of buildings down by the riverfront that felt and even looked like the village where the protaganist was held captive in the old British television series "The Prisoner." . . . On the surface, every need was taken care of—something like 80 percent of the population lives in government-subsidized housing—but you had better be utterly content, or else. . . . Walking down the main drag on Saturday night, the entire street was air-conditioned. The refrigeration spills out of the enormous enclosed shopping pavilions and there are enough of them lined up pumping out enough cool air to effectively climate-control the outdoors.

What can I say about Singapore? A guy I know, whose opinion I trust, had told me that while there is virtually no violent crime in Singapore, the price you pay for living under those conditions is your freedom. Or, freedom as Americans think of it anyway: the freedom to take a leak against a tree, to say what you want about the government, to toss a cigarette butt into the gutter . . . I wasn't there long enough to really evaluate that assessment, or to assess that evaluation, but in the hotel room there was a sign affixed to the wall informing us that short pants were not acceptable attire in the hotel. It was ninety-five degrees outside. . . . And there wasn't a single cigarette butt anywhere on the street. I checked.

Catherine's take was different:

We arrived, appropriately, in the middle of "the Great Singapore Sale," an annual event publicized for weeks around the region. Every

WE ARRIVED, APPROPRI-
ATELY, IN THE MIDDLE
OF THE "GREAT SINGA-
PORE SALE," AN ANNUAL
EVENT PUBLICIZED FOR
WEEKS AROUND THE
REGION....AT C.K.
TANG'S, A LARGE
DEPARTMENT STORE,
A SOUTH KOREAN MAN
SCOOPING UP PORCELAIN
TEA SETS TOLD ME HOW
HAPPY HE WAS, BECAUSE
THE SAME THINGS WERE
A GREAT DEAL MORE
EXPENSIVE IN SEOUL.

THE TANGS
GREAT SINGAPORE SALE

$1.00

hotel was filled, there were lines at every restaurant and coffee shop, as conspicuous consumers from all over Asia flew in for what amounted to a national "50-Percent-Off" festival. Indonesians. Malayans. Indians. Pakistanis. Many of them, the rich ones, have apartments in Singapore. At C. K. Tang's, a large department store, a South Korean man scooping up porcelain tea sets told me how happy he was, because the same things were a great deal more expensive in Seoul.

They're cheaper in New York. By world standards, the bargains were not so great. . . . In New York, you get 50 percent off already reduced prices at end-of-season sales. . . . So you get things at over 60 percent off original price. That's a sale.

While I agree with my sons' perceptions of Singapore, I have long felt that we are not in a position to judge the trade-offs that have been made by Singaporeans. . . . Perhaps if we were asked to trade off certain freedoms to have a healthy, secure, prosperous, clean if somewhat sanitized environment, good schools, and a relatively crime-free city, many of us would make the same choices.

We had a bad getaway on Sunday morning. Fiona, in tears for reasons that were not clear, disappeared from the lobby, crowded wall-to-wall by people moving into airport buses. Already visualizing her sold into slavery, I finally found her sitting outside the door of the room we had already vacated, 1241. Then at the airport, the Business Class crowd, Catherine and I, lingered over coffee and tea in the Silver Kris Lounge, losing track of time after all three kids went on ahead. We ended up running through the terminal hearing ourselves being paged by a thousand or so hidden speakers. Finally making it to the bus to the plane, we encountered our offspring glaring at us. We, the responsible adults, had all the passports, so even if the three of them had gotten on the plane, they would not have been able to get off at our next stop, Kathmandu, Nepal.

"This has got to stop," declared Colin, rising to a power-shifting occasion. He assumed the mantle of Mr. Time as his elders begged forgiveness. Our flight stopped at Dacca in Bangladesh, giving us a good aerial view of that cursed country's ongoing battles with flooding. From on high, coming into the airport, the floods revealed themselves as a great gray-green lake with intricate patterns on the bottom—the fields and roads under water. It is a wretched place, but we are not really there. In our A310 Airbus, we carry our environment and modernity with us as surely as if we were in a space capsule—with safe international flight rules, drinking water, and wine, and our Muzak.

A couple of hours later, we land in the valley that is Kathmandu. But we are still in a wired global village, the archipelago of jumbo jets, international airports, and Hilton hotels. *Beauty and the Beast,* the Disney soundtrack, was piping through the terminal as we disembarked.

Chapter 11

NEPAL

Descending toward the airport in Kathmandu, not so far below us because the valley of Kathmandu is more than five thousand feet above sea level, I was surprised to see what looked like a red-brick Middle American airport. Sitting next to me, Fiona looked, too, and said: "How many countries to Egypt?"

For a moment I thought it was the old, "How long before we get to . . . ?" But she was writing a note, working on a schedule of some sort. "Four," I said and went back to wondering where the bricks came from.

They came from Nepal, of course, which has been using bricks in construction for ten centuries or so, maybe longer. I had a lot to learn. We all did. None of us had ever been there before. This stop was Cindie's idea, but she was going to miss it. Germany was six countries away—and that was when her doctor back in Fort Lauderdale said baby Ian could travel.

The airport did have a suburban mall look about it—there are, alas, few fields anymore with grass landing strips and a hangar at the end. Too bad. But inside, a couple of things gave promise that we were time-traveling. We had crossed a Rubicon, going the wrong way. The Muzak was playing an anthem of Disney's world government. The first sign I saw, however, was not from Orlando. It was hand-painted with letters getting smaller and smaller at the end where the sign painter ran out of room:

"His Majesty's Government informs foreign visitors that they are allowed to bring in the following goods subject to their return on the way back . . . Binoculars—1. Camera—1. Tricycle—1. Perambulator—1. Radio cassettes—10. Disk records—15."

"Why one tricycle?" said Colin. "Maybe too many trekker tourists have been coming in with three or four."

The clock started ticking backwards at the desk where you buy Nepalese rupees, forty-eight thousand to the dollar. The cashier was behind an old big-screen IBM computer terminal, in which he dutifully tapped my name, address, and passport number, the usual stuff. Then he slipped carbon paper between the pages of a tatty old pad and carefully wrote out the information on the screen. I signed in a couple of places, being careful to press through to the last carbon. Then in a ritual brought to South Asia by the British in India, the cashier used a straight pin across the left corner of the sheets, in lieu of paper clips or staples.

"I am your driver and these are my assistants," said one of three men in the front seat of the van Catherine had arranged a long time before.

"Why do they need three?" Fiona asked.

"I hope we don't find out," I answered.

LEPROSY STATION was one of the signs we saw on the drive into the city. A big tan dead dog, legs rigid in the air in rigor mortis, was at the side of the road, the center of a festival of greenish flies. There was almost no traffic, just a couple of the painted trucks and the three-wheel tractor wagon-pullers of South Asia were our only mechanized company. We passed a road repair crew. Men with small hammers were squatting in *shalwar kameez,* the loose-fitting long shirt and pants of South Asia, cracking football-sized rocks into sharp gravel, which they collected on round woven bamboo trays. Teenagers held the trays and then walked out onto the road and shook the gravel into potholes.

Live cows and dogs wandered across and along the roadway zigzagging along between muddy piles of garbage, food for living scavenger dogs and rats. All sacred. The cows are sacred, of course, as in Hindu India, but in Nepal, the dogs and rats are, too. Many Nepalis, Catherine told Fiona, believe that their animals may carry the spirits and souls of ancestors. I noticed the boys, sitting in the back, were listening this time.

"There was a bizarre little golf course just outside the airport," wrote Colin. "The third fairway had a stream running through it where women were pounding laundry on rocks. Fore!"

Looking around, Fiona asked: "If they have a king, why doesn't he do more for his people?" It was the filthiest place she had ever seen, the streets, the buildings, the magnificent but crumbling temples of centuries past, and many of the people. It was, in fact, the filthiest place Catherine and I had ever seen and she had worked in most of the world's refugee camps, most recently in Rwanda.

Yes, there is a king, a British-style head of state now, who went to Harvard for a year or so. And there is a brand-new democracy, controlled at the moment by the Communist Party. I did not read any planetary implications into that. As far as I can tell, the local Communists have won favor by mentioning that the king has no clothes. True, their party symbol is the hammer and sickle, but it is turned so the handle of the sickle is horizontal; it looks like an ancient oil lamp, more religious than what Lenin had in mind.

The world's highest country, a beautiful land under Mount Everest, was the real Shangri-La, a far place where a spiritual simplicity ruled and people never got old—at least if you got old enough to remember the book and film *Lost Horizon*. Unfortunately, I was beginning to suspect that in real life and real time, nonfiction Nepal is a perverse tribute to modernity. The life expectancy of the Nepalese was just twenty-eight years when the kingdom opened itself to the world in 1951. At that time it was believed that only 224 Westerners (white Europeans and all that) had ever been in the valley.

The first of the waves of post-1951 outsiders to come in were United Nations technicians and other good people who tried, with limited success, to persuade the Nepalese to clean up their sanitation act. The country's drinking water begins high in the Himalayas as the purest in the world and is amoebic poison after it passes through a village or two. Then came the mountain climbers, whose efforts complemented the old vision of untouched Nepal, innocent of the wicked and wasteful ways of the outside world. A couple of things about climbers and climbing struck me: they are the litterbugs of Everest, leaving debris all over the mountain; there is a morgue in the U.S. embassy, the only one in the world, to collect fallen Americans.

Then the hippies came and the druggies, puffing away in a country without laws—there are still "Freak Street" signs in the center of Kathmandu—and doing a pretty good job of turning many local young people into dazed walking wounded. Looters came, too, stripping the artifacts of ancient Buddhist and Hindu temples before locals realized the value of the great art of their ancestors.

THEN THE HIPPIES CAME AND THE DRUGGIES, PUFFING AWAY IN A COUNTRY WITHOUT LAWS—THERE ARE STILL "FREAK STREET" SIGNS IN THE CENTER OF KATH- MANDU—AND DOING A PRETTY GOOD JOB OF TURNING MANY LOCAL YOUNG PEOPLE INTO DAZED WALKING WOUNDED.   —RICHARD

The average life expectancy of the Nepalese has reached fifty-four years now. But the mortality rate for newborns is still as high as 50 percent in parts of the country. In some areas of the countryside, more than half the babies die before they reach the age of five. That's related to the fact that mothers in after-birth have traditionally been seen as "unclean." New mothers nursing their babies are often sent to live in cowsheds for two weeks.

Our hotel (brick) was named Shangri-La, too. And it deserved the name, with a beautiful garden and outdoor restaurant. Fiona gave it her coveted "10" rating, writing:

> There was a homemade complimentary chocolate cake waiting for us and in the hour since we've received two complimentary fruit baskets. Anyone who comes to Kathmandu should stay here.

If they can afford $155 a night. There are two more expensive hotels, the Soaltee (a Holiday Inn property), with a casino, and the more famous Yak and Yeti. The name alone attracts people and someone there said our senator, California's Dianne Feinstein, was coming next week with friends to celebrate the sixtieth birthday of her husband, Richard Blum.

Conor's judgment:

The Shangri-La is great. The first thing that happened is we run into Chuck Narchi—a lawyer and sometimes Yale professor—a kind of mysterious guy who got us into the American club in Islamabad when Colin and I were younger and about to die of hamburger deprivation. What are the odds? Mom and Rich were going out with him and a guy from the embassy [David Queen of the United States Information Service] for a drink on our first night here. They told me I was more than welcome to tag along. "Are you kidding?" I just can't make that Third World jet-set name-dropping scene. What do I look like, a stringer from Reuters? . . .

It turns out that Chuck's wife is some kind of tiger expert and even she is not venturing up into the bush because of *leech season!* Apparently, if you go up to where the tigers are you just get covered with bloodsuckers.

▲▲▲

HOW POOR IS POOR?

Nepal has a population of 21 million, about the same as Taiwan. The per capita income is about one-fiftieth of Taiwan's. In Nepal there is one television per five hundred people; one telephone per three hundred and fifty people; one doctor per twenty-one thousand people—overall, there are one hundred *dharmi-jhankri* (faith healers) for each doctor and nurse. The country has thirty-two miles of railroad track. The literacy rate is said to be 27 percent.

Each month, according to the *Kathmandu Post*, the Bank of Nepal issues economic indicators described as "encouraging, positive and on the right path"—but there has been a 13 percent decline in exports, especially woolen carpets and ready-made garments, this year.

The paper says another principal reason is a decline in agricultural exports because of "farmers' ignorant use" of chemical fertilizer.

Freak street,
Kathmandu.

"It's like a drug addiction," said the Director of the Institute for Sustainable Agriculture. "Initially production is high, but the dose has to be increased yearly."

While we were there, farmers demonstrated, demanding fertilizer which was being imported from Lucknow in India and sold the day it arrived. A photograph accompanying that report showed bent older-looking women happily strapping large sacks of the fertilizer onto their backs.

The same day's *Post* quoted the vice chancellor of the Royal Nepal Academy saying on another subject, copyright protection: "We do not have enough publications to meet our demand so we have to depend on low-cost publications to come out of piracy. . . . The country is poor and can only afford books if pirated."

▶ ▶ ▶

Our guide, Kissor Bazar, hired months in advance, was also waiting at the hotel with a Land Rover look-alike. Our first stop was Durbar Square—which means Square Square since durbar is the Nepalese word for "square." He showed us "Freak Street," leading to the square.

"What ended all that?" I asked.

"IT WASN'T ALL THAT FREAKY," WROTE CONOR, WHO DOES NOT CONSIDER THE WORD PEJORATIVE. "I MIGHT HAVE THOUGHT DIFFERENTLY WHEN I WAS ABOUT FIFTEEN YEARS OLD. BUT I DON'T HAVE THE SLIGHTEST URGE TO HANG OUT WITH THE KIND OF PEOPLE THAT WOULD BE DRAWN TO THAT SCENE. IT'S PRETTY CRUNCHY."

"Ronald Reagan," said Kissor. "The Americans forced us to stop the drugs, threatened to cut off our aid." And the aid was essential in a country whose budget is 60 percent donated by richer countries, which include India and China, their neighbors. In fact, almost all countries are richer than Nepal.

"It wasn't all that freaky," wrote Conor, who does not consider the word pejorative. "I might have thought differently when I was about fifteen years old. But I don't have the slightest urge to hang out with the kind of people that would be drawn to that scene. It's pretty crunchy."

Added Colin:

Well, so much for that. Americans and Europeans sat around strumming guitars and smoking hashish. . . . Richard, who was one of the few people at Woodstock who wasn't wasted, he was covering it for *The New York Times,* said Kathmandu reminded him of that: "A lot of garbage and mud. Except there was a lot less garbage at Woodstock." Not nice, Ricky.

This was the rest of Colin's take on the square and the center of the city:

The architecture was incredible. The Pagoda, popularized to the rest of the world by countries farther east—countries with bigger GNPs and bigger bombs—made its appearance in the Kathmandu Valley. The buildings could be called awesome stacks of timber-boxes of diminishing size stacked up precariously. . . . At the top of one tower, Mom was intent on leaning way out onto a ledge for a photo and Richard had to repeatedly

Catherine: "I was not prepared for the architectural beauty of Nepal."

THE ARCHITECTURE WAS INCREDIBLE. THE PAGODA, POPULARIZED TO THE REST OF THE WORLD BY COUNTRIES FARTHER EAST—COUNTRIES WITH BIGGER GNPs AND BIGGER BOMBS—MADE ITS APPEARANCE IN THE KATHMANDU VALLEY. THE BUILDINGS COULD BE CALLED AWESOME STACKS OF TIMBERBOXES OF DIMINISHING SIZE STACKED UP PRECARIOUSLY. . . . —COLIN

grab her and pull her back. He knows a thing or two about ancient timber. . . . Great skyline: satellite dishes sitting atop three-hundred-year-old roofs of sod. . . . Lots of hustlers on the street trying to sell cheap souvenirs, eventually coming down to one-tenth of their original asking prices. . . . Lots of kids peddling wares, or hiring out their likenesses for photographic reproduction. . . . "

Catherine's best line, indignantly, was "Ten dollars? You offered that for nine dollars back there five minutes ago."

She appreciated the look of the city, writing:

I had always thought that the primary reason for visiting Nepal was the trekking. . . . I was wrong. I also thought that Kathmandu had been ruined, that with the influx of trekkers it had lost its own essential soul. Wrong. I was not prepared for the architectural beauty of Nepal. The magnificent carved windows on so many public buildings, religious edifices, and private homes, the multitiered roofs, which seem so unique to this part of the world. The combination of red-brick buildings with wooden roofs and the supportive struts with intricate religious themed carvings supporting the overhanging roofs . . . In all of our travels around the world, I have never seen anything that exceeded in beauty the squares and architectural assemblages of the buildings, palaces, and temples. . . . The most surprising of them all was the palace of the "Living Goddess," the Kumari Bahal—and Fiona and Richard actually saw her.

In the presence of the Living Goddess, Kathmandu.

WHILE MOM WAS BARGAINING WITH A MAN FOR A POSTCARD OUTSIDE THE TEMPLE, MY DAD AND I WENT IN AND ACTUALLY SAW HER. SHE IS FIVE YEARS OLD AND HAD ON A RED SILK DRESS AND SHE LOOKED QUITE AGGRAVATED. SHE STOOD IN A WINDOW LOOKING OUT TOWARD US. SHE STAYED LIKE THAT FOR ABOUT TWO MINUTES, THEN STUCK UP HER NOSE AND WALKED AWAY, PROBABLY THINKING HOW BEAUTIFUL SHE LOOKED, WHICH SHE ACTUALLY DID. —FIONA

So we did. Wrote Fiona:

While Mom was bargaining with a man for a postcard outside the temple, my dad and I went in and actually saw her. She is five years old and had on a red silk dress and she looked quite aggravated. She stood in a window looking out toward us. She stayed like that for about two minutes, then stuck up her nose and walked away, probably thinking how beautiful she looked, which she actually did.

Our own little goddess was fascinated with the idea and the ritual selection of the Kumari by five priests administering thirty-two tests of perfection, which Fiona practically memorized: "Thighs like a deer, chest like a lion, neck like a conch shell, eyelashes like a cow, body like a banyan . . ." The last test is some kind of gauntlet of bloody buffalo heads. The chosen child, installed in the eighteenth-century palace we saw, is believed to be the incarnation of the fierce Hindu goddess Durga. Now the most prominent of the worshipers is the King himself, the fellow who went to Harvard.

Fiona was enchanted. But I was not. My first impression of Nepal was that it was a great place, as long as you didn't look down—at the dogs and the filth everywhere.

That night, *sans* children, we went over to David Queen's home with the Narchis. It was a beautiful house of brick, timber, and glass hidden away behind a wall on one of the dirt side streets near the Shangri-La. The six of us sat with our gin and tonics talking about the

lack of optimism at home and about how Americans seemed to be losing confidence in themselves. It was a sad, ludicrous conversation in
this setting. I remembered that during the day, Kissor, who had once
been to Los Angeles, said, "Now you are the only superpower; every
place and everyone belongs to you. . . . That is your disadvantage."

We all, the family, had dinner at the Yak and Yeti. "Buffet. Great
spread. Mutton. Nice and spicy. San Miguel beer, brewed and bottled
in Nepal," wrote Colin.

As we were leaving, Catherine saw something pass across the entrance. "What is that?" she asked the doorman, who was dressed for the
door of the Connaught in London. His English was accented in that
direction and he said: "That, madam, is a rat. It won't bother you."

The guys agreed that Kissor, our guide, was as good as they come
and Colin wrote this of the next day:

Kissor knew how to handle the strange dynamic that we posed,
seemed able to answer any ridiculous question thrown his way,
and once sold a Nepalese painting to an American for seven-
teen thousand dollars. "I had an exhibition of my collection in
Los Angeles." he said. "Do you know of the hotel there called
Howard Johnson's?"

The next morning we met Kissor at the appointed hour,
and headed out for a look at the areas around Kathmandu.
The first stop was a fifteen-hundred-year-old temple of Vishnu
at the top of a hill village called Changdu. The drive up to the
temple was an experience in itself: a thin dirt road winding
steeply up through terraced rice paddies, farmers bent over, up
to their elbows in paddy . . . people bathing by the roadside in
rice paddy runoff. As we climbed high enough to see distant
hillsides, the terra-cotta farmhouses clinging to the sides of
the hills were remindful of the Italian countryside, except rice
paddy green is an electric shade you'll never see among the
dusty pastels of Tuscany.

He parked the van at the end of the road, from where you
could only proceed by foot up crumbling walkways and stair-
cases, stepping over goats and infested dogs, through a village

that hasn't changed for a thousand years. The only other people inside the walls of the temple were sincere worshipers. A sign above the door of the inner sanctum asked that only Hindus enter the actual chamber, so what goes on inside is a mystery to these gringo eyes.

There were a few enormous old bells positioned around the structure and every so often someone would grab the clapper and shake the hell out of the thing; some sort of announcement to unseen deities looming overhead, or within us all, or whatever. . . . It was an amazing place, caused me to step lightly and respectfully because it was active; people were smearing colorful powders and things onto thousand-year-old art treasures and performing other rites I didn't understand. It hadn't been overrun by curious foreigners with the price of a plane ticket. People lived inside the outer walls of the temple and Kissor told us that those homes are passed on from one generation to the next. And none of them had become postcard shops.

The place is under the protection of some national conservancy trust and there was a hand-painted sign on one wall which read, in English only, SAVE OUR SELF-ESTEEM. DON'T ENCOURAGE BEGGING. It seemed to be working. The same kids who would ordinarily be trying to sell us some crap, or offer to pose for photos and charge by the minute, or just follow us around with outstretched palms, were simply going about their mundane business, gonging the prayer bell and trying to avoid us. I don't know which way they'd rather have it.

Conor's version of the morning's events was a little different:

I didn't catch the name of the first place we went, let's just call it "The Place That Spooked Richard." Colorful scenery—expansive vistas, rice paddies, wild marijuana fields, water buffalo, kids in school uniforms, ladies in saris with red dots on their heads, people showering at roadside spiggots, and the usual festering garbage heaps. We had to walk up through the main and only street of this little hilltop village to get to the temple at the top. It was pretty damn filthy—mangy dogs and even mangier goats and sheep lying around in their own excrement, filthy little naked toddlers covered in snot. By the time I got to the temple I was, let's just say, pretty wary. The temple was incredible, or you could tell that it once was. The carvings, the sculptures, the architecture were all beautiful, but I was mostly impressed by the level of decay. Granted, it is all fifteen hundred years old, but if these people had the drive and ingenuity to create these things, why are they incapable of maintaining them? It just goes to show you what happens when you keep putting off cleaning your apartment for a few centuries.

Now, as I said before, this experience really affected Richard. He would later tell us, "Seeing some of those kids up on that hill really got to me." I thought it was dirty but I wasn't all that suprised by it. What did he expect? I mean, isn't that why we go to these places?

He asked me that question on the hill. My answer was: "I don't do ignorance anymore. . . . People don't have to live this way." I was mad. I probably began reeling off infant mortality rates.

"Take it easy," said Colin. "It's worse in Haiti." He's got me there. I've never been and he has been there a couple of times, producing news reports on the American-protected return of President Jean Bertand Aristide. In his foreign correspondent mode, he lit up a cigarette. Kissor was shocked and said: "Excuse me. I am amazed to see you smoking. I stopped in California when I realized Americans look down on smokers, because they believe they are killing themselves." Colin mumbled that he was down to three or four a day.

Our next stop was Bhaktapur, a small city with a big legacy. A beautiful decaying place. Conor wrote:

Walking into the square at Bhaktapur, Kissor told us that the film *Little Buddha* was shot here. Mom said, "Oh really? I remember seeing that movie and thinking how it would be wonderful to see some of those places in my life." Kissor said: "Well, now they're right in front of you."

She was not disappointed, writing:

Everywhere you look in the preserved town, you see beauty. There are three great squares lined with temples, and palaces with ornately carved wooden windows and doors . . . and the squares have beautiful pagodas with multiple tiers of roofs. . . . We climbed to the top of one of the temples and looked through the carved wooden windows, enjoying the rooftops of Bhaktapur. There are no cars allowed in the city, adding immensely to the pleasure of strolling around. We bought traditional thanka paintings, with slight variations in the design and colors used. A haunting place.

Colin wrote this after we left:

On our way out of the city I wandered over to a group of guys who were clustered around a board playing some spirited game involving dice that were being slammed around with lots of coaxing and cheering. I was standing there for a while before one of them broke away and came over to talk to me.
"From what country?" he asked.
"America."
"Ah! Seattle?" he said, the city where most of *Little Buddha* was shot.
"No, Los Angeles."
"Oh! City of Hollywood! Drugs! Guns! You know Keanu Reeves?"
"No." (We're not related.) Undaunted, the boy from Bhaktapur said: "I also like very much Sly Stallone."

The description of Hollywood had its points. But Nepal was making me think that there are people and times that would be better off seeing more of the worst of American pop culture, beginning with dreary old situation comedies. It is not that "our" values are any better than "theirs," but whatever else it does, lowest common denominator American entertainment shows people how the other half lives. Our films and television show the ways and things of modernity—and as romantic and picturesque and spiritual as Nepal may seem to some purists and romantics, its people will be a lot better off with clean water and electricity.

There was at least one man in Nepal who agreed with me, Angrita Sherpa, who has climbed Mount Everest nine times. In a little magazine called *Attitudes*, a simple English-language version of American city magazines like *New York*, he was quoted as saying in a translation that seemed a little too elegant: "Our village is untouched by any form of modernity. For tourists it is a paradise gained, but to us it is a paradise lost. . . . At least we should have the right to basic modern amenities of which our children are deprived."

Conor wrote:

AN ELABORATE MOM'S BIRTHDAY BALLET: SHE LOVED THESE STYLIZED CIRCULAR THANKA PAINTINGS OF BUDDHA'S ASCENT TO NIRVANA AND IT WAS HER JOB TO DISCREETLY HINT AT WHICH ONE SHE WANTED. SHE'D TELL ME, COLIN WOULD ASK HER TO STEP OUTSIDE FOR ONE REASON OR ANOTHER, I'D TELL FIONA, FIONA WOULD TELL RICHARD, AND RICHARD WOULD BUY IT.
—CONOR

> As we were leaving, Kissor made the mistake of taking us into a thanka painting shop, to show us the difference between the real paintings done by the monks and the cheap imitations that most tourists buy. . . . I'm kidding, it was not a mistake, but an elaborate Mom's birthday ballet: she loved these stylized circular paintings of Buddha's ascent to Nirvana and it was her job to discreetly hint at which one she wanted. She'd tell me, Colin would ask her to step outside for one reason or

Thankas checked out by the phony expert.

another, I'd tell Fiona, Fiona would tell Richard, and Richard would buy it.

Shopping is a joy in Nepal, perhaps for the wrong reasons. It is basically a preindustrial society. Everything is done by hand. Real or counterfeit. The thankas, beautifully colored cloth paintings, are generally inexpensive. The more intricate and the more gold paint, the higher the price. There are also replicas of these beautiful carved windows . . . and small brightly colored purses and hats. We also walked off with those.

The thing that really sticks with me from Bhaktapur are

the faces of the young girls who crowded around us wherever we went, relentlessly trying to get us to buy their touristic knick-knacks, which we did. There was no getting rid of them. Well, they would run off whenever a stick-toting policeman would pass by, but then they were right back as soon as he was gone. They had great responses. If you said, "No, thank you," they would say, "Oh, yes, thank you!" . . . They were poor and they were dirty, but they were also physically beautiful with extremely pretty faces and they were smiling and you could joke around with them and it was cool.

> THE THING THAT REALLY STICKS WITH ME FROM BHAKTAPUR ARE THE FACES OF THE YOUNG GIRLS WHO CROWDED AROUND US WHEREVER WE WENT, RELENT-LESSLY TRYING TO GET US TO BUY THEIR TOUR-ISTIC KNICKKNACKS, WHICH WE DID. THERE WAS NO GETTING RID OF THEM.
> —CONOR

At lunchtime, we headed for a hill town called Dhulikhel, which seemed terrific when Catherine was planning the day six months before back in Los Angeles. She thought it was good enough to schedule it in for July 17, her birthday. So there we were, bouncing up a little road, with the birthday girl up front and her sons in the back doing some more light reverting: "Mom, Fiona won't leave me alone. . . . Make her stop!"

There was a toll gate at the entrance to the village, a sight I will never forget. A long bamboo rod blocked the roadway. It was controlled by six men squeezed into a kind of box on stilts at the side of the road, looking for all the world like the directors of the Triborough Bridge and Tunnel Authority. They watched solemnly as a toll-taker below them accepted five rupees from Kissor. They nodded and up went the bamboo barrier.

Worth a detour. Our chosen inn was as good as Catherine thought it might be, a wonderful top-of-the-world place called Himalaya Horizon, with a view of mountain ranges up to the Himalayas.

I AM FIFTY-THREE YEARS
OLD TODAY AND MY
THREE CHILDREN ARE
WITH ME, AND WE ARE
ALL FOR THE FIRST TIME
SEEING, AND LOVING,
THESE INCREDIBLY
BEAUTIFUL PLACES,
WHICH STILL TEEM WITH
THE LIFE THAT IS LIVED
IN THEM AS IT HAS BEEN
FOR CENTURIES....
    —CATHERINE

Unfortunately for us the highest peaks cannot be seen during the rainy season. But you got the idea and the short-range views, say twenty miles of green valley, were wonderful. If it were in France, Himalaya Horizon, which is also a hotel, would be red rocking chair and *Relais et Châteaux*. But the food and prices were different: curries and local beer and soda and the bill for six of us was: $35.

We sang "Happy Birthday" for the third or fourth time so far in the day and Catherine wrote:

I am fifty-three years old today and my three children are with me, and we are all for the first time seeing, and loving, these incredibly beautiful places, which still teem with the life that is lived in them as it has been for centuries. . . . The view of the valley and the terraced rice fields from this hill town, as well as the street life in the towns, is wonderful and stimulating. . . . In the mornings, I saw a real division of children. Many of them don uniforms, ties, and small backpacks to go off to school. Many walk and many wait on corners, even the six-year-olds, to climb into crowded public buses. But most countryside families seem to have five or six children and some stay home to herd the animals and work in order to augment the family income, which in this country averages less than two hundred dollars a year. (More children are the Social Security of poor countries—the idea being they'll take care of parents in old age.)

Colin and Conor and Kissor talked of Mount Everest, somewhere out there in the clouds. As Eddie back at Borobudur talked of the "discovery" of that wonder of the world by an Englishman, Raffles, Kissor said it was hard to believe that no Sherpa had climbed Everest before

Colin and kids.

Fiona and parents.

After lunch in Dhulikhel.

Edmund Hillary came along from New Zealand with Tenzing, his local guide. "They are the best climbers in the world," he said of his countrymen. "But no one cared that many of them had climbed the mountain before the outsiders came."

"Do the Sherpas climb for adventure or fun?" asked Colin.

"No," said Kissor. "They do it for money. It's a job."

"Ah, another day at the office," said Conor.

He loved the place, writing:

I had local fare—grilled chicken and veggies over a bed of rice and wild mushrooms. The vegetables were fresh and colorful (and, fortunately, cooked or else I probably wouldn't have eaten them). The bread (*naan* and *chipati*) was out of this world. . . . We were reminded of Muree, the hill station in Pakistan where Colin and I had begged to be able to go back to America twelve summers earlier. In response to our pleas Richard had come up with the now classic line, "Fuck 'em, Cath, they're kids."

The memories of parents and children ever amaze me. Ordering at lunch the day before, Conor had said: "What's a day in South Asia without chicken *jalfrazzi?*" We lived on that dish and orange soda, five of us, Catherine and I, Colin and Conor and Jeff, in a small room (with a rumbling air conditioner the size of a Volkswagen) at Dean's Hotel in Peshawar, Pakistan, in 1983.

Moving on again, Colin wrote:

> FIRST WE SAW TWO MONKEYS THAT HAD LEFT THE TEMPLE AND WERE WALKING AROUND IN TOWN DOWN THE HILL. AT THE TOP MONKEYS WERE PLAYING WITH PRAYER BELLS AND ONE BIG ONE WAS SHAKING A WHOLE RACK OF THE BELLS. IT WAS FUN. I HIGHLY RECOMMEND IT.
>
> —FIONA

Our last stop was Kissor's hometown, Patan. There was another awe-inspiring square, thousand-year-old buildings towering improbably into the sky. It began to rain, forcing us to take cover under an eave of one such structure. Sitting stationary, allowing a single vista to burn into my retinas and being able to really absorb it, was a welcome change from our usual strategy of constantly moving through every new place we saw.

We did keep moving; next was Swayambunath, the "Monkey Temple," a twenty-five-hundred-year-old stupa on a hill near the center of Kathmandu. Catherine:

There is a Tibetan Buddhist monastery on the top level of the temple . . . and young novitiates in burgundy robes walked with us. The point of the stupa has a painting of the great all-seeing eye of Buddha.

The eyes of Nepal are upon you . . . .

Fiona was wearing a T-shirt with that same eye—quite in style—and she wrote:

> First we saw two monkeys that had left the temple and were walking around in town down the hill. At the top monkeys were playing with prayer bells and one big one was shaking a whole rack of the bells. It was fun. I highly recommend it.

At the end of a long day, Colin wrote:

> We had a birthday dinner for Mom at Soaltee, the nicest Holiday Inn in the world. The food was delicious, if not hot enough for my liking, and we were entertained by traditional Nepalese dancers. The dancing was less strictly calculated and synchronized than Balinese dance: more casual, rhythmic, sensual grooves.

"The entertainment was terrific," Conor added. "A series of dances with a single obvious theme—flirtation and seduction."

I woke early the next morning and walked the streets of the neighborhood around the Shangri-La. As the city woke, people dressed for work stepped through the gates of their walled houses and threw their garbage into the gutters or out into the streets, rousing the dogs sleeping everywhere. I also saw two dogs on leashes, being walked by their Western owners. This must seem a strange world to those two dogs from Paris or maybe New York.

▲▲▲

ALL THE NEWS

There are two English-language newspapers in Kathmandu, the *Kathmandu Post* and *Rising Sun*. A front-page story in the latter reported that a plane landing at Bharatpur airport the day before bounced back into the air four times before coming to a crashing, nose-diving stop—damages to the plane were recorded but there was no mention of what happened to the crew and people on board. This is a sampling of headlines and parts of some of the stories we read during the three days we were there:

GASTROENTERITIS CLAIMS TEN FROM JUNE 27 TO JULY 13. (*Post*)

"Bhaktapur is starting a program to alert people against a possible cholera epidemic. Residents suspect cholera cases are the result of mismanagement of an army septic tank and unscientific pig farming." (*Post*)

DIARRHOEL DEATHS REACH 90 IN ACHHAM (*Post*)

"The Nepal Communist Party is changing its name to Nepal Samyabadi Party. Its main objective is to put into practice the principles of Marxism, Leninism and Maoism in creative works." (*Rising Sun*)

"Nature's Call," an editorial: "Kathmandu municipal authorities should require 'Pee-bags' used by those stuck in traffic jams in Bangkok (Bangkok buddies) to be used by all those lining up along Ratna Park's barbed fences." (*Rising Sun*)

"A tiger snatched a twelve-year-old boy from home and took him into the jungle. All that was found was his head and parts of his hand. A five-year-old boy was also recently snatched by a man-eater and killed." (*Post*)

"NEPALESE VIRGIN GIRLS EXPOSED TO AIDS IN BOMBAY" . . . "About half of Bombay's 100,000 prostitutes are girls and women who are routinely raped, beaten, exposed to AIDS, and kept in brothels as virtual slaves. . . . Many are young girls from remote hill villages who are lured by local recruiters promising jobs or marriage. Then they are sold to brokers who deliver them to brothels. Their skin is generally lighter than Indian girls and that makes many men prefer them to local prostitutes. Many women are forced to repay the brothel the amount of money paid to purchase them, plus interest. That keeps the poorly paid women in the whorehouses for years. A report by Human Rights Watch blames Nepal for failing to arrest the traffickers even when they are known. Many of the girls are very young, as young as ten years, and are prized as virgins free from AIDS. They often return with AIDS." (*Post*)

▶▶▶

Catherine, Fiona, and I headed for the zoo, which was said to attract a million people a year, half as many visitors as the Bronx Zoo. We walked through a religious festival preparing the way for the beginning of the monsoon season. Two giant carts with wheels about fifteen feet high were being pushed and pulled slowly across a stony and rubble-strewn field called "Land of Beauty." The entrance to the zoo was a gate in a wall near the lot and we paid to go into what at first seemed an oasis inside the city.

But this was no oasis. It was a circle of hell, one of the worst things I have ever seen. It was crowded this school holiday, the muddy-slick paths packed like Tokyo subways. Schoolchildren were throwing stones at the animals and their parents were rattling the cages of the five hundred animals there—including rabbits and squirrels, exotic in these parts. The Nepalese families were trying to get the animals to move, to do something. But they had little luck, because the animals were dying. One died every ten days, we learned. They were not being fed on any schedule, there were no veterinarians, and usually no one to clean the cages and enclosures. The zebra, a listless beast, was in a dark enclosure barely big enough for it to turn around. Fiona just wanted to get out of there. So did I.

Catherine wrote:

> A disgusting experience. All around us, people of all ages kept hawking up what in my childhood in Queens were called "lugars" ("lugies" in Jersey City, said Richard) and spitting on the ground all around us. I must admit it made me yearn for a little of the authoritarianism of Lee Kuan Yew in Singapore.

Our next stop was the home of the American Ambassador, Sandra Vogelgesang. Getting there was an adventure. We had trouble finding the address and a couple of times I got out of our taxi to go into offices or stores to ask directions, with little luck but great wonder on Catherine's part. Yes, I am one of those men who will do anything rather than ask directions. Finally, I spotted a number and said, "Stop!" The driver slammed on the brakes and a young man on a bicycle, a student, crashed into the back of our car, flying over the top. I was sitting

Fiona signs in with Ambassador Sandy.

next to the driver and he landed half on the roof and half on the windshield in front of me.

He was okay, or said he was. But the driver was running in a circle around the car looking for damage, screaming at the kid, yelling that he had to pay for the damage. A crowd was gathering, which can be a very dangerous thing in some countries. But the crowd was not mad at us or at the driver; they started screaming at the bicyclist. It was another manifestation of the rules of the road in most developing countries, if Nepal can claim that status: the bigger and the faster always have the right of way—trucks and buses first, then cars, mopeds, bikes, rickshaws, and, finally, men, women, and children, usually in that order.

"Call me 'Sandy,'" said Ambassador Vogelgesang, who was talking with a man wearing high rubber boots about a plumbing problem he was trying to fix. It turned out that he was her husband, another Foreign Service professional, who was on an official leave of absence to be with her. That is the way we do things—and the Nepalese and others probably think we're a pretty odd bunch.

"Fiona," said Sandy, "would you like something to drink?"

"No, thank you," she answered.

We began talking about the contrasts of Nepal. She said twenty-two hundred of the temples in Nepal were classified by the United Nations as heritage sites, the greatest concentration in the world. But at the same time engineers and health officials were coming through and arguing that it was the dirtiest place on the planet.

Then she stopped and turned to Fiona again, saying, "Are you sure you don't want something, a Coke, water?"

"No, thank you."

"CALL ME 'SANDY,'" SAID AMBASSADOR VOGELGE-SANG, WHO WAS TALKING WITH A MAN ABOUT A PLUMBING PROBLEM HE WAS TRYING TO FIX. IT TURNED OUT THAT HE WAS HER HUSBAND, ANOTHER FOREIGN SERVICE PROFESSIONAL, WHO WAS ON AN OFFI-CIAL LEAVE OF ABSENCE TO BE WITH HER. THAT IS THE WAY WE DO THINGS—AND THE NEPALESE AND OTHERS PROBABLY THINK WE'RE A PRETTY ODD BUNCH.

What worried her most, Sandy said, which meant what worried the U.S. government, was that Nepal was a new democracy—the King ceded power after riots in 1991—but so far the people had nothing to show for their move to the wondrous Western way of governance. Yes, the Communists headed a shaky coalition government now, but they had won only because the Congress Party, winner of the first elections, were now split into two factions. Another set of elections seemed inevitable.

"Fiona," Sandy said, "Would you like . . . "

Suddenly we got it. The Mondale story, Fiona and the "adultists," had gotten around somehow. We all laughed and Fiona said she'd take some Coke. When Sandy brought it in, Fiona, who had been drilled by us, looked at the ice cubes and said, "Is this safe?"

"That's a good question," Sandy said. "Yes, it is, but it's about the only safe water in the country."

It turned out that the embassy had tested all of the country's bottled waters—and found that it was all the same, river water, tap water, water in sealed bottles with fancy names. All of it was alive with gardia and other bugs looking for humans as their next homes. It is not that the United States routinely tests foreign waters, but they did here because so many embassy employees and guards were sick. The eight U.S. Marines assigned to the embassy were all laid low at the same time. Then the advance team for a visit the month before by President Clinton's wife and daughter all got sick. The Reeveses were on their own, but the last thing anyone wanted were sick Clintons.

Back at the hotel, Conor was telling Colin: "My stomach is not feeling 100 percent today. I think I'm going to fast and just drink some water to cleanse the pipes." He finished his first liter of bottled water just as we got back. "Then," he said, "Richard came back and dropped 'The Microbe Bomb,' saying all the water was bad."

Luckily, Conor was fine. We all were, so far. Colin wrote:

In the afternoon, Conor and I walked to a part of town called Thamel. The line on Thamel was that it was the modern Freak Street, the place where all the young foreigners hang out. There were a bunch of low-budget guest houses and some guy offered to sell us some hash . . . English-speaking merchants hawking postcards, T-shirts, and assorted "authentic" souvenirs of Kathmandu that had been stamped out by a huge machine somewhere. A young guy approaches and pulls a bundle out of his pocket, handles it as if it were a precious relic from the Buddha himself, and unwraps it to reveal some knickknack identical to dozens of others on sale up and down the street. . . .

Conor was looking down, and after the Thamel walk he wrote this:

There were huge festering piles of garbage everywhere. Long stretches of stench where you have to hold your breath like you're driving past a graveyard. Huge metallic-green clouds of flies blossoming upon your approach; stray scabby dogs gnawing on unidentifiable crap in the heaps of refuse. Who knows what sinister amoebas lurk within those mounds—what terrible heretofore unknown viruses are incubating in the sweltering Nepalese summer.

Health was on their minds, sort of. Wrote Colin:

Somehow a few mosquitoes managed to squeeze through the screen and into our room. I managed to crush a couple of them against my cheek during the night, but I woke up with a number of bites. The doctor we had consulted before leaving L.A. told us there wasn't much to worry about at Kathmandu's altitude, but she also prescribed medication, Larium, for the malaria we didn't have to worry about. The hypochondriacs in the smart set use Larium, which gives you funny dreams. And both Conor and I have been having very funny and potent dreams, which we've been sharing with each other with varying degrees of bewilderment and embarrassment. I guess we'll never know if it's attributable to the Larium, or to the overwhelming circumstances and conditions of the last few weeks. But just to be on the safe side, we ritually gobble those suckers back every Saturday.

Before leaving the country, I walked the north bank of the Bagmati River with Linda Keatro, an American architect who came to Kathmandu as a student in the 1970s. She fell in love with it and never went home. Now she was trying to get international financing to restore what once had to be one of the most impressive rows of temples in the world, more than a dozen of them built along the river between the thirteenth and nineteenth centuries—structures that are now almost invisible with trees growing through and on them. "The country is a museum," she said. True and sad. "And it's disappearing."

It is. But what is destroying Nepal is not foreigners, it is the

Nepalese themselves—beginning with King Birendra. As we headed for the airport, Conor, writing with more passion than analysis, wrote:

> I hope the Communists take over and move this place out of the Middle Ages.

Catherine wrote:

> A few months ago, crossing the Atlantic on the *QE2*, we had struck up a conversation with a couple—charming people. They had homes in India, Nepal, and London. The man had proudly told me that his wife was a "Princess"—in Nepal. "She is a Rana," he said more than once. That meant nothing to me. Now I know the Ranas are the family of an eighteenth-century soldier-dictator who ran the country for the benefit of a few. The King's wife is a Rana. They still hold great power in Nepal after having accumulated much of the wealth the country has generated over the centuries. And it is still a country with few public services.

The public be damned, we might say. Catherine showed me a year-old clipping from an Australian newspaper, the *Melbourne Age,* which she had collected in her research. She said she really had not believed it could be true.

> The rats outnumber the dogs in Nepal. It is considered a bad omen to kill them. Dogs help to keep their numbers down. Dogs also assist with human excrement as their voracious appetites provide an unpalatable but pragmatic solution to kerbside stools. . . . The canine contingent is so numerous that unofficial estimates run to 40,000, excluding family pets. On any given street in any of the valley's cities one can see blind dogs, lactating dogs, scrawny dogs, lame dogs, bald dogs, copulating dogs, toothless dogs . . . As with many uncontrolled canine populations, the risk of rabies is high.

"The canine contingent is so numerous that unofficial estimates run to 40,000 . . . "

"Now I know it's true," she said as we left for the airport—on our way to India.

▲▲▲

TIPPING

At the airport in Kathmandu, as we were leaving Nepal, after all the formalities and searches, our formidable line of bags remained on a stopped conveyor. Several envoys approached us whispering unintelligibly, nodding back toward the smiling fellow behind the inspection table. Finally we got it. A small tip. A bribe. But we had voided ourselves of rupees. The smallest American currency we had was a five-dollar bill. We turned it over to him and he walked over to an electrical panel and pressed the "Go" switch. And our bags headed for India.

Later, Catherine said: "He's in a country paying virtually nothing to its people. I am checking twelve bags onto a plane. He's entitled . . . ."

▶ ▶ ▶

Conor and Colin settled into their seats on Air India Flight 814. First, Conor's story:

> We were flying over the Himalayas into monsoon country. Luckily we didn't run into any monsoons, but by the way Mom was acting you coulda fooled me. She started off the journey by saying, "You know the last time we took a flight like this was twelve years ago and we were in the monsoon and we were bumping all around and you were terribly ill with your head in my lap. I was sure we weren't going to make it and I felt so guilty that you would never get to grow up and . . . "
>
> I had to cut her off. I mean, it's unsettling enough hearing something like that under normal circumstances but while taxiing before takeoff on Air India? I mean, Qantas it ain't. (Qantas being the only airline never to have crashed, for those of you who didn't get the joke.) During the flight we ran into some routine turbulence and she started wigging out. "Oh my God! He didn't see this coming, the pilot didn't see this cloud! Oh my God, dear God up in heaven we're not going to make it! I hate this I hate this I hate this!"

Colin's version ended:

> "Dear God in heaven above . . . I've lived a good life . . . I love you boys. . . ." She's used to getting a certain amount of sympathy and soothing words from whoever is sitting next to her, usually Richard. [Not true. We rarely sit together. I've paid my dues and leave her dependent on the kindness of strangers.— Richard] But on this flight she was flanked by me and Conor,

and neither of us suffer paranoid delusions gladly. So Mom headed back to the flight attendants' station where she re-mained for the duration, soaking up their cooing reassur-ances. The landing was a bad one, the plane bouncing hard twice and listing to one side. She didn't even look up from the newspaper she was tearing articles from. It's turbulence that gets to her; she isn't bothered by actual impact.

Ah, India! The Delhi airport is much more modern—and efficient!—than I remembered. They have systems now—like uniformed officials in charge of taxi stands and a line more orderly than the ones at Kennedy Airport in New York City. Perhaps India was beyond the old "No problem!" which meant no chance, and "Follow me!" which meant just maybe. But once we were in the van Catherine had arranged, we were blocked by a rusty bus backing up across lines of arrival and departure traffic. That maneuver, part of a lumbering and smoky U-turn, took a little more time than usual. India was indeed trying to meet world standards; in this case, the bus, with a crew of two, was signaling its backing up with backup lights and that quick beep-beep-beep sound. Unfortunately, both backup lights were smashed and the beeper was a man who walked to the rear of the bus, hung out a window with no glass, and toot-toot-tooted on a whistle.

Reported Conor:

> We were met at the airport by a large, jovial Sikh man in a nice big air-conditioned van. "The monsoons will begin in a few days," he announced with great authority. "It is time for rain." Coming from Nepal, I thought to myself, "Ah, back to civilization." I was wrong.
>
> Driving in Delhi is the craziest I have ever seen and ever hope to see. For starters they drive on the left side of the road. But that's

DRIVING IN DELHI IS
THE CRAZIEST I HAVE
EVER SEEN AND EVER
HOPE TO SEE.

—CONOR

not so unusual. What is unusual is
the array of vehicles operating on
any street at any given time. Buses,
trucks, cars (mostly those comical
little Ambassadors), scooters with
up to four people on them, rinky-
dink little motorcycles, bicycles,
bicycle rickshaws, tok-toks, those
tok-tok–style minibuses, tongas
pulled by horses, oxen, water buffalo, donkeys, camels, handcarts,
elephants . . . And, of course, the sacred cows walking around
unsupervised and unmolested.

ANYTHING AND EVERY-
THING IS STREET-LEGAL,
AND I DOUBT YOU HAVE
TO HAVE A LICENSE.
THANK GOD THE
ROLLERBLADING CRAZE
HASN'T CAUGHT ON
HERE YET.   —CONOR

Anything and everything is street-legal, and I doubt you
have to have a license. Thank God the Rollerblading craze
hasn't caught on here yet. At night it's pitch dark because there
are practically no streetlights and hardly anyone uses their
headlights. It's scary. The only saving grace is that there is a
speed limit of 40 kilometers per hour (24 mph) for cars and
trucks, 50 kilometers (30 mph) for motorcycles. . . . But tail-
gating is the norm; the exhausts are like New York City buses.
Street signals are only sometimes heeded. . . .

In fact, that day's *Times* of India said in an editorial: "Are traffic
lights mere decoration pieces meant to add color to the roads? . . . Not
many road users seem to be aware of their significance . . . worse, even
policemen are equally ignorant of their purpose."

The roads into the old Delhi, as opposed to New Delhi with its
government buildings, embassies, and homes for foreigners, were
brightened by hundreds of porters, thousands probably, walking along
in groups and processions carrying elaborately and brightly decorated
pails and cans of water at the ends of long whippety poles on the men's
bare shoulders. Our driver, Mr. Singh, the name used by all Sikhs, said
they were carrying water from the River Ganges. Holy water. They
were transporting the precious cargo several hundred kilometers back
to their villages, walking for seven or eight days.

Hearing that, Fiona said to him, "I have a Buddha from the Buddhist religion."

To which he responded with diplomacy, "That is also a very good religion."

There were more foreign cars than Catherine and I remembered from earlier visits, Toyotas and Suzukis, trucks and minis. But . . . we were beginning to look at each other. Not much at all had changed since the last time we were here twelve years before. There were almost no new buildings in central Delhi. Horns were blaring, chasing away smaller cars and professional porters pulling carts or bouncing along with their poles and headstraps—everything Conor was describing. Among the districts we passed through were the old tire market, where tires were being retreaded or melted down to make soles for sandals. There were giant hand-painted billboards of handsome and smiling couples—the advertisements of sex doctors and therapists.

Catherine wrote:

I had chosen a grand old colonial hotel, the Oberoi Maidens. We had a pair of enormous suites, one for seventy-five dollars a night and the other for eighty-five, both of them larger than some of the apartments I had as a young woman out of college.

The place was a British leftover. Doormen and guards of various kinds saluted us at every step. Fiona adapted immediately, using a royal finger wave to all as if she were Princess Elizabeth visiting before Independence. Room 310, actually two rooms with high ceilings to vent hot air, was large enough for the two of us to run laps, singing "Heart and Soul." She did a somersault each time we sang the words, "tumbled overboard." Madly.

The air conditioning had the room down to about forty degrees. After a call to the front desk, adjustment arrived in the form of a man in a *shalwar kameez,* carrying a long pole. He used the pole to reach a vent at the top of the high walls and reduced the flow of cold air by sliding a board over part of the opening. He came back every few hours as the room temperatures surged up and down and up again. Central air conditioning, Indian style.

As we arrived, we noticed that what looked like an amusement park had been set up on the greensward between the hotel and the walls that separated it from street life, a wall that seemed the highest in the world later that night. Coming back from dinner, driving through the gates, we came into the center of something like a miniature of New Year's at Disney World with a shooting water fountain where a castle would have been—music and lights, fireworks, a little Ferris wheel and other screaming kiddy rides, carnival booths, Mickey and Donald and other animal characters in bulky plod-along costumes, hugging, laughing, screaming children posing with them as dozens of sleek parents focused the latest in Japanese camera technology. Lights of many colors were strung above it all and professional video crews wandered like minstrels taking it all in. We must have taken a wrong turn on the way back to the hotel and somehow driven into Beverly Hills.

"Happy Birthday, Radikah!" read the banner above it all and the banners in hotel ballrooms where more adults ate and drank at long buffet tables or danced to the sounds produced by a small orchestra and disk jockeys. "Opulence" was the word in my mind as I stood in a window overlooking the spectacle and the platoons of guards and drivers outside the walls, protecting the Mercedes and Toyotas of the crowd inside.

Who were these people and where did they get this kind of money? I never found out, but I did check and find out that Radikah was one year old that day. The next morning, everything was gone, water was playing on the grass to straighten it up again as we drove out to see the city. This was "The Return of the Pink Plume!"

◢◢◢

HOT ENOUGH FOR YOU, COLIN?
Colin, master of the universe of Mexican food, was disappointed in country after country in his search for heaven or hell hotter than habanero. Perhaps India!

He wrote:

I told the waiter that when I ordered the mutton curry from room service the previous night it wasn't very spicy. "What's the hottest thing on the menu?" I said.

"Well, we can make anything as hot as you want it," he said with a sly chuckle. "Take the chicken Tikka. We can make that very hot. Are you sure you want it hot?"

"Yeah, man. Do your worst. Tell the chef I'm not British and he can go nuts with the Tikka."

When the chicken arrived, I was pumped. The wait staff was gathered in the door to the kitchen watching me, no doubt waiting for me to break down, maybe flames would shoot out of my ears like Daffy Duck or Wile E. Coyote. . . .

Again I was disappointed. The grub was a little hotter than the Milquetoast fare I had been served previously, but not by any means impressive. Not a single bead of sweat on my forehead, no need to take pause for bread or rice. I'm gonna send that waiter a batch of my chili for Cinco de Mayo next year. . . .

▰▰▰

In the summer of 1983, when Conor was fourteen years old, we went to Pakistan—Catherine and I and our three sons, Colin and Conor and Jeff—because Catherine was writing about the lives of women in the refugee camps as families from Afghanistan fled south from the war in that country after the Soviet Union invaded on Christmas Day of 1979. That August we crossed the border into India at Amritsar, site of the Golden Temple, the holiest building of Sikhdom—and the scene of a bitter and vicious little civil war between the Sikhs and the Indian federal government from that day to this.

Because of the earlier and ongoing Pakistani-Indian wars and near-wars, we had to walk across a mile-wide demilitarized strip to cross the border. There was an Indian immigration and customs station at the end of the walk and we have a wonderful photograph of Colin, then sixteen, being questioned by a line of bearded men in turbans, each

with a nameplate in front of him saying, in the Sikh manner, "Mr. Singh."
So it was:

"Mr. Singh" . . . "Mr. Singh" . . .
"Mr. Singh" . . . "Mr. Singh" . . .

There were, however, no good
pictures of Conor, whom we had to
practically carry in, a very sick young
man. By the time we got to Delhi, he
was better, or so we thought. We were
driving through the wide and modern
streets of New Delhi in one of the
Ambassador taxis he now makes fun
of—the exterior design of the black
cars with yellow trim is not changed
from year to year—when the sweaty-
browed stomach clench hit him again. "Head for the Taj Hotel!"
yelled Catherine, pressing more and more Pepto-Bismol on her boy.

FIRST STOP WAS JAMA
MASJID MOSQUE, SHAH
JAHAN'S HUGE AND
GRACEFUL MOSQUE,
BEGUN IN 1644 WITH
ROOM FOR TWENTY-FIVE
THOUSAND WORSHIPERS.
RICHARD, WEARING
SHORTS, WASN'T
ALLOWED TO ENTER
BECAUSE THEY DIDN'T
LIKE HIS EXPOSED
KNEES.... —COLIN

She figured if you need a bathroom, why not the best? Mocking
her best efforts, Conor began throwing up—violently but, luckily, out
the window of the speeding cab. As mother and child raced toward
one of the many marble toilets of the great Taj, I paid and watched the
cab drive away, newly decorated with a giant plume of Pepto-Bismol
pink.

Conor was back. The cabs looked the same and Colin and I got
our kicks saying: "Look at that one! He knows it's you. Oh God, here
he comes. Is that a sword?"

Not only the kids were reverting.

Our first morning in Delhi this time was described by Colin:

We piled into a car for a tour of some of the city's sights. The
standard configuration of three in the back, with Fiona
squirming around on top of the bench of thighs, and the
quickest to act riding shotgun next to a driver. . . . First stop
was Jama Masjid Mosque, Shah Jahan's huge and graceful
mosque, begun in 1644 with room for twenty-five thousand

worshipers. Richard, wearing shorts, wasn't allowed to enter because they didn't like his exposed knees. . . . The next stop was Delhi's Red Fort, again the work of Shah Jahan. The Mogul (Muslim) emperor Shah Jahan, one of the great builders of world history, ruled much of what is now India and Pakistan in the mid-seventeenth century. The walls of the fort of red stone run for more than a mile, enclosing warrens of marble rooms and pavilions, hearing rooms, and royal baths.

On the walk from the ticket booth to the entrance, Conor almost decked a woman who pinned something to his shirt, saying, "School fund, school fund!" He reined himself in and settled for tearing the thing off and throwing it at the woman's feet. This might seem like a rash response, but it didn't seem at all unreasonable at the time. Tempers were running short all around, thanks in large part to Fiona's traveling style. . . .

The work of Shah Jahan.

Fiona obviously had a root-canal gift for getting to Colin, but that was not all that was happening. The guys were angry at India, as I had been at Nepal. Catherine caught part of the reason:

> The impact of the day was heightened by the severely maimed people who work public monuments and train stations. There was the small boy with elephantiasis of the foot—a foot that was about three feet long, gargantuan in size. Floppy. There was a person whose thigh bones appeared to have been driven at right angles into his hips, leaving him to walk on all fours in the manner of a monkey—and in fact was called "Monkey Man." . . . You didn't know what the humane response was, and with a child, you were worried about physical contact, because you were worried about disease.

The guys reacted to all this differently. One of the questions on the little quizzes handed out by Catherine as we left each country was this: "What was most difficult?"

"Desensitizing myself to the poverty and suffering," answered Conor.

"Realizing I was immune to the suffering of the poor wretches hounding me for handouts—deformed beggars purposely maimed as infants in order to make a better living," wrote Colin. Then he went on:

> There were a huge number of hawks and vultures constantly circling overhead in Delhi. A plentiful supply of rats keeps the birds of prey population flush. They're part of the cityscape, perching on branches directly above main traffic thoroughfares, sailing by second-floor windows, oblivious to the noise and other distractions of civilization. Gotta go where the rats are. There are many people in India who make their livings as rat-catchers, getting paid per rat. I wonder if they view these big, taloned birds as competition, and wage campaigns of extermination similar to California sea urchin farmers' policy toward the rebounding sea otter . . . or cattle ranchers and wolves . . .

We went next to Chadni Chowk, the great bazaar of old Delhi, described by Catherine:

> The entire range of human endeavor is here, jammed together with the cows, rickshaws, motorbikes, bikes, trucks, cars, and pedestrians in saris, turbans, dotis, Western dress, all crowding each other for space.

But there was trouble in this shoppers' paradise. The day we arrived, a page-one headline in the *Delhi Times* asserted: CHADNI CHOWK HAS LOST ITS SHINE. Said the report: "The street is beset with crime and civic problems. In the last six months, six people were killed as two houses collapsed. Major fires damaged hundeds of buildings. . . . Illegal, unauthorized, shoddy construction . . .

What could be worse? A sign of prosperity, reported by the *Times:* "The importance of Chadni Chowk has been dwindling with the lack of parking spaces."

After that, Catherine, Fiona, and I went over to the United States embassy, a complex so large it includes an enclosed softball stadium used by an eight-team league of embassy people, to talk with officials there about the "Indian Miracle" and such. One of them came up to me and said, "Hey, Reeves. Remember me? I'm Bill Kelly. Van Reypen Street in Jersey City. Frank's brother."

Unbelievable. Frank Kelly was about my closest friend in the world once upon a time. I knew he had become a Foreign Service Officer, in Beirut for a long time, and I knew his little brother, Billy, had been a Navy pilot. It turned out that Bill, too, had gone into the Foreign Service when he retired as a Navy commander. Now he was the embassy's operations director, which he described as being "mayor of this small American town." Fiona immediately got it: Daddy's friend was in charge of the ballfield, the big swimming pool, the bowling alleys, and the people who made hamburgers and pizzas here in the middle of New Delhi. "Wow!" she said. "I'm going to be Billy Boy when I grow up." I said we'd be back.

▲▲▲

AS OTHERS SEE US

There were joint Indian-American naval exercises while we were in Delhi—and that was a very big deal. Relations between the world's two biggest democracies have been up and down, mostly down, since the partition of Indian and Pakistan in 1947.

The Indians were socialists, they were protectionists keeping out American products and businessmen, they were friendly with the Soviet Union, they believed we favored Pakistan in regional disputes (which we did). That said, I've never seen any personal animosity toward Americans outside of ordinary suspicions about foreigners in war zones like Kashmir and Amritsar.

The real problem, now that Soviet-American problems are history, is that both India and the United States tend toward national sanctimony—both countries greatly enjoy preaching and telling other people what to do.

The day we arrived in Delhi, the *Times* of India published an editorial titled "American Doubletalk" saying:

> It is incumbent on the Indian government to make it clear
> to the international community that India will not join any
> test ban treaty which divides the world into haves and have
> nots. . . . This once again brings home the truth of nuclear
> hypocrisy. The United States talks of disarmament while con-
> tinuing to stockpile nuclear weapons in its own arsenal.

Four days later, the paper, India's best, writing in the context of continuing Indian-Chinese tensions, said this of the American role in Asia since World War II:

> The United States' short-sighted policies are creating obstacles
> for a natural balance of power to emerge in Asia. Previous
> U.S. errors in Asia including pouring arms into China to sup-
> port [Chiang Kai-Shek's] Kuomintang, arms that went to the
> Communists . . . Between 1970 and 1990, the U.S. supported

The Agra train station.

China to counter the Soviet Union, which was already declining. The result—China's power today . . . The U.S. did not understand Vietnam was a dike against expansion of Chinese influence and engaged it in a ruinous war. . . . The present U.S. Administration has not learned from history.

▶▶▶

We were up at 5 A.M. the next morning for the trip to see the Taj Mahal in Agra, a first for all of us. (Colin didn't make the cut, rolling over instead of out.) We figured we had to be at the central railroad station by six o'clock to make the 6:55 A.M. train. We figured wrong. We could have gotten there at 3 A.M. and I doubt we would have gotten a ticket, but that's getting a bit ahead of the story.

The ride to the station in the hour of dawn shook both Catherine and Conor more than I would have expected, but one of the things that made this family adventure exciting was learning more about the minds and ways of the people you love—and think you know best. Catherine wrote this:

It is hard to describe the number of sad things we saw in India. For me the saddest was during that morning cab ride. . . . We passed literally thousands of rickshaws along the streets of the city center, all with their drivers, mostly young men, sleeping in the tiny backseats. Some were waking, going to public fountains to wash, carrying what must be the one rag they owned, blanket and washcloth and clothing all combined. For these young men, this was what they had to do— leave their village to come to the big city to make money to send home to their families. My college-educated son beside me, I felt a wave for sadness for the general unfairness of life.

He, in turn, wrote:

We saw hundreds of people sleeping in the streets. Drivers crashed out on their rickshaws, others just on the sidewalk or on the medians with their shirts pulled up over their faces to block out the dawn.

Again, this is normal? . . .The train station was chaos. We had a rough time trying to figure out where to get our tickets, what platform to go to, etc. Some people tried to help us; I trusted no one.

We were turned away from what seemed to be the central ticketing office by a man who first ignored us, or tried to, and then pointed in disgust to a sign we obviously could not read

AT 5:30 A.M., WE PASSED LITERALLY THOUSANDS OF RICKSHAWS ALONG THE STREETS OF THE CITY CENTER, ALL WITH THEIR DRIVERS SLEEPING IN THE TINY BACK SEATS. SOME WERE WAKING, GOING TO PUBLIC FOUNTAINS TO WASH, CARRYING WHAT MUST BE THE ONE RAG THEY OWNED, BLANKET AND WASH-CLOTH AND CLOTHING ALL COMBINED.
　　　　　—CATHERINE

or had willfully chosen to ignore: COMPUTER RESERVATIONS WILL BE CLOSED 4 HOURS BEFORE DEPARTURE FOR PREPARATION OF CHART.

He was obviously preparing chart and we were obviously not going to be on chart. Catherine saved the day, not for the first time in an unfair world where pushing ahead is just pushiness—unless it works, then it's breakthrough or shared triumph. She described what happened this time:

> Heat, disorder, crowds, inefficiency, and flies are the hallmarks of the Delhi station. We arrived at 6:15 A.M. on the wrong side of about twenty-five tracks. Once we had made our way across those tracks, and after asking several people where to buy the tickets for Agra, we finally got in the line. It did not move. The windows next to the Agra line were staffed and had no customers, but only one window sold tickets to Agra. There seemed to be only one other foreigner in the station, an American businessman who was several people ahead of us on the line. He got his ticket. We inched up. Richard took my place and I went looking for the train, which was right on the platform nearest us. There were plenty of seats, but no longer plenty of time.
>
> At ten minutes to seven (five minutes before departure), the entire line surged for the windows, leaving us at the end. Forget the line. We raced for the train, got on, and took empty seats, me sitting next to the adventurous businessman. The train left precisely on time, with the people at the window still jumping and yelling. When the conductor came for tickets, I tried to tell him. . . . It didn't work. He charged us 50-percent extra for getting on the train without tickets—No, he could not sell us return tickets. Those we would have to buy in Agra.
>
> On the eighty-mile, three-hour ride to Agra, I talked with the other American on board the "Tourist Class," (or First Class) car, the only air-conditioned one on the train. He lived in Wisconsin and his job involved selling high-technology in-

dustrial equipment. Although he had dealt with Indian companies for years, this was his first trip to their country and he had been in India for a week. He said that he had been surprised at the lack of infrastructure—roads, electricity, transportation, or the lack of such things—but that he also had found some excellent work being done. He described a factory he had visited at the end of a tiny, rutted-out dirt road outside of Bombay. He said they were making some state-of-the-art machinery, using some parts made by his company. He wondered how they ever got the machines out to and out of the factory, given the road they had to travel on . . . but he had secured a million-dollar order by showing up. . . .

He also told me that he had flown into Bombay the day before and the engine had ingested one of the giant vultures that hover over much of the country. No problem, said the pilot, this was the eleventh one so far during the year. He noted, too, that in the time he had been in Delhi, he had seen no fast-food franchises. That registered with me as well, McDonald's et al. had not yet penetrated Delhi. . . .

Catherine had another observation, or complaint, recorded by Conor: "'You can't see anything. The First-Class train to the biggest tourist attraction in the country and they can't wash the windows?'"

Conor continued:

We got to Agra, and at the station it was a total scene—would-be guides and cabdrivers screaming and literally fighting over us, women pushing trinkets, an array of wretches. The Kid with the Feet, whom we saw at the mosque the day before, was there, too. Military-style cops with big sticks were trying to regulate the hustlers who served as our welcoming committee. . . .

The Taj Mahal was really cool and I'm glad I saw it but other than that the day was basically a nightmare. It was a hundred degrees and filth was everywhere; I was getting hassled by beggars. Mom was stressed and venting. I couldn't deal. So not

only was I tuning out all the wretched Indians, I was also tuning out my traveling companions. . . . I was totally isolated
and I just wanted to get back to the safety of the hotel in
Delhi. But I knew that was impossible due to what I call "the
Brindisi Principle." Brindisi is a port city in Italy where Eu-
railers catch ferries to the Greek Islands. The trains get there
in the morning and the ferries don't leave until the evening, so
if you go there you are forced to spend a whole day, beefing up
the local economy.

Conor cares; he is a very likable man and he wrote this as we left
the country:

The thing that is so intense about India is not just the poverty.
We saw plenty of poverty in Nepal and it didn't strike me as
all that bad because the whole country is stuck in the Middle
Ages. But that's not the case with India. In India there is a
total clash of centuries, and for me it was overwhelming. The
really rich and sophisticated living side by side with the really
poor and ignorant. Businessmen with expensive watches and
cell phones walking down the street past ancient emaciated
holy men swaddled in rags with bare feet and painted faces.
And for them this is normal, but for me it's depressing.

There are also a lot of wretches—deformed, diseased, and
starving beggars everywhere you go . . . there seems to be a
place for these people in society. They are just there, in your
face, at all times. And this is normal? The two that stand out
the most in my mind are "the Kid with the Big Feet" (ele-
phantiasis? gigantism?) and "the Monkey Man." These people
were like sick cartoon characters come to life, very disturbing.
Walking down the street is like walking through a sideshow,
and nobody bats an eyelash. Being accosted by these people
was really upsetting and got to me so much that on our first
day there, I found myself balling up my fists in rage at some
poor eyeless old man who was tugging at my sleeve. The only

At the Taj Mahal.

way for me to deal with it was to completely tune out. . . .
I learned to just look right through them, and it didn't feel good.

Fiona's moment of the day came at my expense. She wrote:

Today we went to the Taj Mahal. First, at the train station, I
saw a bunch of policemen ready to hit people with bamboo
sticks [canes]. When we went downstairs, we saw two tombs
and they were Shah Jahan and his wife. They made us walk
around the room and when we got to the end there were two
plates for offerings, one with flowers and one with money.
The man asked my dad to put some money on the plate. He
put down a hundred rupees and took fifty back. He told me
he was mad because he didn't want to walk around the tomb
and was trapped into paying. "You're not supposed to take
change from the gods, Daddy. Something bad is going to happen to you, Daddy," I said.

   "Nope, nothing bad is going to happen to me," he said,
laughing and tossing back his head. He tossed it right into a
marble doorway. Crack!

Her parents, however, will remember the beauty of the Taj and the
moment when two Indian girls about her age came up to Fiona and
said, "Are you ready for walking?" Fiona seemed nervous, but she said
"Yes," and the three of them walked the pavilions, around the walls,
chattering about their schools and friends, more animated each time
they passed us.

Catherine wrote:

The building does not disappoint. It is graceful and serene. The
marble smooth and the inlay preserved. This building, too, was
Shah Jahan's work, a tomb for his wife, Mumtaz-i-Mahal, who
died in 1631 giving birth to their fourteenth child. It took
twenty-two years to build. Shah Jahan planned to build a second Taj for himself, but before he could he was overthrown by
his own son and now he lies beside his Mumtaz. . . . Just down

Richard, Fiona, and Conor leaving the Agra fort.

"Something bad is going to happen to you, Daddy. . . ."

the wide Yamuna River was another Red Fort, the Agra residence of Mogul emperors, with magnificent pavilions over the water. . . . I ran into my friend from the train. He was carrying a small inlaid marble tabletop, done in much the same style as the inlay at the Taj Mahal. He insisted we go and buy one, since it was a specialty of Agra. I thought for one second about my family's growing displeasure with my treasure trove, and decided that adding a marble table might lead to revolution.

There was not much else to Agra; the center of the town was crowded with camels used as beasts of burden. The tourist express back to Delhi was not scheduled to leave until 7 P.M. The temperature was over a hundred degrees back at the ticket office in the Agra station and the ticket office was temporary home to a dozen or so local folk taking siestas on the marble floor. We found out there was a 2:30 P.M. train coming through and asked for tickets. "You don't want to take that train. Wait," we were told more than once. But finally we got the tickets and went out into the main part of the station.

A small victory, or so it seemed. I overheard someone saying, in an odd way: "They're giving up seats on the Taj Express for the two-thirty?" I wondered what he meant.

Catherine wrote:

> I RAN INTO MY FRIEND FROM THE TRAIN. HE WAS CARRYING A SMALL INLAID MARBLE TABLETOP, DONE IN MUCH THE SAME STYLE AS THE INLAY AT THE TAJ MAHAL. HE INSISTED WE GO AND BUY ONE, SINCE IT WAS A SPECIALTY OF AGRA. I THOUGHT FOR ONE SECOND ABOUT MY FAMILY'S GROWING DISPLEASURE WITH MY TREASURE TROVE, AND DECIDED THAT ADDING A MARBLE TABLE MIGHT LEAD TO REVOLUTION.
> —CATHERINE

It is hard to describe the dirt and flies and general lack of sanitation at the Agra train station. I put down a bottle of orange soda I had bought and in seconds it was full of drowned flies. When the train pulled into the station, a buzzing storm, a gray-green storm of flies rose from the tracks where they had been feasting on feces and garbage.

Added Conor:

The flies, the heat. Our train was late so we waited for what seemed like a minor eternity, first down on the platform but then up on the pedestrian overpass because it had a breeze. Mom bought us all sodas. She of course immediately got out her alcohol swabs and thoroughly wiped down her bottle before putting it to her lips. On this occasion I gratefully did the same. . . .

IT IS HARD TO DESCRIBE THE DIRT AND FLIES AND GENERAL LACK OF SANITATION AT THE AGRA TRAIN STATION. I PUT DOWN A BOTTLE OF ORANGE SODA I HAD BOUGHT AND IN SECONDS IT WAS FULL OF DROWNED FLIES. WHEN THE TRAIN PULLED INTO THE STATION, A BUZZING STORM, A GRAY-GREEN STORM OF FLIES ROSE FROM THE TRACKS WHERE THEY HAD BEEN FEASTING ON FECES AND GARBAGE. —CATHERINE

The only thing I could say was, "Oh, the humanity!" like the guy doing the play-by-play on the *Hindenburg* crash. The whole scene was baffling to me, it made me punchy. "I don't get it, they got this huge piece of land and all these natural resources, they got close to a billion people, why can't they get it together? What's going on in this country?" I asked Richard. "Not enough or not a hell of a lot," he replied. When the train pulled in, late, it sent up flies that covered the platform like a black blizzard. They had all been on the tracks, breeding in the pools of stagnant water and human shit.

There was a mad scramble to get on the train, complete with bad directions, confusion, shrieking, and panic, but we eventually made it onto our car. When we got on we realized why nobody wanted us on this train. It made the morning train look like the Orient Express. We were the only nonlocals; even the Eurail types weren't messing with this.

It was totally dark inside what was or used to be a sleeper car with bunks lining the walls. Now the bunks were filled with fellow passengers stacked in concentration-camp style, unseen but felt as we came through the narrow center aisle. Finally, at the end of the tunnel, we were squeezed into a dark compartment with two groups of surprised men sitting on the beds. In a while, a man from the front of the car, just another passenger, came back with gifts for us, a Hindu calendar and two mangoes. I was touched.

Back to Conor:

It all worked out, I guess. Richard even managed to fit in a two-hour nap, God bless him. . . . I was actually the one who lost my cool. Toward the end of the ride, which took more than four hours, I snapped. I couldn't take it anymore. India had worn me down and I took it out on my traveling companions, going into one of my famous "funks." But as I've said you can't take anything anyone does or says in these situations personally and that goes for me too.

Famous as they are, Conor's funks don't cause trouble. He glares and doesn't talk much—occasionally to himself, but that's all. Colin was triumphantly refreshed when we got back, having swam for a while, read Kurt Vonnegut, and watched a BBC documentary on a young woman who had walked around the world.

▲▲▲

SHOPPING

India is people, not things. The only thing I ever bought there were cricket bats, made from trees in Kashmir and hung from those same trees along miles of roads, and pirated copies of one of my own books. Catherine's more expert commentary follows:

Connaught Circle is still the central shopping stop in Delhi and it has not changed much since the British left in 1947. I saw only one "modern" building, which I think had a Citibank office. . . . But in central Delhi there are no shopping malls or office towers of the standard of Jakarta, Kuala Lumpur, Bangkok, Singapore, etc. The Indian Miracle has not yet happened. And after this visit I'm less sure it will.

The one exception was the entrance to the Red Fort, a vaulted arcade filled with shops, once for the ladies of the Mogul Court, now selling all manner of souvenirs. I fell in love with the hand-painted pages of old Islamic texts with tiny detailed drawings of Shah Jahan and his court. Five hang framed on our walls back home now. They cost about fifteen dollars each and are virtually weightless, thus causing no trouble with my big, strong men.

▶▶▶

And India certainly can wear you down. There is nothing that is not true about India. We and all our countrymen have been told, by the *New York Times* and the United States government, that the country is on the verge of an economic miracle. That reads better than it shows in the country itself where the real miracle may be that it gets through tomorrow. The telecommunications giants of the world are impressed by the skill (and low pay) of computer programmers in Bangalore and dazzled by the size and potential of the Indian market. But that is another way of saying that there is only one telephone for each 120 Indians—and it may not be working right now.

Ah, India! The conventional wisdom is that all this is changing already as India phases out of more than forty years of protectionist socialism taught them by incompetent economists sent by the Soviet Union during the years the United States and India did their best to ignore each other. Mahatma Gandhi, fighting British colonialism, persuaded his fellow citizens that India could and must stand alone, blocking the merchants and the goods and the ideas of the Europeans and the Americans. After Independence in 1947, the Indian government subsidized the manufacture of everything from cotton thread to automobiles—and now many Indian products seem to be about twenty-five years behind the state-of-the-art world.

"This is the last of the emerging big markets to open its doors to international commerce in a significant way," says Jeffrey Garten, then-Undersecretary of Commerce and now Dean of the Yale School of Business. "It's ready for a gigantic leap."

"Emerging" is the emerging conventional wisdom. Catherine's trusty clipping bag produced this December 1994 *Los Angeles Times* headline: U.S.–INDIA TRADE POISED FOR TAKEOFF. The *Independent* in London the same month reported: "Indians are doing the clever computer jobs at a tenth of the cost of programmers in the United States, Europe and Japan." While we were there, *Business India* added this: "Global tastes are increasingly governing Indian spending patterns. Taboos like borrowing to buy, have taken a back seat. Sixty-percent of consumer purchases are bought on credit. . . . Industrial wages have risen faster than prices. There is vast and continuing growth of purchases."

"Emerging market" then is the new jargon, the emerging market of 70 million Indians. Reading that number in a magazine one day, my wife the former official of the International Monetary Fund said, "That leaves a 'poor class' of about 700 million Indians."

▲▲▲

SACRED COWS

For some reason we had the impression that the sacred cows of Hindu India had been sort of pushed out of the center of the cities, at least in Delhi. Wrong! They were still there, everywhere.

The reason, from a 1994 *Sunday Telegraph* (London) article Catherine pulled from her magic file bag when someone asked, is: "The cow is venerated for its five products: milk, curd, butter, urine and dung (fuel). All five are used in the Hindu ritual of penance and purification. . . . Killing a cow is forbidden even though bulls and oxen can be used for religious sacrifice."

India's hundreds of millions of Muslims eat beef and they oppose the laws which outlaw the killing of cows in a country that is officially secular.

In an odd coincidence, a month after we left India, Catherine and I happened to have dinner with Jeffrey Garten, a U.S. official who was so optimistic about India's future. I said that I was not so optimistic and thought some things were getting worse.

"Like what?" he asked.

"Well, the railroads," I said.

The next day, an express train coming into Agra at night was derailed and more than thirty people were killed. The cause: the train hit a cow on the tracks.

▶ ▶ ▶

There is, no doubt, an emerging modern elite class and it was being heavily covered by the very lively press of India, an understandable phenomenon linked to the fact that most of the poor millions cannot or do not read newspapers and magazines. Here are a few of the stories that appeared while we were there:

AMONG THE MIDDLE CLASS: NOW CHILDREN CALL THE SHOTS read a headline in the *Times* of India—remember there is only one television set per twenty-eight people in the country—over this copy: "The MTV generation is ruling the home terrain. One family's children control the remote control for the TV and screech whenever the parents try to watch. BBC market research shows that 40-percent of the decisions involving choice of consumer brands are influenced by the children in the family. Ads have begun targeting children, with children even modelling washing machines."

TEENAGERS GETTING BIG ALLOWANCES was a *Delhi Times* headline over a story of teenage demands for new clothes and money for restaurants. "Most parents interviewed," reported the paper, "testified to a helplessness in the face of rampant consumerism. . . . After working hard to give their children a 'decent' lifestyle, they do not want their children to be left out of their 'peer group.' Parents become an easy target for emotional blackmail."

Another *Times* of India story said: "The Indian Academy of Pediatrics has called for a crackdown on the television culture. Time spent in front of TV is equal to that spent in school. By end of high school, children will have watched 18,000 murders and as many rapes, bombings and suicides, and semi-nude sequences by the tens of thousands. Effects include 'aggressive behavior, acceptance of violence, trivialisation of sex, and increased passivity.'"

A typical American comment on all that came from Senator John Kerry of Massachusetts, who had been in Delhi a few months before, saying, "If India continues down the road on the economic reforms, there will be almost more interest in doing business here than in China, because of the democracy, the legal system, and the lack of a language barrier."

That would be nice, and so are the advertisements in *India Today* magazine for a gated community in Delhi called "Malibu Towne." But I wonder how much pretty pictures mean. Per capita income in the country is still only $310 a year. All conversations about India's once and future economy have to begin with population growth. There are 900 million Indians now—one-sixth of the human race—and though the female fertility rate has been reduced from 6.0 births per woman to 3.6, that lower figure produces projections that India, already the world's most crowded country, will surpass China as the world's most populous by the year 2025. And beyond the gates and the drivers sleeping in the streets of Delhi, half the residents who sleep under roofs do not have toilets or electricity.

The *Asian Wall Street Journal* reported that for foreign investors, India is the riskiest country in Asia, riskier than China, Indonesia, or the Philippines, because "the social situation is much more volatile." There can be political problems, too. The biggest business story in India while we were there involved an American energy company called Enron, which had a $2 billion contract with the government of the state of Maharashtra to build an electrical power plant, a contract that was canceled when the governor who signed it lost the next election. In Bombay, when the Securities and Exchange Board of India announced it intended to computerize the stock exchange, three-thousand clerks and messengers went into the streets to block the conversion—and the loss of their jobs. When the national government proposed allowing America's Cable News Network into India, opposition parties said: "Tie ups like the one with CNN will allow multinational corporations to control the Indian mind."

The Ministry of Labour, while we were there, announced a plan to try to eliminate child labor in the carpet-weaving industry, where six-hundred thousand children under fourteen are said to be paid fifteen cents a day. Yet in Agra, our driver proudly showed us carpet-making factories where children worked. He could not understand that some people thought children should not work.

In a government survey of truckers in Calcutta, 90 percent visited at least one prostitute a week and 5 percent were HIV-positive. In prosperous Bangalore, another survey reported that 81 percent of the doctors said they believed that a syringe could be reused if you changed the needle. In all, India is believed to have more HIV carriers than any other nation and could have 30 million HIV cases by 2010.

On our last day in Delhi, the rains came. The monsoon began, just as Mr. Singh had said it would. Conor and Colin were at the house of Conor's friend from Vassar College, Madhavi Menon, who lives in New York but was back visiting her family in Delhi. Conor wrote:

It was good to see Madhavi and meet her relatives. Her grandfather sort of clarified Hinduism for me. We asked him how many gods there are. He explained that there is really just one god, one divine force that flows through everything and everyone and that all these other "deities" are just examples of this divine force working in different ways. They are used to teach certain morals or what have you in a sort of allegorical way. "Kind of like saints?" someone asked. "Yeah, kind of like that. It's not idol worship." Anyway, I think that's what he was saying.

Colin's take was edgier:

It was nice to see an old friend so far away from home, and her grandfather was all too happy to give us a lecture on Hinduism: not pedantic, just a helpful introductory lesson. He gave me some literature and recommended that, because I seemed to be spiritually wandering in a godless daze, I should really look into Hinduism as a possible solution to what he perceived as my dilemma. I listened politely, and refrained from telling him that his solution seemed as imbued with the same sort of leaps of faith and hard-to-digest dogma as other popular religions. Instead I just told him that I had a Buddha from the Buddhist religion. He did not volunteer that "That is also a very good religion."

Then while we were sitting on the balcony, the monsoon began. Very abruptly. Just as our tolerant Sikh driver, Mr. Singh—the man who assured us that "Buddhism is also a very good religion"—had said it would. It was time to rain. When the first drops started coming down, the stains on the driveway looked like somebody was dropping water balloons. Huge wet circles quickly overlapping and bleeding into one another, this year's advance troops . . . When the rain let up, Conor and I jumped into a cab and headed over to the American embassy, where Richard was having lunch with a guy he grew up with. After a quick meal of burgers and fries on American soil we loaded up our minivan and headed for the airport and our flight to Pakistan.

Fiona, Bill Kelly, and I were swimming in the big pool at the embassy when the rains came. It is one of the great experiences. Catherine and I had seen it once before, not far away, in the house we had had in Islamabad in Pakistan in the summer of 1983. Walls of water, lakes of it, came down all at once at speeds and power defying Galileo and the laws of gravity. I love big weather.

Just before the rains, a sixty-five-year-old man named John Joseph Chari reached Delhi after walking from his home in Assam to protest his dismissal from a good government job as a road inspector. He began the walk on April 13, 1973, was on the road for more than twenty-two years. That is the way some things are done in India. This is true.

It is all true. Everything. It is India.

Chapter 13

ISLAMABAD

After all these years we were back on PIA. Pakistan International Airlines to the world, but known locally as "Perhaps It'll Arrive." This was Flight 271 from Delhi to Lahore, Pakistan, where we would change to a smaller plane for the short flight from Lahore to the airport serving Rawalpindi and Islamabad. We had come this way before. In fact, Catherine's flight anxiety really began on a Lahore-Islamabad flight during the monsoon season of 1983. For some reason the pilot flew straight into a thunderstorm and the plane, a small Fokker turboprop, was overmatched, being bounced around inside this great pinball machine in the dark sky. Passengers were screaming, praying, and vomiting.

The woman behind us, a veiled Muslim lady, remained remarkably calm through the ordeal. As we finally broke into the clear, Catherine turned to her and said: "Why weren't you frightened like the rest of us?"

"I have great faith," said the woman.

Catherine leaned closer to her and said: "Tell me about your religion!"

This time in a larger plane, a Boeing 737 on the Delhi-Lahore leg, she noticed all the Business Class seats on the other side of us were empty. "VVIP," she said, meaning "Very Very Important Person." In Pakistan, and in India, airports and railroad stations still retain the old British colonial system (with the original rough hand-painted signs) of separate waiting rooms for the masses, VIPs, and VVIPs. And, we knew, a certain number of seats were kept open on every flight on the chance a VVIP, a general or a minister, might show up at the last minute. We had long ago learned the hard way how cavalier PIA could

be about honoring reservations and seat assignments—VVIP prefer-
ence was only part of it—but there were ways to beat the system.
Draining and unpleasant ways. Once, trying to get out of Peshawar,
Catherine had said to me: "God, what I'd give to be someplace where
you don't have to burst into tears and throw a fit to get your seat on a
plane."

But tears usually worked. There was something about a crying
Western woman that made PIA officials glance wildly about and then
give up, saying: "Please, madam. Follow me. You will be on this
plane." And so would her husband.

This was Flight 271, a few minutes after the scheduled takeoff
time from Delhi, as recorded later by Catherine:

> In walks a group of men, the obvious leader of them a bulky,
> bearded man in the robes of a mullah. He sat down directly
> opposite us. "That's Faz-le Rehman," Richard said. Oh, great!
> This is a Pakistani "extremist" in India, if you believe what
> you read in the Indian papers, offering to negotiate the release
> of six European and American tourists seized by Muslims in
> Kashmir demanding that Indian-controlled territory there be
> turned over to Pakistan. . . . My normal airplane anxiety was
> reaching new heights. This is a man with real enemies, power-
> ful enemies, multitudes of them. I kept peeking over at him to
> see if he looked relaxed. He calmly read all the papers, while I
> thought about the assassination of Benigno Aquino as he
> stepped off a plane in Manila.

The coincidences and the ironies of life are amazing. I knew
Rehman, by reputation in Pakistan and personally in New York.
Catherine and I also knew Pahalgam, the Kashmir village where the
tourists were captured—and where the kidnappers left the head of one
of the foreigners, a Norwegian. It is one of the prettiest places on the
planet; I had once written an article for *The New York Times Magazine*
about its views and the beauty of its silver mountain streams running
through high meadows of wildflowers. Through mutual friends,
Rehman and I had met one afternoon in 1984 in the backroom of a

discount souvenir and variety shop on East Fourteenth Street in New York. Relatives of his owned the shop near Union Square. One of the things he said to me that day eleven years earlier as we talked about democracy and Islam was: "Your Constitution, which I have read, emphasizes 'rights.' If you buy a ticket you have a 'right' to a seat on the bus. That is fine, but we emphasize human values. Vacating that seat for an old lady is a human value. Do you understand?"

All of us, except for Fiona, had a history with Pakistan, an Islamic republic with a population of 130 million. Catherine had worked and studied here and I had come carrying her bags—along with Jeff, Colin, and Conor. That part of our lives began in 1982 when she was studying for a Ph.D. at Columbia University's School of International Affairs.

At Columbia, Catherine became friendly with a group . . . Well, she can tell you:

> I was approached one day for some help on something by a classmate, a smiling twenty-six-year-old named Farwa Zafar, from Lahore, Pakistan. We became friends. A few days later in a seminar on Indian Ocean issues, a diminutive, feisty, brilliant woman, Shireen Mazari, a professor living in Islamabad, happened to sit next to me. We became friends. . . . I was (and still am) in awe of her clarity of thinking and force of personality.

As I remember it, vividly, Catherine came home from Columbia one night in February of 1983—we were living on East Sixty-second Street in Manhattan—and said: "What do you think about spending the summer in Pakistan?"

"I think you're crazy," was my answer. Actually it was me who went crazy, saying I had to make a living and I sure as hell could not do it in Pakistan. I was just warming up, but Catherine said: "Okay. I brought it up too soon."

"No, no, no," I said. "It doesn't matter when or how you bring it up. We are not going to Pakistan. Never. Never."

We got there three months later, toward the end of June 1983, as soon as the kids were out of school. Catherine was a director of the International Rescue Committee, the largest American refugee organization, founded by Albert Einstein to help Jewish refugees and others to escape from Hitler's Europe before and during World War II. In Islamabad and parts north she began the work that led to the creation of the Women's Commission for Refugee Women and Children with Liv Ullmann, the actress, who was also on the IRC board. I ended up writing a book about the experience, *Passage to Peshawar,* and the next year went back to Peshawar to make a *Frontline* television documentary called "Red Star Over Khyber."

The three boys seemed to get less out of that hot and hectic summer—we have a photo of them in the hills above Islamabad bowing before Catherine, begging to be put on a plane back to the U.S.A. But a few years later, I noticed they all used the trip as a centerpiece of their college admission essays. That was the trip during which Conor compared living in Santa Monica with life in the villages of the Hindu Kush. It was also when Jeff, then twenty, caught a bug of some sort that plagued his stomach for years and significantly diminished his enthusiasm for Asian travel.

I began to realize that I was wrong about how much that first trip meant to them when I read their notes this time, beginning with Conor's:

> I had a sense of foreboding about Pakistan more than anywhere else on the itinerary. I felt as if I were going back into the belly of the beast. . . . I found that I kept making nervous quips about it before we even got there, sort of preparing myself mentally for the experience, I guess. In Bali in the outdoor market I'd say, "You think this is something, wait till we get to Pakistan," or, "This hat is perfect for Pakistan," as if the rest of the trip was just a preface and an epilogue.
>
> The flight from India to Pakistan had the heaviest security I've ever seen on any plane flight. Before checking in, they X-ray your checked baggage and put a "Security A-O.K." sticker on it. Then, after check-in and after they stamp your passport, you go to a little room and identify your checked bags out of a

lineup. While your bags are getting X-rayed, you are getting frisked, or patted down as I like to call it. Then, on the tarmac just before boarding the plane, there is another, more intimidating security squad who actually open each person's carry-on baggage and rummage through it just to be sure. I happened to be carrying the film/medicine/Mom's makeup bag so we had a pretty good time with that. The guy was totally baffled by the disposable cameras. He had never seen one before.

All the security made me a little nervous but I was glad once I got on the plane and saw who I was traveling with—a whole lot of bearded, turbaned, shifty-eyed men who were speaking a language with a lot of a's, l's, and that "kh" sound they make where it sounds like they're clearing their throat. I know it's probably racist but I've seen too many of the *Delta Force* and *Iron Eagle* movies to not get a little fearful in a situation such as this.

We were met at Lahore this time by a cousin of Farwa's. That was a surprise, stopping our run for the Islamabad flight. (Islamabad, a new city of modern architecture built beginning in the 1960s as the country's capital, is twenty miles from Rawalpindi, an old city on the Grand Trunk Road that runs west through the Khyber Pass to Kabul, Afghanistan.) Farwa, it seemed, had arranged an overnight train trip to Rawalpindi for us. A private VIP car on the train was actually being held for us. But because we had meetings scheduled, including one with Prime Minister Benazir Bhutto, we decided we had to fly. In the confusion we lost track (and possession) of Catherine's garment bag, with her fanciest traveling duds.

Fiona's carry-on shopping bag also seemed to be gone and with it her dog "Sandy," a stuffed animal that was beginning to seem real to some of us, the silk kite she bargained for on the beach in Bali, and the *wayang golek* puppets she bought in Yogyakarta. She was taking it like a trouper—the family rule is don't bring or buy anything you can't afford or bear to lose—but the rest of us just wanted to cry for her. At least I did.

And the gods were waiting once again. There was a tremendous thunderstorm between Lahore and Rawalpindi. This got Colin's attention:

Incredible. Unlike any lightning I had ever seen . . . enormous, thick, jagged bolts dividing the sky. When clouds were between the plane and the lightning, the sky would flash uniformly, the light diffused so no source was discernible. I was happy not to be sitting next to Mom.

Her comment was: "I have aged five years in the last three hours."
"*Inshallah* ('God willing') in a few minutes we will be landing at Rawalpindi . . ." We had heard that for the first time twelve years before. He or She was willing and we did.

Wrote Colin:

We were met at the airport by the Pakistani Ladies Mafia Auxiliary Committee, Mom's friends when she was at Columbia over twelve years ago. They were waiting in their Dior *shalwar kameez,* with a small fleet of foreign cars—a Jeep and a Honda Accord—and a couple of menservants to help with the bags.

We packed into the cars as a monsoon squall began and drove through the wide and empty streets of Islamabad to Shireen's house, where we had stayed in 1983. (Shireen was in New York most of that summer.) A few things had changed. Shireen was now married with a kid. Her neighborhood, E-7, was more developed and actually seemed more like a neighborhood and less like an E-7.

It was all immediately familiar to me. Even Khan, the *chokidar,* who met us with a British military salute, his hand palm forward against the right side of his face. The last time we had seen him, Richard asked if there was anything he would like us to send him and Khan made circles with his thumbs and forefingers and held them in front of his eyes. Assuming he meant binoculars, Richard later mailed him a nice pair of field glasses. Khan seemed happy to see us, so we knew that

Richard probably got that earlier request right. It was strange though, Khan looked younger this time, as if he had been living in a time warp. But the neighborhood had definitely undergone changes: there was now a huge house on the lot next door where there had been a field of wild marijuana, and trees had grown tall enough to throw shade onto the streets.

Wrote Conor:

We were treated to a healthy dose of Pakistani hospitality. The cook made us a big meal when we arrived and the local fare was a lot better than I remembered—a lot like Indian food but with some unrecognizable vegetables and not as spicy. For dessert there was a bowl full of mangoes from "our village." I was going to pass on dessert, not thinking myself much of a mangoes person, but Shireen's husband, Tabesh (one of the nicest people I've ever met), insisted and even went so far as to cut one up for me so that I could eat it the way it's meant to be eaten. They were so good I ended up having three.

▲▲▲

A COUNTRY WITHOUT TOURISTS

Pakistan is a country virtually without tourists. It has the Hindu Kush, including K2, the second-highest mountain in the world, and the Khyber Pass; it has Arabian Sea beaches and ruins from the time of Alexander. The Kalash Kafir in the north still live much as they did when Rudyard Kipling wrote of them and their remote life in *The Man Who Would Be King.*

But no one comes to visit them. Nor do many people take the trouble to visit the incredible sultanates of Swat and Gilgit or the rugged land of the Pathans in the North West Frontier Province. There just are not that many foreigners in the country.

It has been dangerous at times. The politics are volatile almost all the time—Prime Minister Benazir Bhutto was deposed and put under house arrest a year after we saw her—but civil disorder has usually been confined to one part of the country. While we were there this time, the troubles were in Karachi, hardly a tourist attraction at any time. Colin tried to put something in his ironic perspective, writing: "We were in Karachi twelve years ago, but things were a little too tense this time around. It was almost as dangerous as Los Angeles."

True. Peshawar, on the Afghan-Pakistani border, was the most dangerous part of the country in recent years after the 1979 war against the Soviet invasion of Afghanistan. Pakistan then was filled with foreigners. But they were more likely to be spies, relief workers, or arms salesmen than tourists.

The rest of the world has lost interest since the war ended in 1989, though that could change depending on the course of continued civil war in Afghanistan. It's a more complicated world than many Americans think. The principal foreigners' hotel in Islamabad, the Marriot, has the usual lobby board of photographs of famous visitors being greeted by the manager. The one of Hillary Clinton and her daughter Chelsea is next to the one of President Rafsanjani of Iran. When we came by to rent a car, the dining room Muzak was playing "Ave Maria!" There were a few men in suits having breakfast, but it was business and money that brought them to a country most care nothing about.

▶ ▶ ▶

Some definitions and explanations are in order here. Islamabad, like Brasilia in Brazil or Washington in the United States, is a "new city," a planned capital built on a treeless plateau, laid out by the Greek architect and city planner Constantine Doxiades—and sections were designated by letters and numbers in the original plan. (The Presidency was designed by an American, Edward Durrell Stone, and looks quite like another of his buildings, the Kennedy Center for Performing Arts in Washington.) It is an enclave of the rich and powerful and foreign, unlike anything else in Pakistan. In layout, the city could be compared with prosperous California neighborhoods, but many homes are bigger because two or three generations of families live together. They have real "family values" in Pakistan. And the edges are

The Ladies' Mafia: Shireen, Farwa, Catherine.

rougher because landscaping is rare outside the walls around many houses and *chokidars,* soldiers, and policemen congregate at corners and gates, gossiping or sleeping. A *chokidar* is a watchman, guard, and handyman, who lives in a house or outside on a rope-bed. Most urban Pakistanis are identified by home villages, where they return for holidays. (Their less fortunate relatives, the villagers left behind, rarely travel more than a few miles in a lifetime, living in a feudal world in the sense that they have no real freedom because they are tied to the land.) The Mazaris, Shireen's family, are rich and powerful, among the large landowners in the country, controlling and also responsible for many villages. Farwa Zafar's family is not of that class, but her father is a prominent diplomat and civil servant who was the director of the national railroads when we first met him.

"Why do they do so much for Mom?" Conor asked me. I said that I thought she had done a lot for them, too, but the reason was probably that most foreigners find America a cold place and Americans too busy to bother with them. "Your mom's not like that," I said.

Lives had changed over time. For one thing Fiona had been born on our side and Shireen had married Tabesh, a pediatrician, and they had a two-year-old daughter, Iman. Shireen had become the chair of the Department of Strategic Studies at Quaid-i-Azam University and then founded a weekly newspaper, *Pulse.* Most everyone in the country who counted politically knew of her strong opinions—including Benazir Bhutto, whom we knew during her years of exile in London. And the Prime Minister did not like Shireen's opinions one bit. Farwa was involved in a nonprofit economic development commission financed by the United Nations and the government of Pakistan.

Catherine wrote:

> We have taken up in mid-conversation—as though we had just left off yesterday. We don't always agree, but there is a caring bond. . . . Farwa cleared her calendar for us. She organized the first large dinner since she moved into her own apartment—a big thing for a single woman in this society—and hosted an evening with her family, whom we had met over the years, and her friends, now members of parliament, poets, and leaders of

the arts in Pakistan—and women activists. We talked about whether or not Simone de Beauvoir had led the full life because she had not married, had not had children, and had not worked in an organization where she had to adjust to male bosses. A leading poet talked of her new autobiography, *Story of a Bad Woman,* and complained that Betty Friedan, my dear friend, had backed off on feminism too much in her book, *The Second Stage.* Needless to say we disagreed. . . .

We talked about Benazir, which immediately divided our friends and their friends. . . . They talked of their belief that the West was selling out Bosnia because they did not want a Muslim state in the heart of Europe—and they wanted to know why the world was not focusing on Indian human rights violations in Kashmir.

COLIN AND I WERE THE ONLY NON-PAKISTANIS IN SIGHT. THE LOCALS HARDLY PAID ANY ATTENTION TO US AT ALL. THE PLACE JUST SEEMED ORGANIC AND FUNCTIONAL...THERE IS SOMETHING VERY WILD WEST ABOUT RAWALPINDI. DUSTY STREETS, PEOPLE TRAVELING BY TONGA CARTS, LOTS OF EXCEPTIONALLY RUGGED-LOOKING CHARACTERS. IT COULD ALMOST HAVE BEEN SOME BORDER TOWN DURING THE MEXICAN REVOLUTION. VIVA ZAPATA!

—CONOR

In the morning, Farwa picked up Colin and Conor for a tour of Rawalpindi. It was Sunday, but as Muslim sensibility rose after partition and the founding of the Islamic Republic of Pakistan in 1947—the name means "Land of the Pure"—the Pakistanis rejected the Christian Sabbath, choosing to rest on Fridays. This was Conor's account:

The bazaar in 'Pindi seemed "authentic" to me in that it catered to the needs of local people and there were no tourists. Colin and I were the only non-Pakistanis in sight. The locals hardly paid any attention to us at all. The place just seemed

THE TRAFFIC IS NEARLY
UNNAVIGABLE, LOTS OF
HORSE-DRAWN CARTS
CROWDING OPEN-AIR
MARKETS, STRANGE
SMELLS WAFTING AS
WOMEN CARRIED HUGE
PARCELS BY ON THEIR
HEADS. IT IS SOMEHOW
A LOT MORE CONVINCING
THAN ISLAMABAD WHICH,
BY CONTRAST, FEELS
LIKE TUCSON.   —COLIN

organic and functional. . . . There is something very Wild West about Rawalpindi (and about Pakistan in general I remembered from our 1983 trip). Dusty streets, people traveling by tonga carts, lots of exceptionally rugged-looking characters. It could almost be some border town during the Mexican Revolution. Viva Zapata! It's low-tech, I like it.

Colin approved, too, writing:

The traffic is nearly unnavigable, lots of horse-drawn carts crowding open-air markets, strange smells wafting as women carried huge parcels by on their heads. It is somehow a lot more convincing than Islamabad which, by contrast, feels like Tucson.

Farwa had a little business to take care of while we were there, and it was a treat to watch her work. She needed to pick up a small pitcher that her mother had left with a polisher some months before. The guy had been evasive on earlier visits and when Farwa caught him in his shop, she found out why. He had been commissioned to put a handle on this pitcher and the quality was not up to spec. Farwa is a tiny woman living in a country where women are second-class citizens, despite the gender of the Prime Minister. . . . Well, Farwa has seen the future and she proceeded to lay into this guy, berating him for his incompetence and making him very nervous. So much so that he tried to assuage her ire by giving me and Conor a polishing demonstration and pulling a laminated letter of recommendation from the wall of his shop. It was written in 1988 by a U.S. Naval officer who swore to this polisher's professionalism and skill. Farwa continued to lambast him, threw some money at him, and stormed off in a huff, Conor and I at her heels.

The Wild East: low-tech Rawalpindi.

Colin in 'Pindi.

Catherine and I, meanwhile, were off to see that woman Prime Minister for lunch at her official residence on a hill overlooking the city. It was not, of course, Benazir Bhutto's gender but her name that was most important—and her courage. The Bhuttos were major landowners in the province of Sind, the lands behind the port of Karachi, and her father, the country's first elected national leader, had been overthrown in 1977 and later executed by General Mohammad Zia-ul-Haq, a man both Catherine and I got to know before he was killed along with the American ambassador, Arnold Raphel, in a mysterious plane explosion in 1988.

The slim and beautiful young woman I had met in 1985 had become larger in every way since being elected Prime Minister in 1993, heavier in body but now with her own gravitas, moving at the center of a crew of fluttering assistants as we sipped orange juice before lunch. (It was suggested later that part of her bulk may have been a bulletproof vest. Perhaps). She was in command, introducing us to an eager assistant for foreign affairs and saying: "I invited him to lunch because I had to pass over him in announcing promotions this morning. I told him to have confidence in me. After the election he will get his posting."

Richard, Catherine, and Benazir Bhutto.

The *Daughter of the East,* as she had titled her autobiography, written with a friend of ours, Linda Francke, was now the very model of the modern national leader. She must serve two hard constituencies (or masters): her own people in a poor, brutal country, and the economic demands of the new money-driven world dominated by the United States and its sidekick, Japan.

Catherine, as is her wont, asked whether Pakistan's heavy military budget could be cut to fight illiteracy—above 75 percent in many places. "We have our security to think of . . . ," began the Prime Minister. Then she said, "Please, let's eat before we talk

OVER COFFEE AND TEA, CATHERINE ASKED WHAT WAS THE MOST IMPORTANT PART OF BEING PRIME MINISTER. WE WERE SURPRISED BY THE ANSWER OF THE YOUNG HARVARD AND CAM-BRIDGE SOCIALIST BECOME A MIDDLE-AGED CAPITALIST: "MY JOB IS TO PROMOTE THE COUNTRY, TO SELL IT TO INVESTORS.

—RICHARD

about such things." So we talked of friends and children. She has two, now. Having seen the same thing with Zia, who continued to live in his military quarters during the years he ran the country, I was amazed again to see gold-trimmed wine flutes filled with a touch of ceremony by servants pouring Diet Coke. Islam.

Over coffee and tea, Catherine asked what was the most important part of being Prime Minister. We were surprised by the answer of the young Harvard and Cambridge socialist become a middle-aged capitalist: "My job is to promote the country, to sell it to investors. Today's chief executive has to market his or her country. There's limited investment capital in the world and it can go anywhere. If we don't market this country aggressively and successfully, we're not going to get our share.

"Economic growth is essential to political respect," she said, articulating the link between her roles as national leader and international saleswoman. Pakistan is a big and very poor country—per capita income is less than four hundred dollars a year—and a very disorderly one. In this post–Cold War world, Bhutto and other leaders of poor countries are now charged with making the world safe for capitalism—at least if they want its economic benefits.

Not so long ago, anything Pakistan did or wanted or had, including the development of nuclear weapons capability and military dictatorship, was tolerated and subsidized by the United States as long as the country was the base for the war against the Soviet occupation of Afghanistan. Now she must march to a different drummer, a sort of benign Western tyranny. "To be a respectable international player," Bhutto said, "one is judged on a range of global interests"—pretty much American interests—"democracy . . . human rights . . . open markets . . . narcotics control . . . population planning . . . environmental awareness."

"As a Muslim," asked Catherine, "do you feel events in Bosnia-Herzegovina would have been different if the people being attacked were Christians rather than Muslims?"

"Perhaps," she said, then gave a harsher answer than we expected, bringing up Kuwait, where Americans did aid Muslims. "When it's oil, yes. When it's human lives, no. . . . I think Europeans are uncomfortable with Muslims in their midst."

CAN SHE SAVE PAKISTAN? was the headline across Bhutto's face on the cover of the current *Asia Week* magazine. She did not. Instead, she was removed from office in a bloodless *coup d'etat* in November of 1996. Perhaps no one can save the Land of the Pure. Can anyone? It is a country of people living in many centuries who happen to share the same geography.

As always, when Pakistan is not at war with India, it seems on the verge of war with India. There was political killing every day we were there in the streets of Karachi. "Mohajirs," the Urdu-speaking descendants of Indian Muslims who fled India during the Hindu-Muslim massacres after Partition, who believe they have been systematically discriminated against from the beginning and were in the streets—in open rebellion against Sindhi-speaking natives of the country's principal port and economic capital. Foreign investors run from street-fighting, especially when Westerners are targeted, like the three American consulate employees gunned down in Karachi as they drove to work four months before we arrived. And in both Karachi and Peshawar, almost a thousand miles to the north, men with weapons left over from years of anti-Soviet warfare in Afghanistan are engaged in the profitable but bloody business of drug-trafficking.

▲▲▲

THE MOST DANGEROUS SPOT
ON EARTH: KASHMIR

The struggle between India and Pakistan for control of Kashmir will soon begin its fiftieth year of overt and covert war, sometimes political, sometimes military. The lovely and bloody valley divided between them under a United Nations resolution calling for a plebiscite may be the most dangerous spot on earth.

Not that outsiders care anymore.

"What are Americans saying about Kashmir?" an American is asked by officials in the capitals, New Delhi and Islamabad. The honest answer is nothing. Terror and rearmament in South Asia have long since passed through the attention span of foreigners.

Unfortunately, if things in Kashmir go on as they have been for the past couple of years, there is the possibility of war on a scale the world has not seen for a very long time, if ever. The status quo—military occupation, official and unofficial terrorism, the occasional kidnapping or beheading of tourists—is probably the most optimistic of scenarios.

The more pessimistic scenarios include:

1. A fourth war between India and Pakistan, with casualties in the hundreds of thousands.
2. A fourth war that includes the use of nuclear weapons.
3. A fourth war that brings China in on the side of Pakistan, with a potential for casualties in the millions as the world's two biggest countries, China and India, collide—the battle of the billions.

Indians and Pakistanis (or Hindus and Muslims) slaughtered each other after Partition in 1947—the division of British India into the countries of India and the Islamic Republic of Pakistan in 1947—and since then South Asia has developed as almost a separate world of distrust and unresolved questions, particularly the question of who runs Kashmir.

In that first year, 1948, the United Nations managed to broker a cease-fire and a division of Kashmir into Indian and Pakistani sectors—with agreement by both sides for a plebiscite to determine which country Kashmiris wanted to join. There is no doubt that for almost all the years since then, the people of the great valleys, most of them Muslims, would choose Pakistan.

But there never was a UN-sanctioned vote, because India had the will and the might to prevent Pakistani dominance—and the Indian position now is that Kashmir is forever and inseparably a part of India.

The Pakistani press runs headlines and commentary like this in the *Muslim:*

INDIA DETERMINED TO HOLD FAKE ELECTIONS IN KASHMIR . . . "Ever since Pakistan has come into being, the Indian factor has predominated in our thinking and politics because India has not let any opportunity slip without causing maximum damage to Pakistan."

In India, where "trans-border terrorists" are blamed for the troubles in Kashmir, the concern has reached the point that senior military officials are saying things like these two separate quotes from generals in the *Times* of India:

"Our boys are battling in Pakistan. Why are we not unleashing our full fire-power on foreign invaders? What we are seeing is a full-fledged war in which the defending side has been told to function as though they were policemen armed only with lathis [canes]."

"When Pakistan is showered with sophisticated armaments by the Clinton Administration, it is criminal neglect on our part not to press ahead with the development of crucial technologies."

Finally it would be a mistake for either country to think the world is watching—and might save them from themselves. No one is watching closely. The Indians and Pakistanis seem to have permission to kill each other forever.

▸▸▸

In that day's newspapers, the *Pakistan Times,* the *Muslim,* and the *Nation,* there were stories of "drives"—the drive to reduce illiteracy, the drive to persuade villagers to let their daughters be educated, the drive to reduce child labor in carpet factories, the drive to stop horrific crimes like an eighteen-year-old strangling his sister and a boy because he found them in "a compromising position." There was a government announcement that four hundred teachers and headmasters were being assigned to remote districts because their students had not done well in national testing. Other teachers were being given free "Haj," trips to Mecca in Saudi Arabia because their students won high scores.

Monsoon flooding was washing away villages; already more than six hundred Pakistanis were dead in flooding and another ten thousand had lost their homes and were marooned, waiting for Army rescue helicopters. In a mixture of anger and frustration, a local writer looked at the flood stories in the morning paper as we had breakfast and said to me: "This is Pakistan. We've known these floods were coming for almost a year, but no one did anything. That's what 'developing' country means. . . . We haven't built a mile of railroad since the British left. We haven't maintained a mile either, the concept is foreign. We wait until things break or the floods come. It's 'God's will.'"

The *Frontier Post* in Peshawar reported on the pronouncements of Qazi Hussein Ahmed, a leader of the fundamentalist party, the Jamaat-i-Islami:

Only Muslims are being crushed and killed throughout the world today, but our politicians of both parties are claiming to fight against "fundamentalism" to win the blessing of the United States. America is afraid of increasing Muslim populations and that is why attempts are being made to restrict their population on the pretext of family planning. . . . Corrupt politicians and bureaucrats are the root cause of rampant corruption, oppression, lawlessness and injustice. . . . Smugglers have made their way into assemblies. Foreign loans are obtained by those at the helm of affairs and then heavy taxes are levied on the masses to pay for them. It is time for the masses to unite against feudals and capitalists.

Back at Shireen's house, we reconnected with the family, as described by Conor:

> Mom warned us that "This party is very important for Farwa"—something about how this is the first time she's had company at her new place. So we put on our Pakistani outfits—Farwa gave Colin, Richard, and me embroidered vests and beautiful *shalwar kameezes* for Mom and Fiona—and we were on our best behavior. The party started out very awkwardly. There was just a very stiff vibe . . . unlike most American cocktail and dinner parties this one never really loosened up for the very reason that there were no cocktails. Booze is forbidden in the Islamic Republic of Pakistan.
>
> It is. But there are ways. There was liquor around when we were there before, but we tried to avoid drinking with Pakistanis. It was more dangerous then, during Zia's dictatorship, but also because people who were not used to the stuff were more likely to get sick or pass out—creating a whole new set of problems. Anyway, our young men did learn that there were simple codes for ordering whiskey and wine from local smugglers—talking about a pair of brown sparrows could mean two bottles of scotch, that sort of thing.

A TWENTY-FIVE-YEAR-OLD WOMAN ASKED ME IF I WANTED TO MARRY A PAKISTANI GIRL. I EXPLAINED THAT I WASN'T SPECIFICALLY TARGETING THAT NATIONALITY, BUT NEITHER WAS I EXCLUDING IT. SHE THEN SAID: "WELL, I THINK IT'S FAIR TO TELL YOU, BEFORE WE TALK ANY FURTHER, THAT I AM ENGAGED. I JUST THINK YOU SHOULD KNOW THAT."...SHE'S MET HER FIANCÉ ONLY TWICE. I ASKED HER ABOUT ARRANGED MARRIAGES AND SHE SAID, "I THINK PARENTS KNOW BETTER ABOUT SOME THINGS."

—COLIN

Whatever Conor thought, I found the evening fascinating. Elegant women would casually talk of two weeks in a Class "C" jail—like airports, prisons were segregated with "A" cells, including air conditioning and servant rooms for VVIP prisoners—during the days of military rule. Engineers repeated the frustration that the idea of preventive maintenance was not part of South Asian culture: things were not fixed until they broke. A lady of some influence who loved golf explained to me that all of the country's courses, built by the British, were in Army cantonments: to play golf you had to play ball with the military. (In much of Asia, institutions often provide a complete life: for instance, Army housing, Army hospitals, and Army schools for children.) Colin, a golfer, joined us and the two of them began using language I did not understand. They have, it seems, a universal language that begins with "Fore!"

Colin also told me:

A twenty-five-year-old woman asked me if I wanted to marry a Pakistani girl. I explained that I wasn't specifically targeting that nationality, but neither was I excluding it. She then said: "Well, I think it's fair to tell you, before we talk any further, that I am engaged. I just think you should know that." . . . She's met her fiancé only twice. I asked her about arranged marriages and she said, "I think parents know better about some things."

Conor described a conversation with Farwa's twenty-seven-year-old sister, Amina, and another young woman:

We compared our cultural differences. I asked them about arranged marriages, they asked me about rock 'n' roll, drinking, and freedom of the press. Amina is dying to be an American but doesn't know it. She is into Elvis, the Beatles, Tolstoy, Sinatra, and Phil Collins. She also really likes the song "Abracadabra" by the Steve Miller Band. She said she would not have an arranged marriage. She has a sister who lives on Long Island and I got the feeling that if she went over to stay with

> THERE IS REALLY A
> UNIFORM NATIONAL
> DRESS FOR WOMEN: THE
> FLOWING, LONG TUNIC
> TOPS, LOOSE PANTS, AND
> LONG SCARVES DRAPED
> IN FASHIONABLE AND
> VARIED WAYS AROUND
> THEIR THROATS AND
> SHOULDERS. THE
> FABRICS AND PATTERNS
> AND THE WAY THEY ARE
> WORN TOGETHER BY
> UPPER-MIDDLE-CLASS
> WOMEN CREATE SOME OF
> THE MOST ATTRACTIVE,
> FLATTERING, AND
> FEMININE ENSEMBLES I
> HAVE SEEN WORN BY
> WOMEN ANY PLACE IN
> THE WORLD. . . .
>   —CATHERINE

her for a few months that would be the end of it.

Fiona's mother wrote:

Fiona was lovely in her pale blue *shalwar kameez* and was busy accepting compliments. There is really a uniform national dress for women: the flowing, long tunic tops, loose pants, and long scarves draped in fashionable and varied ways around their throats and shoulders. The fabrics and patterns and the way they are worn together by upper-middle-class women create some of the most attractive, flattering, and feminine ensembles I have seen worn by women any place in the world. . . . It is hard to "out-generous" our friends here. We arrived with damask tablecloths and napkins we had bought for them in Hong Kong and with presents for little Iman. Shireen gave Fiona a gold neck pendant with a good luck scripture from the Koran and had marble bowls for us.

Back to Conor:

Apparently there were some big shots at this party—a film director, a couple of senators, progressive intellectuals. I don't know if it means anything but I thought this was interesting: of the two senators who were there, the one whose party is in

Party time in Islamabad.

power was a total stiff, and the one in the minority party was a nice guy. The food was good, served buffet-style just like a barbecue back home except instead of burgers and corn on the cob there was lamb curry and *naan*. The whole thing gave me a strange feeling of foreignness and familiarity all at once. Just like some dinner party in the Hamptons but different. Mom seemed to be totally at home: under the stars on a warm summer night, decked out in a *shalwar kameez* and chattering away with the Gail Sheehys and Betty Friedans of the subcontinent.

And Colin:

I enjoyed the food. I learned that the only way to get any heat was to eat home-cooked meals and even then people worry about offending tender Western tongues. . . . My evening was capped off by being cornered for forty-five minutes by a man who explained at great length how wise he had become over the years. After Mom finally came over to rescue me he told her that I would be a "great man in America" because I was a good listener. The in-crowd is the in-crowd is the in-crowd all over the world.

After the short walk home, Conor and I, giddy with our freedom, were greeted by a welcome sight. Khan and his apprentice, Imron, eleven-year-old son of Selena, the house-cleaner, were sitting out front, listening to the radio, chatting about the art of the *chokidar*, the monsoons, neighborhood gossip, the clutch of eggs laid by some lucky bird in the front yard, the latest field hockey scores. . . . [Until reading this, I never realized Colin could speak Urdu.] They both smiled warmly and I wondered just how deliciously hot their dinner must have been.

The next morning, in bright sunlight, we were off to the American embassy. We hired a car and driver to go across town to meet with the U.S. Ambassador, John Monjo. The whole group piled in, partly because among Colin's and Conor's warmer memories of Pakistan in the 1980s were meals—breakfasts and water buffalo hamburgers, mostly—at the American Club inside the embassy. Actually, back then it was a temporary embassy, all of it in a large house rented by the United States Information Service. It was a cozy arrangement; it was like a club. But the reason for the coziness was that Pakistanis had stormed the old U.S. embassy in 1979, killed a couple of people, and burned everything to the ground—with Zia's soldiers standing by and watching. The destruction was in reaction to a false rumor that the U.S. Central Intelligence Agency was somehow involved in a hostage-taking at Mecca, the holiest place of Islam.

I'll let Colin pick up this tale:

For the ride over to the compound we abandoned our usual seating configuration. Richard usually sat in the back with Fiona on his lap, but today he was wearing a suit, his only one, and wanted to avoid any unsightly rumpling, so he cried out "Shotgun!" as the car pulled into the driveway. A little startled by his outburst, we honored the rules of the game and relinquished the front seat. Shortly into the ride, however, he became the victim of some ancient tenet from Greek literature. The monsoon made its morning visit. We were driving through a furious deluge, visibility was not much farther than the hood of the car, an unbelievable volume of water. It wasn't long before a hard left-hand turn conspired with a perfectly placed leak in the sunroof to dump a quart of water into the lap that was being spared a rumpling. Cats and dogs in the front seat, nowhere to hide or squirm to avoid it.

He emerged at the embassy sporting a stylishly mottled look—destined for a couple of hours in the sort of air conditioning that can be found only in U.S. embassy compounds in the tropics. An imperial, chilling blast. Gone are the days of ceiling fans hanging in high, shuttered rooms. The Brits are out, disinfecting their wounds with gin and quinine, and there's a new imperialist in town, wired on Larium and throwing dollars around, bringing his own Bud and keeping his rumpus rooms icy.

By the time we got to the gate, the rain had stopped. The first checkpoint was Pakistani. An obviously uncomfortable Army sergeant showed me a piece of teletype paper that said "REEVES and Party, 10 A.M."

"Is this you?" he said. Clearly he could not read English.

"Yes," I said. They waved us on. Great security. The paper could have said "CLINTON" or "JESSE JAMES" and they would have done the same thing. We drove up to the American checkpoint and the car was searched. Guards there were talking about a murder. It seems that after we left the Prime Minister's residence a constable shot and killed one of Bhutto's servants—no one knew why yet.

Conor:

> Breakfast was awesome. Bacon, eggs, hash browns, real American coffee with free refills and everything, and half of Fiona's waffle. In the club, technically on American soil, I was overcome with the same sense of patriotism that I had felt twelve years earlier. "I love America!" I proudly proclaimed. After breakfast, while Mom and Rich were talking with the ambassador, Colin and I shot a few games of pool and watched ESPN in the upstairs bar. I was moved truly to tears, it was a beautiful thing.

Ambassador Monjo was finishing up after three years in Islamabad. He ran off a string of mostly discouraging facts: Seventy to seventy-five percent of their budget is defense costs and debt payments because they're locked in cold war with India. . . . This is still the most likely nuclear flash point in the world, but the generals on both sides are rational. . . . They see the United States as a fair-weather friend. . . . Benazir is trying. . . . But the birth-rate is still above 3 percent."

It struck me that there were 20 million more people here than there were when we came twelve years before.

Catherine and I both went shopping then, each in our own way. She went to carpet shops with Farwa. I roamed bookstores in Islamabad.

Catherine's account began:

> I am a weak person and my friend Farwa is strong. I knew I could not buy a rug. The family would kill me. But Farwa took me to a building behind the local version of a strip mall. Up some dark stairs and at the top . . . *Voilà!* There were a dozen or more shops all selling gorgeous rugs, hundreds of them piled one on another. I kept telling her, "We're just looking."
>
> We sat on a pile of rugs. She started ordering around the young man who was alone in the shop to "Show this one . . . no not that one." I was getting even. weaker. But if I got a rug, it would have to be small, so we could carry it. Then I remem-

bered that some of those heavy damask tablecloths we had been carrying since Hong Kong were being left here as presents. . . . I imagined how each rug would look in my front hall. After Farwa talked down the price, I settled on a hand-made old one in tones of brown and green. It was sixty-seven dollars and I slipped it into one of our bags without telling anyone. Well, I did tell Fiona, but she understands these things. (It looks lovely now in our front hall.)

Books aren't light either. And you can learn a lot in bookstores. Islamabad's best—Mr. Books and the London Bookshop—are like attics, wonderful surprising places filled with dusty volumes and magazines left by the British and the Indians who went south at Partition. *The History of Khyber Medical College* was next to *I'm OK—You're OK.* Random information, no time line—perhaps that accounts for the computer-programming brilliance of so many young people in South Asia.

The very best sellers all seemed to be about one man, the world-class cricket star Imram Khan, retired now at 42, the country's most famous and most handsome player. Adding to his fame, he had returned to Lahore that very week with a bride, twenty-two-year-old blond and beauteous Jemina Goldsmith, daughter of one of the richest men in the world, Sir James Goldsmith. She had converted to Islam and it was rumored that Khan was interested in politics and that the happy couple would soon be visited by her great friend, Diana, the Princess of Wales. (Diana did come and joined Mrs. Khan in charity work at hospitals funded by her husband. And Mr. Khan formed a political party, Movement for Justice. When Benazir Bhutto fell, he began a national campaign tour, saying in cricket talk: "Let me be the bowler, and you take catches. We can bowl them all out and rid Pakistan of this political mafia!")

Pakistan's *Newsline* magazine ran a headline saying THE BRITISH PRESS EXPLOITS THE IMRAM-JEMINA MATCH TO INDULGE IN ITS FAVORITE EXERCISE, "ISLAM BASHING." One headline cited: DON'T THEY MECCA LOVELY COUPLE?

The new thing at the bookstores were New York City newspapers. I saw the *New York Daily News* and *Newsday* everywhere. Why? I finally figured out that not only are there large numbers of Pakistanis in New York, including in my mother-in-law's building in Woodside, Queens, many of them are in the newsstand business, selling them in candy stores and street kiosks they are buying from the city's elderly Jews. I bought two books, one a small volume of columns by a Karachi newspaperwoman named Zeb-un-Missa Hamidullah, written during a 1956 trip to Hollywood and points East in an exotic place called America, and the other *The Zia Years,* by my friend Mushahid Hussein.

Mushahid and I had met in 1983, when he was editor of the *Muslim,* an Islamabad daily, the best of them. There was a photograph of the Ayatollah Khomeini in the paper's conference room, not something an American saw every day. We had kept in touch over the years. He was an international affairs graduate of Georgetown. A lovely man, very smart. "He is a Shia," said more established Sunni Muslims, the majority in Pakistan, who did not like his politics or his paper or maybe him. (Without going into the whole thing, it was something like an Episcopalian dismissing the opinion of someone because that someone was a Baptist.)

We had lunch with Mushahid and his wife, Dushka, another classmate of Catherine's, the day before we left Islamabad. He was still a man of some prestige, essentially the shadow foreign minister of the Pakistan Muslim League, the union of parties in opposition to the Pakistan People's Party, the more secular and leftist party created by Benazir Bhutto's father. Between Benazir Bhutto's two terms, Mushahid had served as chief of staff and national security adviser to Prime Minister Nawaz Sharif from 1990 to 1993.

We had a wonderful time—Mushahid mixed talk of politics with talk about the doings of his eight-year-old son, Mustafa—talking about families and about the issues that divide the worlds of an American writer and a Muslim intellectual. I sensed, not for the first time, that there is an anger in Mushahid, beyond the personal, against what he sees as the unfairness and gaps between the rich and the poor nations. What I see as reasonable or capable of being worked out, he does not. We are friends, I think. But he is, as the Irish might say, ready for the troubles. More than I am, which of course is natural, because he wants more fundamental change in the world than I do.

That night, we said our good-byes to everyone. We have known these people almost all of our married life and, though we live so far apart, feel close to them. When we were alone, Catherine and I talked long into the night and the next day about our bonds to this place— and about those troubles the future might bring.

Our flight out was long delayed by monsoon storms. So we decided to see whether there was anything we could do about our lost bags. Catherine, usually a match for any bureaucracy in the world, lived to tell this story:

> I went to file a report and see if either bag had shown up, but I wasn't allowed to go past airport security guards. They told me that it would be "much better" if a male member of my family were to make the baggage inquiry. Richard gathered all the old tickets and went off to test the old ways, not only sexism but systems still prisoner to the archaic procedures and paperwork and carbon copies of the British Raj. He returned with no bags, but surprising news. He had had tea with the person in charge of domestic lost and left luggage. A woman.
>
> Then he went off to International Lost and Left, but came back totally frustrated. He had made the mistake of telling someone that the bag was his wife's and they immediately seized on the *sahib*-error; he was not allowed to file a claim for another person. Only I could do that, but the guards would not let me out of the "Secured" area because I was a woman.
>
> Richard went back, determined to get into the rooms and cages where they kept found luggage. And he did, coming back to report that nothing we owned was located, but that for some reason there were hundreds of baby strollers, all different, all covered by the dust of months if not years. The final word was that we should file a claim with PIA in New York. Right.

On the plane finally, Catherine sat next to a woman, not young, who would look at home in most any village in the farther reaches of Pakistan. This was her story:

Wearing a long one-piece covering and a scarf wrapped around her head, she was in her late fifties. . . . Her husband had "land," she said, over a thousand acres with cotton, wheat, mangoes, and other products. Her son was studying at George Washington University in Washington, D.C. Her older daughter was married to a Pakistani boy she, the mother, had selected and they were living in Pennsylvania. Her younger daughter had been married a month ago in Karachi and that was where she was going, to celebrate the one-month anniversary. That marriage, she said, was not arranged. She had allowed the younger daughter to talk to the young man on the phone, then allowed them to see each other in the presence of many adults so that they would know each other before marriage. She thought arranged marriages were preferable but that the children should have the right to veto their parents' choice.

Of her country, she said she worried that people spent too much money on the wrong things—weddings and shows of pomp. The founding fathers of the country had had the interests of the nation at heart, she believed, but too many of the new breed of politicians thought only of themselves and not of the national interest. She said she thought that the country should spend more money on making life better for its people. . . . People were leaving the farms. She said that the children of her husband's farmworkers were becoming educated and some were going to college. That was good, but she thought that in order for farming to survive in the future it would have to be mechanized.

She also told me that she felt that women the world over had a lot in common. They had it harder than men and there was a bond among them. She mentioned then that she had a master's degree in political science.

We exchanged cards and she promised to send me a Christmas card.

I have always envied my wife's ability to talk to strangers. I read. Desperately curious introverts like me become reporters so that we have a cloak, an institutional cover, that allows us to ask questions. We work in *purdah*.

In each country, we asked each other whether we expected to come there again. We decided we would come back for another visit—a longer one next time.

Chapter 14

DUBAI

Catherine will now explain why we went to Dubai and spent thirty hours there:

> For years, alone, together, or with the family, we and millions of other Americans and Europeans stopped at the Dubai airport for a one-hour fueling layover on the way to Asia and points east. We'd have a coffee, tea for me, pick up the two English-language newspapers, the *Khaleej Times* and the *Emirates News,* stroll through duty-free shops, and, for our trouble, end up with a heavy pocketful of dirhams, the coin of this realm and no other. I'd think of those stops every time I noticed the dirhams and the distinctive engravings of Arabic pitchers on them each time I was in Richard's office—because he has never learned to void himself of local cash before moving on. . . . So, I just wanted to see what it looked like and how people lived in the incredibly rich United Arab Emirates.

It looked ugly and Emirians live well.

The 350,000 of them, citizens of the UAE, use the revenues from the oil under them—a humorous God's joke on the rest of the world—to bring in a million-and-a-half foreigners to do their work for them. That leaves them free to look at their deserts, camel races, and the listless waters of the Persian Gulf.

Wrote Catherine after they let us out:

> It's a place which celebrates money. It does not welcome visitors, but does import workers—maids, garbagemen, engineers,

soldiers, whatever they need. Eighty percent of the people living in the nation are not citizens . . . and can never be. After all, the actual citizens, though they have no political rights, do get a share of the oil money, about $17,500 per capita each year, after the emirs of the seven emirates take their cut off the top. There are no income taxes and the citizens get free medical care and schooling through college.

For anyone interested in watching them be rich, the seven emirates, which were sleepy British protectorates until oil was discovered in 1966, are: Abu Dhabi, Dubai, Sharjah, Ras-al-Kaihmah, Ajman, Umm al-Qaiwain, and Fujairah. They are enclosed as an enclave on the Gulf by Saudi Arabia and Oman. Just across the water is big, bad Iran.

Dubai is run by a family named Maktoum, whose members seem to spend a good deal of time meeting with other Emirian princes, at least judging by pictures in the *Times* and *News*. The population of the city is 206,000 and they are not looking for any more.

Continued Catherine:

They rob you before they let you in. You must have a "sponsor" to get in and that costs one hundred dollars a head with your two-hundred-dollar-a-night hotel as the sponsor. . . . Then we were at the airport for quite a long time because Colin had to get a twenty-four-hour visa. He had been working in Moscow (and so was his passport) when the rest of us delivered our passports to get visas in Los Angeles.

This is what happened next, according to him:

The rest of the family was ushered into the express Right-This-Way-Keep-Moving line, while I was singled out and told to wait indefinitely in the You-Might-Be-Sleeping-in-the-Airport line. They wanted my passport, so I handed it over. . . . I was admitted to the country under some kind of passportless house arrest. An airline guy who had taken my ticket did hand that over or tried to. The thing, the whole around-the-world thing, slid out of his hands and piled up at his feet. It was about eight feet long with an impenetrable system of creases and folds; a code that gives it some kind of meaning at check-in counters. Every attempt at folding it ended with the thing slipping through his fingers or squirting out the sides and hitting the floor again.

Finally, he just scooped it up into a pile and held it out to me in his cupped hands like a white flag, hoping for mercy. I rolled it up and stuffed it into my shirt pocket. . . . At the hotel there was a sticker on the bedside table with an arrow pointing to Mecca. I peeled it off and rotated it a couple of degrees, setting a heading for Philadelphia and thinking of Salman Rushdie. . . .

Catherine wrote:

The rest of us were sponsored by the Dubai Intercontinental because I thought we should be in the city center, instead of lounging at some fifty-acre hotel resort. It didn't matter, because there was no one on the streets anyway in the blazing double-hundreds summer heat. People moved from door to door by car—52,000 automobiles were bought last year, 42,000 from Japan, 5,000 from the United States, and 4,000 from Germany. Whether they have drivers or not, Emirians leave their cars running while they are shopping or whatever, so that the air conditioning will stay on. . . . Dubai is a collection of three- and four-story shopping malls . . . with nondescript modern buildings in between.

The shopping malls have some foreigners in Western dress and more black-robed women, peering through their veils to try and see what the shoe they are considering looks like. There is a wider assortment of black fabric than I imagined existed in the world. The shopping emphasis is on the fabric and on gold.. . . . I went to the gold souk in the afternoon. I went to store after store looking at jewelry filigreed in very

Catherine: "Dubai is a collection of three- and four-story shopping malls. . . ."

The chosen—by oil.

delicate patterns—in one shop, a man dressed in white robes was looking at bracelets for three women dressed head to toe in black robes. What was astonishing to me is that they wore gloves to cover their hands, which did not stop them from trying on bracelets. In one perfume and incense shop, they sold bottles of packaged European brand-name perfumes. Next to each bottle were glass vials with numbers. I was given a sheet on which each number corresponded to an international perfume. Chanel, Poison, etc. I tried a few, and am now the possessor of a five-dollar vial of perfumed oil called Coco Chanel. Since I do not normally invest in perfumes, I have no idea how close the scent is to its namesake.

While I was in the shop, three women, two quite young and one much older, came in dressed in black with eye-slits about three inches wide. This allowed wrinkles—or the lack of them—to be observed. The older woman had tattoolike marks on her hands—no gloves on this group. They sampled incense and talked loudly and aggressively to the shop helper, probably a shopping expedition of a family from the country.

I went into a gold shop which displayed crowns and immense gold belts and filigreed gold breastplates, all of the pieces encrusted with jewels. I asked the proprietor who would buy these and what would they wear them for. "Very rich people, madam," she answered. "For weddings."

I also noticed that a number of shops displayed tiny gold charms with Christian themes, then realized that with all the Filipina maids who have been imported to take care of the homes and children of the emirate, this was a way to get back some of the foreigners' hard-earned money. Sure enough, while I was there, young women, foreign maids and nannies, appeared to admire the crucifixes.

That captive retail market is not so small. There were 21,400 Filipinas in the UAE—and others from Indonesia, Sri Lanka, and Kenya—most of them quite young. The courts had just sentenced one of them to seven years in jail for murdering her employer after he raped her. But, whatever the working conditions, the economic reality is that maids in Dubai are paid about 200 dollars a month and school-teachers in Manila earn less than half that much.

Catherine continued:

Other than buying a few black veils, which I thought would be attractive as scarves, I left the gold souk empty-handed. I did try to take a few photos, but even though the women were veiled and across the street, they turned and yelled at me when they saw the camera. The veils can be seen through when pressed to the wearer's eyes. But an observer cannot see the face underneath.

I also visited one of the large shopping malls. . . . It carried a full range of Western women's wear. The foreigners in the mall were dressed very casually. Dubai is among the most lib-eral of the Arab states, considered a "foreign-friendly" emirate. Women from other countries are allowed to drive and wear their own "national costume" on the streets. . . . I was also sur-prised to see liquor in the minibars in the hotel, and on restaurant menus. In Pakistan, you had to show a foreign pass-port and swear that you were not a Muslim before you could buy alcohol by the glass—or eat (behind screens) during Ra-madan, the Muslim month of fasting between dawn and sun-down.

The UAE may be more friendly for businessmen, but local women still are not allowed to work or travel without written permission from their husbands.

I was not crazy about the women in black. While we were sitting in the hotel lounge, where the usual ranges of liquor were available, they came through in what may have been Islamic slumming. Though you could not see their eyes, or any other feature, they stood and ap-peared to be staring at us—as if the Intercon were a museum of deca-dence, or a zoo. The food, however, was great. One hotel restaurant served fresh fish laid out with vegetables and condiments; we chose our own dishes, they were weighed and priced, then prepared to order.

سيدات
Women

Fiona: "Hey, look at this sign."

Conor in the Persian Gulf.

Fiona, on the other hand, loved Dubai. Our plan was to check out early in the afternoon, then hang around the pool, have dinner, and go out to the airport for our 3:40 A.M. flight to Cairo. She had headed for the pool first thing in the morning, hooked up with a French girl her own age, named Sonya, and the two of them splashed and played happily around until sunset, testing the energy and creativity of pool-side room service. Afterward, she informed me that she had decided to change the title of her book from *Fiona's World* to *Room Service Around the World.*

She also got a kick out of ladies' room doors marked by a woodcut of a woman wearing a veil. And she got a needle into Colin when he enlightened all with a reference to the date John Lennon or someone died. Said his little sister: "He knows when every famous person died and how, but doesn't know when anyone was born."

Leaving her to the lifeguards and Sonya's family, the rest of us rented a car and went out to see what passed for countryside in those parts. It was, noted Colin, the first place we had been since Japan where all the traffic was automobiles. No scooters or bicycles. There were housing developments behind walls in the distance. The landscape was dreary, rubbley desert without color or any signs of life beyond the warehouses and gas stations. And the camel track! There was a grandstand and a club, substantial and well-maintained on an artificial oasis (irrigated and sprinkled even in the off-season)—all familiar to thoroughbred lovers except for the fact that the track itself seemed miles long—it went out as far as the eye could see on flat land. Camels, cover a lot more ground than horses.

But, wait! Crown Prince Mohammed bin Rashid al-Maktoum, who is the Defense Minister of the UAE, is also the owner of more thoroughbred horses than anyone else in the world and he had just put up the money for a four-million-dollar Dubai World Cup, which was expected to draw some of the world's best horses (or their owners) to his desert track. They did come, and the race was won by the great American horse Cigar. In tennis there is a Dubai Open and in golf, the PGA Dubai Desert Classic.

In that desert, we drove past fashionable neighborhoods with large houses along Jumeirah Beach Road to a park at the water's edge. There were parking lots there and a refreshment stand. Our only companions on the sugary sand were a small tour group of Eastern Europeans, wearing the kinds of bathing suits you see in old pictures of Odessa—and, in fact, I learned later that the locals call this "Moscow Beach." The beach was quiet and so were the waves, more like a bay than open water. But the sand was as hot as a stove top. The waters were clear and green and Conor, the only one of us to swim out, reported back:

> The high point of my visit was swimming in the Gulf—as warm as pee and ten times as salty. Other than that there's not much to tell.

There were other Americans around, too—young men with short haircuts. Military. The United States Navy has fifteen ships, including an aircraft carrier and two nuclear-powered submarines in the Persian Gulf, manned and protected by ten thousand sailors and Marines. After going to the markets, Catherine wrote:

> The young Americans, apparently off-duty for an afternoon, cruised the souk looking at gold chains. I would hate my sons—or anyone's sons and daughters—to have to risk their lives to defend selfish, unjust Emirians. Since the Emirate cannot survive without oil sales, why does it matter to us which family or group controls the oil? They will have to sell it to sustain themselves . . . and the next group is unlikely to be worse than the present group.

Tough lady. But that subject, which is really the United States role in the Gulf War, is also being talked about nervously in the UAE—from the top down, like everything there. The princes of Araby have absorbed the obvious: Kuwait, a country of 650, 000 people but only 100,000 citizens, would now be part of Iraq if American sons and daughters had not come to preserve that particular monarchy in the name of King Oil. On the day we visited, the commander of the UAE armed forces, which is made up mostly of Pakistani and Indian Muslim troops, was in Washington, discussing "military cooperation." That is a euphemism for come-save-us-if-the-Iranians-invade. Of course, at the same time, the princes, in the name of Islamic solidarity, complain publicly about United States efforts to contain their big and belligerent but still Islamic neighbor to the north.

One of the lessons the emirates seem to have taken from that international rescue of Kuwait was the disgust of Americans like Catherine (and me) at the thought that our boys and girls risked their lives to preserve a medieval lifestyle in which young women are kept behind walls and the young men not only don't fight for their country, they don't even work.

On our day in town, the lead story in both UAE newspapers was a speech by the President under the headline: SHEIKH ZAYED URGES YOUTH TO SHOULDER RESPONSIBILITY. The report began: "His Highness President Sheikh Zayed bin Sultan Al Nahayyan yesterday said work is an honour to every human being and the right path towards civilisation, welfare and prosperity. . . . 'The more work and effective role the UAE national has in his society, the more respect he will receive from his people, Government and homeland.'"

The papers are censored by the government. Foreign publications must pass through the Ministry of Information and are allowed to circulate only after being checked for pornography and criticism of Islam or the royal families of the emirates. Television and radio are owned and run by the government, although the number of local advertisements for direct satellite-to-dish repairmen indicated that the same people who regulate what others can see are treating themselves to censored fare.

I felt as if I were locked in a bank overnight. Catherine concluded that we had seen the best of it before this trip: "The liveliest, most diverse and interesting place in town is the passenger lounge at the airport."

That was literally true. When we had arrived the day before, there was an immigration booth for American and European passports, but no line. Just us. There was another for UAE citizens. No line. Citizens were probably on vacation in Europe to beat the deadly heat. But there were long lines of young men at the booth marked "Foreign

Passports," workers coming here from the countries we had just visited in order to make money to send back to their families, perhaps even to earn enough for a bride back home.

At the airport, on the way out, Conor wrote:

> Our flight out didn't leave until 3:40 A.M. . . . We lounged around the Intercon pool well into the night, then had dinner at the Hyatt and went to the airport. Mom and Rich and Fiona went to the Singapore Silver Kris Lounge and promptly fell asleep. Colin and I sat wide awake in the crowded public waiting room with the peons. . . .

Colin, worried about trouble over his twenty-four-hour visa, was a little more stimulated—lucky for all of us as it turned out. This was his story:

> I was tense, not knowing whether my disregard for Dubai's laws was going to land me in the proverbial back washing dishes . . . or if I would have to spend a couple of years beating carpets and feeding camels for some Bedouin warlord. I've seen *Midnight Express*. I know how it works. . . . At the immigration office, an armed officer talking on the phone threw my passport across his desk and dismissed me with a wave of the hand.
>
> I fell asleep listening to a Russian man next to me as he gave repeated loud demonstrations of a walking stick that exploded into an umbrella at the push of a button. Just one of the nifty little numbers available at the world's largest duty-free shop downstairs. He offered a test spin . . . no doubt a symbol of his free-market liberation, and I did not want to risk offending him. So, I popped it open and said "Wow!" . . . The thing was a shoddy piece of crap, furthering the symbolism in a way that was lost on the beaming new capitalist. . . .
>
> I woke up, glanced at my watch, and realized that our flight left in twenty minutes. I woke up Conor and then went to the Business Class lounge where Mom, Rich, and Fiona

were curled up on modular couches. They each had to be
awakened. . . . The sight of my mother suddenly coming to,
and looking around in momentary confusion was something I
had seen in other people, but never in her. The roles had always been the other way around. Dazed, half-asleep, unclear
about her surroundings, maybe slightly panicked for an instant. It didn't seem like her, and made me feel old. . . .

On the plane I grabbed Richard's Walkman, which he
bought somewhere along the way—India maybe—in order to
transcribe an interview with Fritz the Cat Mondale for a column. Conor had a cassette of early mixes of some tracks he's
been working on. One of the tracks, when played fast, sounds
like an old pop song by the Cure called "The Stranger," after
Camus's classic about the death of an Arab. In fact, the chorus
includes the line "killing an Arab!" . . . I yelled to him, loud
the way you do with earphones on, "Is this the killing the
Arab song?"

Conor looked around at our companions on the packed
plane, looked at me, and said, "Are you completely insane?"

Conor wrote:

I didn't sleep a wink on the flight. It was the up-to-date version of the overnight train across Java. At one point I looked
over to Fiona, who was sitting one row up and across the aisle
from me and she was sobbing uncontrollably. "I can't sleep,"
she cried. I took her up to Raffles class and dumped her on
Mom and Rich.

Catherine's forms asked about the future of each country. Conor's
answer this time was: "One day the oil will dry up. I hope I live to see
that."

Chapter 15

CAIRO

The first person we talked to on the walkway outside the Cairo airport was a young Egyptian soldier wearing a "Military Police" armband. He asked: "Are you Americans? Do you know where Oklahoma is?"

He was headed there for training with the United States Army and his question was one of many signs that the United States more or less adopted Egypt after it signed a peace treaty with Israel in 1979. Since then the United States government has been pumping more than $2 billion a year into Egypt, an annual award for not invading Israel anymore. But we were to find that Cairo also had its growing share of problems. Coming back for the first time since 1983, it seemed to Catherine and me at first glance that the Egyptians had spent their bounty relatively well. Driving into the city before 7 A.M., we were impressed with new cars, newer and wider and cleaner streets and overpasses—they call them "flyovers" in the English manner—a new subway and new suburbs along the way.

Our hotel was on Gizera Island in the river Nile across from the center of one of the oldest of world cities. The Gizera Marriott. (In this wired world, almost all international hotels, even the oldest and remotest, must become part of the big chains because the Marriotts and the Hiltons and the rest control electronic international reservation systems—it's as simple as that in the global village.) The Gizera, however, does not look like a Marriott. It struck me as something like an Arab Grossingers, the most famous of the Catskill mountain resorts that thrived north of New York City before the jets expanded vacation options. Huge Arab families, rather than New York Jewish families, vacationing weeks at a time to escape the summer heat of Dubai and other oil states in the relatively cool ninety-degree heat of Cairo—and in the relative social freedom of a country that is Arab, but also distinctly Mediterranean.

Within an hour or so of our early arrival the restaurants, the pools, the shops, and even the hallways were clogged and alive with running and yelling children, fast-moving Filipina servants, and slow-moving mothers, many of them veiled. Later in the day, teenagers and younger parents would appear, first tennis-ready, then the women disco-ready in short skirts and high heels. Then came the cellular-ready fathers in traditional white robes and red headbands, and now, little gray phones. Nice folks all, *en famille,* maybe they leave the grumpy ones back in Dubai.

The Gizera is a big place, 1,250 rooms, growing out in every direction from the French-style palace built as a guest house in 1869 for Empress Eugénie of France when she came for the ceremonies opening the Suez Canal. Our rooms were on the ninth floor of the tower, with balconies overlooking the great river and the life of the hotel itself.

We were a pretty grumpy bunch ourselves by the time we settled in for naps. Overnight flights were saving hotel bills, but we were beginning to pay in other ways. Catherine and I were up and out first, having scheduled meetings with government officials, both Egyptian and American, and some Egyptian journalists.

The Minister of Information, Nabil Osman—his title is an indication of the limits of press and political freedom in Egypt—proved to be a charming fellow who has spent a good deal of his life in postings in the United States and has children living there now. "Egypt is the brain trust for the Middle East," he began. "We carry the cultural torch. With 60 million people, we are the largest market."

His official pitch was that President Hosni Mubarak was enormously popular. But the 1993 "reelection" of the President with 96.4 percent of the vote was an indication of the limits of democracy in Egypt. It is said that he had more mummies in his cabinet than King Tut. Mubarak's job after the assassination of the peacemaking President Anwar Sadat in 1981, Osman continued, was to mobilize one generation of Egyptians to sacrifice while the country's infrastructure was rebuilt or built new so that future generations would not live in the poverty that has plagued the country since the glory days of centuries long past. Mubarak had put aside such things as higher wages, better education, and modern health services to build up the highways, railroads, public utilities, and modern telephone systems—the things demanded by international business. And, though the minister did not mention it, build up the military. The official goals for what is called Mubarak's third term (1993–96) are "a friendly investment environment"; protection of low-income classes, and a higher level of security in Egypt.

"Now," said Osman, "it is the people's turn. We want to build a workforce trained for the twenty-first century."

That there had been significant progress during the fourteen-year tenure of Mubarak, a former Air Force officer, seemed obvious to us. Government statistics recited by Minister Osman, pretty much confirmed by officials at the U.S. embassy, reflected that, too:

Life expectancy—from 56.5 years to 61; infant mortality—from 70 deaths per 1,000 births in the first year of life to 34; population growth—from 3.04 percent (1985) to 2.13 percent; telephone lines—from 500,000 to 4 million; paved roads—from 16,027 kilometers to 38,470; inflation rate—from 19.6 percent to 9.7; budget deficit as a percentage of gross domestic product—from 24.7 percent to 2.6. Per capita income has doubled, but it is still only $635 a year, with the rich keeping as much as they can get their hands on or hide overseas.

The American Ambassador, Edward Walker, and his people also listed some of the problems Mubarak and Egypt face, beginning with the fact that he is sixty-seven years old now and has no apparent successor and vicious enemies. There have been several attempts to kill Mubarak. The most recent occurred only a month before we arrived. The Muslim Brotherhood, the fundamentalists who assassinated Sadat and have attacked foreign tourists, are believed to have some quiet support from 10 percent of Egyptians. Part of the reason is that, with money coming from Saudi Arabia, the Brotherhood has had some success in providing the kinds of health and education programs Mubarak's government has largely ignored. Thousands of fundamentalists have been jailed (without charges) and others are being hunted down by the government.

▲ ▲ ▲

SHOWING THE FLAG

Both Catherine and I have worked with or interviewed United States Ambassadors in dozens of countries over the years and only two or three times have we been embarrassed or unimpressed by the men and women who show the flag around the world. This time Catherine wrote:

> During our trip, we met with six American Ambassadors. Two were political appointments and the rest were career Foreign Service officers.
>
> Our overwhelming impressions were positive. They were intelligent, informed, and quite direct about the situations in the countries where they were assigned. They understood the complexity of the problems facing the country, they understood United States policy and goals in their regions. They did what they could to improve the quality of life for the people in the places they worked—particularly in poorer countries.
>
> We met the Ambassadors in their homes, in their offices, and even in a hotel suite. The spouse of one Ambassador greeted us in high rubber boots. He was off to fix a plumbing problem in an embassy building. On two occasions, Fiona was with us and she was received warmly, as though it was perfectly normal for a ten-year-old American with a notepad in hand to arrive as an unannounced guest for a meeting with an Ambassador.
>
> Many Americans may think it is all parties out there. But it is not; it is more often than not demanding and dangerous work—differences with local leaders, war, and disease are part of the job description. With the end of the Cold War many Foreign Service officers have had to forget a lot they learned about security issues and learn a lot they did not know about economics—and most have.
>
> They do us proud. In general, the worst thing about our

Ambassadors is that officials back in Washington do not listen to them as much as they should.

▶ ▶ ▶

Back at the hotel, we had our own problems. Because Cindie and Thomas had been hoping to meet us here, we had reserved three rooms (each at less than a hundred dollars a night). So we gave Fiona her own room for the first time. "We woke up to a crisis," Conor wrote:

> Mom and Rich were going to some meetings and Fiona had hit the wall, nothing could please her. . . . Later that night Fiona admitted that she was acting badly. "Probably," she told me, because she didn't get her ten hours. . . . I think the pace of the trip had finally caught up with her. Hell, I was damn close to snapping myself.

She seemed to have had it with grown-ups—or with trying to act like one. The problem, I thought, would be solved in a few days. In Berlin, she was going to be joined by a friend, Molly Weiss of Sag Harbor.

That evening, Catherine and I had tea with the editor of one of the city's newspapers and a columnist from another at the apartment of the press chief at the U.S. embassy. The building near the center of the city did not look like much; it was stained with the black rot that grows in unpainted concrete in high humidity—the aesthetic curse of poor countries. But the apartment itself was a different story, a wonderful bright place with high ceilings, floor-to-ceiling windows, and parquet floors, fit for a warm Paris. The Egyptians loved to talk and smoke and laugh. I don't smoke, but I liked the rest and these people, too.

We all went on for hours, telling reporters' "war" stories at length, some of them true—and I was reminded again that no matter how different the circumstances under which they must work, newspaper people have the same kinds of personalities the world over. What bothered them most, I thought, was what they called "The Wahabi Virus," a social disease transmitted by Saudi Arabian money to promote a stern and puritan kind of Islam called Wahabi. The Saudi operations in many parts of the world could be seen as bankrolling fundamentalists intent on destroying secularism in Egypt or other Muslim countries—or as payoffs to buy internal security in Saudi Arabia itself.

Catherine wrote that night:

> We talked about life and work. . . . I was surprised to find out that all the newspapers, by law, are sponsored by political parties, so when you know the paper, you know the slant it will take. The journalists were convinced that the West was not helping Muslims in Bosnia, because it does not want a Muslim state in the heart of Europe. They also believe that fundamentalism develops supporters because it provides needed social services to families. The woman columnist I spoke with said she was surprised to see some of her well-educated young nieces taking up the veil, and that to her it was a form of fashion—almost a fad. "Putting on a veil, imagine! It is not my drama," she said with a flair, waving her cigarette in the air.

Having said that, there was some very interesting writing in local papers. I was taken with "A Day in the Life," a feature of the *Egyptian Mail.* That day's story was on a street sweeper named Karam Naguib. Street sweeper by day, car washer at a garage by night. His ambition: to learn to drive so that he could get a job as a parking valet. He said: "I start from bed at 7 A.M. to begin with my colleague at 8 A.M. We are either distributed in posh areas where the streets do not really need cleaning or are shuffled to any site where we have to scrub the streets because a certain official is paying a visit to the place." He gets three hours off at midday and goes home for lunch, the only time he sees his wife and three children for more than a few minutes. "My children are growing up and I do not think they like my job. Well, I don't blame them. I am not crazy about it either," said Naguib. "The worst thing is that I feel I am so tied to my job. I am neither smart enough nor young enough to take chances. . . . I get home about 11 P.M. and turn on the television because it makes me drowsy and I immediately fall asleep."

WE PILED INTO THE CAR
FOR ANOTHER ADVEN-
TURE, FIONA YELLING AT
MOM, MOM YELLING AT
FIONA, MOM YELLING
AT THE DRIVER, FIONA
YELLING AT RICHARD,
RICHARD YELLING AT
FIONA…. WE WALKED
AROUND THE PYRAMIDS
IN THE BLAZING HEAT
FOR A WHILE, TRYING TO
AVOID THE HASSLES OF
THE WOULD-BE RIP-OFF
ARTISTS. "YOU KNOW
THE STORY OF ALI BABA
AND THE FORTY THIEVES,"
SAID OUR DRIVER. "WELL,
THERE ARE MORE THAN
FORTY HERE."   —CONOR

I will remember the next day in my life, Friday, July 29, as one of the best. Conor wrote of a rocky takeoff:

We piled into the car for another adventure, Fiona yelling at Mom, Mom yelling at Fiona, Mom yelling at the driver, Fiona yelling at Richard, Richard yelling at Fiona. . . . This dynamic combined with the surroundings had a strange effect on me. Here I was in this incredibly compelling setting (the pyramids at Giza are the most magnificent structures I've ever seen), but I was having an incredibly tough time relaxing and really appreciating it because of the tension all around me. It made me feel like an ingrate. I ended up just walking away from the car off into the desert the first chance I had.

So did Richard. We walked around the pyramids in the blazing heat for a while, trying to avoid the hassles of the would-be rip-off artists. "You know the story of Ali Baba and the forty thieves," said our driver. "Well, there are more than forty here."

One guy trying to get to us was a real Anglophile: "English? English? Cheerio! England number one!"

"No," Richard answered. "England is about number eighteen.

Colin picked up the story:

Another epic moor tour today . . . After the short ride out to the pyramids at Giza, during which Rich achieved critical mass, breaking out of character and exiting stage-left, straight across the Sahara sands in heat that has been known to quickly reduce men to twitching, fetal forms, seeing spots, and bleeding from the lips. . . . The fate of the overland team of Richard and Conor was out of our hands, so Mom, Fiona, and I drove back to the entrance of the main pyramid, somewhat calmed by our own knowledge that Richard always travels with a portable sextant and that Conor is pretty handy with his fists.

At the entrance, we were stopped by the camcorder police. They informed us that video cameras were forbidden, but made it clear such things could be arranged. Gesturing at my Bolex, each of them had a visible wad of various currencies. . . . Fortunately, one of the cops knew that the Bolex shoots film and not video, appreciated the difference, gave the Bolex the reverence it so richly deserves, and allowed us to pass.

I have never before been especially uncomfortable in tight, enclosed spaces, nor am I superstitious. So it is difficult for me to find an explanation for the panic attack that I had, other than the obvious explanation of Pyramid Power. Hunched over, ascending to the tomb through a long, narrow passageway, I definitely had a few moments of real panic, heart racing, short of breath. But I was shamed into continuing by the steady stream of elderly Japanese couples coming down through the same passageway. . . . They indirectly prodded the American auto industry back up to its toes, and me to the inner sanctum of the great pyramid. The ultimate destination of this climb, the sarcophogus chamber, smelled of urine. . . .

During our descent, Mom snapped a flash photo, which was promptly met by a reprimand from an angry usher on the landing below. "No flash!" Mom was several people behind me and may not have heard or understood him, so she popped another flash. This really set the guy off. At about this point I reached him and he began to yell at me. I told him that he would have to take it up with Madam, thinking to myself, "Unless you're comfortable with sucker-punching a

The beginning of Fiona's adventure . . .

The pee-police inside the great pyramid.

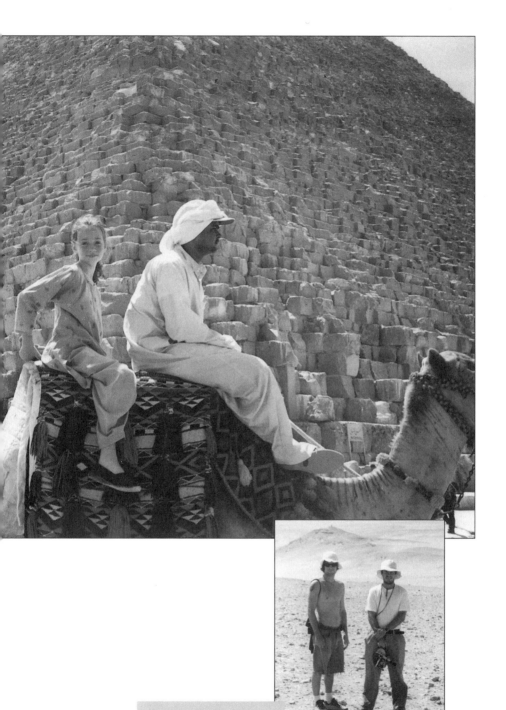

Guys in girl hats.

> THE PYRAMIDS WERE
> OKAY, BUT THEY WEREN'T
> AS MUCH AS I EXPECTED.
> THERE WERE NO DRAW-
> INGS, NO JEWELS, NO
> GOLD, NOTHING INSIDE.
> WE HAD TO CLIMB A TON
> OF STAIRS AND WHEN
> WE FINALLY GOT TO
> THE TOP IT SMELLED
> LIKE PEE....BUT AFTER
> WE LOOKED IN THE
> PYRAMIDS I GOT TO RIDE
> ON A CAMEL, IT WAS
> FUN, THE CAMEL MADE
> THIS WEIRD SOUND LIKE
> A FART THROUGH HIS
> NOSE.　　　　—FIONA

middle-aged American woman and laying her out cold, you are really in for it. . . ."

Then one of the Japanese popped off a flash. It seemed that nothing would contain the guard's fury, that is until Mom stepped down to his level and shot him a look. I've seen the look before and it isn't so much what she does with her eyes. . . . She sets her jaws and lips in a way that triggers a primal understanding. It is not the response of a cornered beast, it is the warning of a confident aggressor. . . . The guard decided to go after one of the Japanese instead.

The overland team, Conor and Richard, were waiting for us at the entrance to the pyramid. They were laden with exotic riches and fabulous tales of their wanderings.

Fiona's report was shorter:

The pyramids were okay, but they weren't as much as I expected. There were no drawings, no jewels, no gold, nothing inside. We had to climb a ton of stairs and when we finally got to the top it smelled like pee. . . . But after we looked in the pyramids I got to ride on a camel, it was fun, the camel made this weird sound like a fart through his nose.

When he was out of sight of the museum park guards, the camel driver slipped off the saddle of Michael, that was the animal's name, and left Fiona on top of the world. She was grinning from ear to ear. So was I, the concerned father running behind the damn camel. . . . Sensing that I had overpaid Michael's driver, the family tried to get the actual figure out of me, but I would not be moved—even when the driver joined in the taunting of "How much? How much?"

Colin continued:

Next stop was the Sphinx. Mom grabbed a passing sleeve to take a photo of the whole group, and with the sleeve came a passerby. A German. As we were all standing side by side, squinting into the sun, and the conscript was dutifully lining up the shot, Mom broke ranks and charged at the man. He took a couple of steps backward but Mom was on him before he could fling the camera at her and run away. She grabbed it out of his hands, rotated it vertically, handed it back to him, walked back to the rest of us, turned, and smiled. . . . The guy's hands were shaking as he clicked the shutter, returned the camera, and hurried off into the desert.

MOM GRABBED A PASSING SLEEVE TO TAKE A PHOTO OF THE WHOLE GROUP. WITH THE SLEEVE CAME A GERMAN. THE CONSCRIPT WAS DUTIFULLY LINING UP THE SHOT, MOM BROKE RANKS AND CHARGED AT THE MAN. HE TOOK A COUPLE OF STEPS BACKWARD BUT MOM WAS ON HIM BEFORE HE COULD FLING THE CAMERA AT HER AND RUN AWAY. SHE GRABBED IT OUT OF HIS HANDS, ROTATED IT VERTICALLY, HANDED IT BACK TO HIM, WALKED BACK TO THE REST OF US, TURNED, AND SMILED. . . . THE GUY'S HANDS WERE SHAKING AS HE CLICKED THE SHUTTER.

—COLIN

[P.S.: THAT PHOTO IS THE COVER OF THIS BOOK.]

Nearby was, the Mena House Oberoi, where we decided to stop for lunch. Because Conor and I had to pay for all our own meals from stipends we received, my strategy for the pricier places was to order light, and then devour Fiona's meal, which she rarely ate herself. I ordered a cup of lentil soup for myself and sat back to hear Fiona tell the waiter what else I would be having. It turned out to be pasta in a rather good tomato sauce.

Great hotel. I felt no need to tell the kids that terrorists had shot up the place, killing a number of tourists, in 1992.

Back on the road for the twenty-mile ride to Memphis, the once-upon-a-time capital of ancient Egypt, we spotted a billboard that read: GOOD NEWS, IMMORTALITY AND HAPPINESS ARE TO BE FOUND IN EGYPT. Two out of three, I'd say for sure. The good news is peace and an improving economy. The happiness is in Egyptians themselves, or so it seems to me. We liked the people we met.

Fiona said this of our stop at Memphis, now just a crossroads, and beyond:

> They had a bunch of Ramses and Nefertiti stuff. They had a statue of Ramses laying down with his forty-two wives holding him up. I didn't like it too much. Then we went to Saqqara and when I was getting out of the car, I saw some men saying, "Hey, look at the foreign kid in the *shalwar kameez.*" I looked at them, they waved, and I waved back. Then we went in. I didn't think it was much, but my mom thought it was absolutely marvelous, that there wasn't another thing in the world like it. Then when we were walking out of this tunnel, some guy said to me, "Hey, you. White kid!" I turned around, waved, and he waved back. That's about all that happened today.

Saqqara knocked me out—somehow it was more comprehensible to me than Giza, which I had seen before. The Step Pyramid of Zoser was built more than 2,600 years before the birth of Christ, and a hundred years or so before the Pyramid of Cheops at Giza—all this before the invention of the wheel, of iron tools, or the block and tackle. Saqqara, only a bit more remote geographically, gave me a sense of chronological distance that Giza no longer did. Colin, Conor, and I walked out into the desert again, behind the Step Pyramid and up a small rise. At the top, we could see twelve pyramids, including Giza. There was nothing else there and for a moment I thought time stood still.

It didn't. Said Colin:

Conor, Richard, and I walked around the back of the pyramid and were treated to a full-blown, Foreign Legion, wandering nomad, Sahara-scape. There was an endless sea of sand getting wavy and fuzzy toward the horizon line. . . . We were a good distance from the area that seemed to be ordinarily occupied by white men with cameras and cash. Then like a leopard who has cut off a single, hapless springbok from the rest of the herd, a guy on camelback was closing on us. "My friends. My friends!" came the familiar call. He wanted us to ride on his camel, take pictures of his toothless mug, or simply lay out some dollars for the privilege of standing on this hill in the heat. In any case, our reverie was broken and we successfully broke back to the safety of the rest of the herd.

Walking back toward the car and the road to Cairo, we saw this sign: GUARDS ARE STRICTLY FORBIDDEN TO GIVE ANY INFORMATION.

Colin was on a roll:

That evening everyone except Conor went out to dinner at a fantastic little restaurant called Felfala Garden. There was an 8-by-10 photo of Jimmy Carter just inside the front door. The food was exceptional. Fava beans in garlic, stuffed pigeon, strange, tasty wads of meat. . . . Fiona was unhappy with the fare and was relentless about letting everyone know it, so Mom took her to the Hilton for some ice cream, leaving me and Rich to drink a couple more beers while he told me Dwight Eisenhower's life story.

After we had settled the tab, Rich and I walked into the street to find a taxi to take us to meet the women at the Hilton. There was a guy waiting in an early 1960s Mercedes and we began the negotiation ritual: "How much for a ride to the Hilton?"

"How much you want to pay?"

A bit disadvantaged by not knowing the distance, or even his inflated ball park figure, we threw it back to him: "How much would you charge?"

"My price is one hundred U.S. dollars. What is your price?"

"Our price is two U.S. dollars."

"Very good, sir," he said, and we climbed in.

I was won over forever that midnight driving through Midan el Tahrir (Liberation Square) near the Egyptian Museum. Families were scattered all over the grass of the traffic circle in the square, picnicking, sleeping and talking, talking, talking through the hot and humid summer night. It reminded me of distant recollections of Central Park in New York when I was very young and air conditioning was very rare.

We could not find our ladies at the Hilton, but I was fascinated looking at *hookahs* (water pipes) almost three feet high burning what looked like chunks of charcoal. They were being delivered in bunches to men at tables in the café behind the hotel. I should have tried one. Later Catherine said the same thing: "I wished I had tried one of the water pipes. But as someone who has never inhaled, it might not have been my cup of tea."

Colin and I decided to walk back to Gizera. The streets were lined with vendors selling food cooked over open flames; dented old zinc ice cream carts; racks of pungent flower garlands; blankets spread with displays of paintings and crafts. Colin's account began:

As Richard and I walked over the bridge to Gizera Island, we were approached by a couple of guys about my age who looked as if they were selling something. Actually, they just wanted to talk—in English and French. They were cousins, both of them language teachers in private schools. The four of us, leaning out over the bridge, talked for almost an hour.

The older one, Mohammed, who was twenty-six, was the son of a tenant farmer three hundred miles to the south. "What is your work?" he asked me.

I told him I was a writer, which impressed him, which it usually does in countries that do not begin conversations by asking how much money you make. He said he was an English teacher and I decided to wait before asking him how much he was paid.

"Are you like Charles Dickens?" he asked.

"Not quite," I said, but we talked about Dickens and London for a bit. Then he said: "I have read *Death of a Salesman.* Is that what America is like?"

"Yes," I said. "That is not all that we are like, but part of it."

He was obviously well read, but he did not yet have a context to understand what he knew. He was not an angry man. He loved teaching, he loved Cairo, Mubarak, and Egypt. But he was frustrated. His pay was 100 Egyptian pounds a month (less than 30 dollars) and his rent for the room, which he shared with another teacher, was 105 pounds. He made ends meet, barely, by giving individual English lessons to the sons of rich men.

"Though it is in my country, I can't go in there," he said, pointing toward the Nile Hilton. "I mean I can go in, but a coffee costs almost more money than I make in a week. The dollar is all that counts now, money is king. But it is hard for someone like me to exist here. I want refreshment, to sit with my friends, to marry, to have a flat, but how can I do those things?"

I don't know. The economic changes in Egypt have caused many dislocations. Fifteen years ago, Egypt had an enormous government bureaucracy and its factories were able to sell shoddy goods in the captive markets of the Soviet Union and Eastern Europe. Now unemployment may be as high as 25 percent and social services are almost nonexistent. And more and more people, like Mohammed, move to

THE GLORIES ARE HARD TO OVERSTATE, PARTICULARLY WHEN YOU SEE THEM IN MORE MODERN LIGHTING AND SKYLIGHTS. MANY OF THE JEWELS AND THE OBJECTS FROM AN EMPEROR'S LIFE THAT FIONA HAD HOPED TO SEE AT THE PYRAMIDS WERE RIGHT HERE IN FRONT OF US NOW.

—CATHERINE

Cairo after seeing the city's new prosperity on new television channels. The population of the city has apparently passed 14 million.

The next morning, Catherine and I went to the Egyptian Museum, one of the most interesting places in the world. We were dazzled once again. But not only by exhibits, which include the King Tut exhibit that thrilled the world years ago, but by a new order that no longer abandoned priceless relics haphazardly in dusty corners and back rooms.

Wrote Catherine:

The glories are hard to overstate, particularly when you see them in more modern lighting and skylights. Many of the jewels and the objects from an emperor's life that Fiona had hoped to see at the pyramids were right here in front of us now. So, too, are the dollhouses, miniatures of aspects of life in Egypt two millennia or more ago, which were found in the tombs of other kings. There are miniatures of kitchens, houses, funeral boats with rowers, and all manner of wondrous things.

The family has a history with this museum. Twelve years before, Colin and Conor had opted for television in the room and the familiar pleasures of the Americanized coffee shop in the Hilton rather than crossing the street into the amazing world of Tut and such. Catherine and I may have forgiven them, but we certainly never forgot. From his perspective, Conor recounted what happened next:

Mom and Rich called and told me how incredible the museum was . . . a once-in-a-lifetime experience. They knew exactly

*Mubarak's Cabinet—
just kidding. It's the
museum. . . .*

what it took to get me to go: cash. Richard offered a bribe and
I accepted. Is that pathetic or what? . . . Actually it was twice
in a lifetime because the last (and only) time we had been in
Cairo, I was a wee lad and I opted to stay in the hotel. . . .

It was not a bribe, only an offer to pay the admission fee.
Anyway, I was glad they called and glad Colin and I went. We
checked it all out, the gold and lapis lazuli, scarabs and
scepters and coffins . . . a lot of cool stuff but not like the museum in Taipei.

Onward and downward, we went to "The City of the Dead." For
years the American press had written of the poverty of Cairo, which is
real enough, and focused on people living in the elaborate cemetery

begun centuries ago. Cairo families built housing, from bungalows to elaborate villas, for deceased loved ones.

"The tombs! The tombs!" said our driver.

"Are you sure?" asked Conor. "Those houses look just like the rest of the city."

They did, but only from the outside.

We saw no squatters, the dead seemed to be at peace. "Some are giant and some are just the size of little huts," wrote Fiona of the house graves. "I know poor people live in them, but I think I'd be too scared to do that."

Next we went through the old Coptic Christian neighborhoods and churches—the country is 10 percent Coptic, and those Christians live around a pleasant walled garden where, it is said, Joseph, Mary, and Jesus stopped on the way back to Nazareth from Bethlehem. The story makes no sense geographically, but the garden itself was a pleasant oasis in a big city. Ironically, in Cairo it is the Christian neighborhoods that are most remindful of old Casbahs with narrow, winding streets. I have always had low-level curiosity about Coptic Christianity, but never did anything about it. As we should have expected, the altars and paintings inside the churches were similar to the Greek Orthodox.

Then we went to the citadel overlooking the vast city, the fort of Saladin, the greatest of Islamic generals. He began construction in the twelfth century—and the magnificent Mohammed Ali Mosque, built inside the old walls in the late nineteenth century.

Finally, we went to the Khan el-Khalili Bazaar, evaluated first by Fiona:

MOM AND RICH CALLED AND TOLD ME HOW INCREDIBLE THE EGYPTIAN MUSEUM WAS...A ONCE-IN-A-LIFETIME EXPERIENCE. THEY KNEW EXACTLY WHAT IT TOOK TO GET ME TO GO: CASH. RICHARD OFFERED A BRIBE AND I ACCEPTED. IS THAT PATHETIC OR WHAT?...

—CONOR

It had all the trinkets and baubles you could imagine. It had giant robes that covered your whole body and it had shirts and skirts made of sparkles that had holes on them. It had purses, it had leather camels, it had camels made of camel hair, it had carvings of different men with the same face. It just had everything.

My dad and I went into a lot of stores and when we were walking down one alley, a man whose store we hadn't even looked at yelled to us: "I give you cheaper price. OK, OK, you choose price. I go low. I go low. You go in my store." He introduced me to his wife and I went to his store.

When I got in, their seven-year-old daughter was behind the counter. She asked me whether I wanted a T-shirt and I said no. Her mother walked in with a white robe and put it up against me and then put a scarf on my head with a red crown type thing over it. I thought it was okay and wanted to get out of the store, so after some bargaining I bought it.

Then we left and I saw some leather shoes. They were blue with gold trim and I decided I wanted them. So my dad got them for me and we went to the café because it was time to see Mom.

She had spent less than ten dollars for the whole outfit. Not bad.

We found Catherine at the wonderful Fatwali Café, sort of the *Deux Magots* of the bazaar. "Did you buy anything?" asked Fiona. Catherine blinked her eyes innocently in silent-movie style and said, "Did I buy anything?"

Said Fiona:

I looked and I said, "You got a new purse." Then she asked my

A MAN WHOSE STORE WE HADN'T EVEN LOOKED AT, YELLED TO US: "I GIVE YOU CHEAPER PRICE. OK, OK, YOU CHOOSE PRICE. I GO LOW. I GO LOW. YOU GO IN MY STORE." HE INTRODUCED ME TO HIS WIFE. THEIR SEVEN-YEAR-OLD DAUGHTER WAS BEHIND THE COUNTER. HER MOTHER WALKED IN WITH A WHITE ROBE AND PUT IT UP AGAINST ME AND THEN PUT A SCARF ON MY HEAD WITH A RED CROWN TYPE THING OVER IT. I WANTED TO GET OUT OF THE STORE, SO AFTER SOME BAR-GAINING I BOUGHT IT.

—FIONA

Into the bazaar. . .

Tea in Khan-el-Khalili.

dad, who had been inside for a moment, if he noticed anything. After he stood there about five minutes looking blank,
she finally put her hand on her head, and said, "I got a new
purse."

We sat and watched the world go by, sipping mint tea while Fiona
made out a list of bargaining techniques around the world. We went
back to Gizera to organize our bags for the night flight to Israel. As we
piled into yet another taxi, Fiona walked over to a doorman and said:
"You have a very nice country."

We all agreed.

◀ ◀ ◀

FIONA'S RULES FOR BARGAINING

Wrote Catherine:

Fiona and I discovered that we were soulmates under the skin
when it came to shopping and bargaining. I had given her fifteen dollars a country to spend on purchases. . . .

She started on the streets of Taipei, bargaining for a little
Buddha, continued through the street market in Guangzhou,
China, where a jade-colored Buddha was added to the collection. On it went, to a silk kite in Bali, carvings in Ubud,
wayang golek puppets in Yogyakarta, Chinese porcelains for
my birthday present in the antique market in Jakarta, thanka
paintings and embroidered purses in Nepal, and on and on.

She gained enormous confidence and a sense of personal
power when she realized that the essential trick to bargaining
was not to pay what was asked for the item . . . but to pay
what it was worth to you. Even if it is a bargain, if you do not
want it, don't be intimidated into buying it.

After a couple of hours in the Khan el-Khahili Bazaar, Fiona herself wrote out Fiona's Rules for Bargaining:

1. Always look disgusted when they tell you the price.
2. When someone is selling something in the street, never make eye contact with him/her or anything they're selling.
3. Always say, "Your best price."
4. Always mention that another person had a lower price—even if it's not true.
5. When you walk away, always flick your hair and give a rich lady wave.
6. Spend a long time getting in your car. They think you're leaving and finally lower the price.

▲ ▲ ▲

Chapter 16

JERUSALEM

Fortified with many little glasses of sweet mint tea and a hope and a prayer for the future of Cairo, we woke up early on the morning of July 30 and piled into an overloaded Peugeot for the drive to the airport. It was very reassuring to know that, in a pinch, with enough ropes and bungee cords, we could actually manage to cram the entire expedition and its supplies into one normal-sized vehicle.

So began Colin's account of his excellent adventure flying Air Sinai across the desert and the ages and endless wars from Cairo to Tel Aviv. He continued:

Compared to a lot of the cultural and religious rifts currently raging in the world, the Egyptian/Israeli conflict is almost a civilized relic. But it does have an undeniable high-profile legacy, along with some extreme activists still very active on both sides. So I was relieved to find that I would be sitting next to a nun in full Sally Field battle regalia for the trans-dogma flight. Not that nuns have proven to be any more im-mune to political terrorism than the rest of us—see Central America—but it definitely seemed like an edge. Then I real-ized that the book I had spread on my lap had just entered a twenty-page stretch involving blow jobs and the like, graphi-cally described. I'll never know if she looked down and read along, but if she had been reading anything, I certainly would have checked it out. . . .

Pilots trained in this part of the world have a habit of staying as high as possible for as long as possible. So when our free fall into Ben Gurion airport began, I was especially glad to have one of the good Lord's pawns in the seat next to me.

Conor had his account of the adventure:

I was sitting alone next to this giant, fat, bearded Arab and his wife. I didn't like the way he smelled and he probably didn't like the way I smelled. Landing in Tel Aviv is a freak show. It felt to me kind of like we were going to crash. I was scared. Everyone was scared. It was scary. (Actually I don't think it scared my mom, who said, "Landings don't bother me.") So I'm clutching my armrest and biting my nails and holding my breath and the guy next to me is working his beads faster and faster and his prayers are getting louder and more insistent— and then there is a deathly silence in the cabin except for the whine of the engines and it felt as if we were going on a kamikaze run at the bridge of the USS *Arizona* (antiaircraft artillery fire would not have seemed out of place at this time) and then all of a sudden *WHAM!* we were on the ground. When I realized we were safe I started laughing, letting go of all the fear and anxiety that built up inside me. I looked at the man next to me and he was laughing just like I was. We were so relieved. He looked at me and we laughed in each other's face. We didn't speak the same language, came from totally different backgrounds, were as different as two people could be, but at that moment each of us knew exactly how the other felt. It was really cool. And let me say that I became very grateful for that guy's prayers and his prayer beads.

However steep the landing, arrival in Tel Aviv can have the feeling of coming home. Israel is many things to many people, but it is essentially a Western country. You could feel a relaxing of some of the tensions in our little party. We had baggage and customs pretty much down to a science and we knew the way to Jerusalem.

Then Colin and Conor disappeared.

We had seen them in another immigration line and now they were gone. So was some of the luggage. The airport was emptying around us.

"I had them paged," said Catherine. "But there was no response." I decided that they must have forgotten the carry-on photo bag on the plane, which we never trusted to check-in. . . . We figured they had gone back on the tarmac to retrieve the bag from the plane.

We retraced that route and an Air Sinai rep tried to call the plane. It had already left, heading back to Egypt. By now, the airport was filling up again, mostly people getting off planes from the former republics of the Soviet Union. The airlines were new to us, and to the world, Kazakhstan Airways, etc. The exodus of former Soviet citizens claiming Jewishness and right of return to Israel is the largest immigration influx Israel has had since the founding years and the exodus of European Jews in the late 1940s and early 1950s.

We were getting frantic about Colin and Conor. I walked over to an area of unmarked doors and asked a guard of some sort if he knew anything about young Americans or luggage. "No." In fact, our sons were behind the door he was guarding. This is what happened, according to Conor:

I had just passed through customs, where my passport was stamped by a beautiful young paramilitary Israeli girl, and was pushing a luggage cart through the airport to catch up with Mom and Rich at the baggage claim carousel. I had made it through the hell flight safely and was feeling pretty good about being in the Holy Land. I was dressed in black wraparound sunglasses, long sideburns, and a T-shirt that said, "Unsane" on it. I was whistling a Led Zeppelin tune.

"Hello! Hello!" Out of the corner of my eye I saw a rather anonymous-looking, clean-cut guy in his early thirties trying to get my attention. Another pesky porter or limo driver, I figured, and kept strolling past him. But he kept coming at me. "Hello! Hello! Passport, please." I stopped and looked at the guy. He was pulling something out of his back pocket, some kind of ID or something. "I'm with the police," he said. "Your passport, please."

I gave him my passport, he opened it, looked at it, and when he looked up at me again he was giving me the Cop Stare. Anyone who has ever had to deal with the police in any sort of adversarial way whatsoever knows the Cop Stare. This stare is a more effective law enforcement tool than a gun, and it is exactly the same wherever you go. They do it in America, they do it in Indonesia, they do it in France, and they do it in Israel. I knew I was in trouble. . . .

Just then Colin walked up and asked innocently, "What's going on?" The cop turned his attention to Colin. "Are you with him? How do you know him? Passport, please. . . ." He then asked Colin the same questions he had been asking me as well as a bunch of questions he threw at both of us. I just clammed up and let Colin do the talking.

The talking brother picked up the story:

Performing my usual *sherpa* function, I watched as some young guy approached Conor and began talking. He was wearing a Don Johnson uniform—an open Hawaiian-print shirt over a tank top and at first I thought he was offering the services of his minivan or his brother-in-law's tour company. Then I saw Conor reach into his pocket and hand the guy his passport.

At this point I realized why the person was decked out in circa 1986 *Miami Vice.*

I sidled up to the two of them and asked, "Hey, fellas, what's up?" The cop asked me if I was traveling with Conor and I told him yes, in fact we were brothers. He explained that he was very interested in our passports, and in the exotic locales we had recently visited.

"Did you bring anything from Nepal?" he asked us.

"Yes, actually a ton of stuff. My mom is a little obsessive."

"Any hash?"

"No, sir. Mostly just cheap plaster things my mom likes to call carvings, along with some other heavy stuff she refuses to ship home. Oh, and some baseball caps."

Leafing through Conor's passport, he asked me what my occupation was.

"Well, it's kind of a funny story. I used to be a TV producer but I quit my job because I really didn't feel that good about my employer. . . ."

"Yeah, okay," he interrupted. "What about you?" he asked, turning to Conor.

You would think that by now Conor would know when to lie to a cop, but to give him the benefit of the doubt, he had a momentary lapse and told the guy the truth: "I'm a muscian."

That was all the cop needed to hear. "Will you two please follow me?" Though it was phrased as a question, he was not waiting for an answer.

He led us into a small windowless room with two desks and a bench along one wall. He told us to put the bags on the bench. He told us to take off our shoes and socks, which we did. And when he was through examining our wholly uninteresting socks, he looked up and said: "Okay, now take off your clothes."

It wasn't a "bend over and grab your ankles," latex-gloved affair, just a casual pirouette, and then back on with the drawers.

While he went through the bags, he asked occasional questions.

Q: What is this prescription?

A: Whatever it says on the label. I've never seen it before.

Another cop walked in with an older Arab man. This man was carrying boxes, jars, and woven bags full of incredibly suspicious-looking dried plants and strange opaque liquids. When the second cop began to question the man about his various flora and elixirs, the old guy became irate, waving his arms around and yelling at the cop in some foreign tongue. After a sufficient amount of raising his voice indignantly and thrusting his suspicious cargo in the cop's face, the Arab man was simply waved out of the room. He left the room muttering and pointing his fingers at the two cops, and he left without having to hoist his robe up to his chest. The best defense . . .

Conor added this:

All I can say is that for having nothing to hide, I sure was nervous. I attempted to use humor to ease the tension: when he told me to drop my boxer shorts I quickly whipped them off, grabbed myself, and said, "Made in the U.S.A., mother . . . ! You can't keep the black man down!" Well, maybe that wasn't exactly it. Because he didn't seem too amused, I decided not to start chanting, "Attica! Attica! Attica!" which at that time seemed like the natural thing to do. Anyway, moving on. . . .

Later, in Jerusalem, the American Ambassador, Martin Indyk, told us it happens all the time, particularly with guys that age who had been in India, which is a drug-transfer country to the Middle East.

We hired a minivan for the thirty-mile drive to Jerusalem, where we had last been twelve years before. Approaching the city, we were surprised both by how far the suburbs had moved into rocky hills and dales and how much farther they were moving in a landscape of cranes and other construction equipment. Israel was booming, its economy growing at 6 percent a year since signing peace accords with the Palestine Liberation Organization. There was a "Peace Dividend": Israel was now doing profitable new business with almost all the world—selling to all the countries that had been treating Israel as an outlaw nation as long as it militarily occupied the villages and cities of Palestinians in Gaza, in Jerusalem, and in the lands west of the Jordan River.

We were staying at one of our favorite hotels in the world, the American Colony in Arab East Jerusalem, occupied by Israel since it drove out the Jordanian Army in the Six Day War of 1967. The hotel

"The economy is booming. . . ." U.S. Ambassador Martin Indyk.

was built by American Christians, a community of prosperous and very religious Swedish-Americans who came from Minnesota and Wisconsin in the mid-nineteenth century because they believed the world was coming to an end. Now it is staffed by Palestinians and has had more than a touch of John le Carré about it in this city of intrigue upon intrigue. For us it also has a touch of Dorothy Reeves, my mother, who told us about it after spending time on archaeological digs outside the city.

The American Colony sort of revolves around a lovely interior courtyard for eating, reading, and chatting, and the swimming pool one level below. Fiona was in the water in a splash.

It's a lively neighborhood. Jewish settlers from the West Bank were demonstrating between the hotel and Orient House, the new head-quarters of the Palestinian Authority, protesting the official Palestinian presence in Jerusalem since the Peace Accords signed in Washington. Catherine wrote:

I walked a block from the hotel to a local beauty salon, and on my way heard sirens, saw police cars and blockades. As I entered the salon the woman who was the proprietor, a Palestinian, complained for all to hear: "They won't let us walk down our own street and yet they let those people (Jewish) demonstrate there. It's not right."

That in a nutshell was what was going on in Israel when we were there. There were about 150,000 Israelis living in 144 settlements on the West Bank, many of whom had been encouraged to settle on old Arab lands by the conservative government of Menachem Begin. Now they were being told they had to leave by the liberal government of Yitzhak Rabin. We arrived as the Israel Defense Force (the Army) began forcibly removing Jewish settlers who had refused relocation.

The lead headline of the day's *Jerusalem Post* was: 213 SETTLERS HELD AS GIVAT HADAGAN CLEARED. Television news showed young women Israeli soldiers carrying off screaming Israeli women who could have been their grandmothers. On page two, the paper reported: "An 11-year-old was pounced upon by three soldiers and kicked in the groin. The arm of a 67-year-old Holocaust survivor was a bloody pulp after he had been kicked by soldiers."

These were Jews being roughed up by other Jews. Peace can sometimes seem worse than war. It is more complicated. As for us, at the moment, we were interested in earlier trials of the Holy Land. Catherine continued:

WE WALKED THE WAY OF THE CROSS ALONG THE VIA DOLOROSA FROM WHERE JESUS WAS CONDEMNED TO DEATH TO THE SITE OF HIS CRUCIFIXION AND BURIAL—UP TO THE CHURCH OF THE HOLY SEPULCHRE. I STOPPED AT THE SIXTH STATION—VERONICA WIPES THE FACE OF JESUS—I TOOK VERONICA AS MY CONFIRMATION NAME WHEN I WAS TWELVE. I ADMIRED HER COURAGE IN STEPPING OUT OF THE CROWD TO DO WHAT SHE THOUGHT WAS RIGHT.

—CATHERINE

We walked the Way of the Cross, the fourteen Stations of the Cross along the Via Dolorosa, from where Jesus was condemned to death to the site of His crucifixion and burial—up to the Church of the Holy Sepulchre built in about 324 A.D., said to be where His body was laid to rest. I stopped at the Sixth Station—Veronica

WHAT SURPRISED ME MOST ABOUT JERUSALEM WAS ITS MELLOWNESS. I WAS EXPECTING HORDES OF RELIGIOUS ZEALOTS AND MARTIAL LAW, A CROSS BETWEEN BEIRUT AND LOURDES. —CONOR

wipes the face of Jesus—I took Veronica as my Confirmation name when I was twelve. I admired her courage in stepping out of the crowd to do what she thought was right. In Jerusalem, you find yourself in the places you have heard about since childhood. Even Colin and Conor seemed impressed.

They were. Conor wrote:

What surprised me most about Jerusalem was its mellowness. I was expecting hordes of religious zealots and martial law, a cross between Beirut and Lourdes. But it wasn't like that at all. Just before dusk we walked from our hotel into the Old City. All the shops were closed, the light was beautiful. There were a few Middle Eastern types hanging around doing their thing. Very picturesque. And then the next thing I knew we turned a corner and we were on the street where Christ carried the cross. And it was just another mellow street, a beautiful street with the cobblestones and buildings made out of matching alabaster or whatever—all the streets in the Old City looked like that. But there were no religious fanatics, no commandos, no protesters, no beggars, nobody trying to sell me ten-dollar postcards or pieces of the true cross. It was very peaceful, dare I say spirtual?

It does not matter what your religion is, if any, because it all happened here within a few square miles. The Wailing Wall, sacred to Jews,

Fiona at the Wailing Wall.

is part of the foundation of the Dome of the Rock, the second holiest site of Islam. "One prayer in Jerusalem outweighs a thousand elsewhere," or so Mohammed is supposed to have said.

Conor's mother wrote:

> Conor put on a yarmulke and prayed at the men's side of the Wailing Wall (or as it is also called, the Western Wall of King Solomon's Second Temple) and Fiona and I prayed at the women's side. Fiona wrote the name of a family friend, Marcia Herman, on a piece of paper and stuck it in the wall, saying a prayer for her. I wanted my children to see and know this, but I was sad thinking of the war and suffering over the centuries that have come from what happened in these places thousands of years ago. . . . The United States of today is a miracle of religious tolerance.

CONOR PUT ON A YARMULKE AND PRAYED AT THE MEN'S SIDE OF THE WAILING WALL AND FIONA AND I PRAYED AT THE WOMEN'S SIDE. FIONA WROTE MARCIA'S NAME ON A PIECE OF PAPER AND STUCK IT IN THE WALL, SAYING A PRAYER FOR HER.
—CATHERINE

For security reasons that were not clear at the moment, we could not walk up the ramp that leads to the Dome of the Rock, the great gold-roofed temple enclosing the rock where, it is believed, Abraham was prepared to sacrifice his son Isaac and, most important to Muslims, the spot from which the prophet Mohammed ascended to heaven. Just looking up, the power of faith and religion overwhelms you here. I was not surprised that night when Fiona asked her Protestant father if he would write out the Catholic and Protestant versions of "The Lord's Prayer."

Catherine, as she had been in the past, was struck by the number of Orthodox Jewish families in the great plaza in front of the wall, writing:

> As I had been by the women in purdah in Muslim countries, I was jarred by the number of Orthodox men, walking around

in the ninety-degree heat in long frock coats and heavy felt
hats or ornate velvet hats. There were always hundreds of
them there, some with women but most of them alone. But I
was not surprised to hear other Israeli Jews complain about
the tough fundamentalist talk of men spending their lives as
students of the Torah—leaving, with legal blessing, other men
and women to do the work and fighting that created the
country and made the desert bloom. . . . Many of the most
militant of such men are actually Americans and there seemed
to be hundreds of them, walking around Jerusalem with their
wives and three or four preschool children and babies. Often
Orthodox young women wore clothes in the Western style,
but extremely modest, long skirts and blouses, and opaque
stockings, so that only their hands and faces showed. Again,
we found more than a touch of resentment from Jews who do
not have American passports and Israeli citizenship. Like the
rich of Hong Kong, some of the most chauvinistic Jews did
have a way out if war came.

▲▲▲

ISRAEL: THE FIFTY-FIRST STATE?

The big movies playing while we were in Israel were *Forget Paris,
Dumb and Dumber, While You Were Sleeping, Free Willy, Forrest Gump,*
and *Casper.* All American. But on the day we left, the government announced it was creating a $50 million fund to finance homemade
movies.

President Ezer Weizman said in speech while we there: "The Israeli people are infected with Americanization. We must be wary of
McDonald's, we must be wary of Michael Jackson, we must be wary of
Madonna." Cheeseburgers were part of the problem. When McDonald's opened on Ben Yahuda Street, Orthodox rabbis protested against
selling cheeseburgers because meat and milk products cannot be mixed
in a kosher home. One of the rabbis said: "When a Jew, a pure soul,
eats an impure animal, it destroys his soul and he becomes a jungle
man, an impure animal."

Look at it a certain way and it is easy to see Israel as some kind of faraway part of the United States, the fifty-first state. For years, American aid to the country has been almost five thousand dollars per family per year. But that is inevitably changing. For one thing, the end of the Cold War means that the Israelis are not as essential to United States military and intelligence operations. For another, the Israel peacetime boom has raised the Gross National Product to $85 billion, making the $3 or $4 billion in aid from the United States less important than it once was.

Now, more and more, the world is coming to Israel. The American International School in Jerusalem, once almost exclusively the preserve of the children of Israel's American patron, now has American enrollment of only 15 percent.

Finally, many Israelis are not totally comfortable with the politics and aggressiveness of militant Orthodox immigrants from the United States. A line in an editorial in the *Jerusalem Post* while we were there took note of who is resisting peace with Arab neighbors, saying it is: "The settlers, with their women and children, their songs and American accents."

▶ ▶ ▶

The difficulty of dealing with religious fundamentalists most anywhere was dramatized that day at an Orthodox hospital, Shaare Zedek. The rabbis controlling the hospital ordered doctors not to perform in vitro fertilization on a non-Jewish woman who had married a Jewish man in a secular service. As far as the rabbis were concerned there was no marriage and a child of the union would not be Jewish, because traditionally the faith passes through mothers. To them it did not matter that the fertilization procedure was guaranteed and financed by Israeli's universal health coverage.

The scene on Ben Yahuda Street that night was decidedly secular and possibilities of war seemed far away. Young men and women of the Israel Defense Force were laughing and gossiping and flirting at ice cream counters in T-shirts and slacks with Uzi machine guns clanking across their backs. "Wow," said Conor in stand-up comedy style, "a lot of babes with guns."

LOOKING OUT THE
WINDOW, CONOR SAID:
"I DON'T KNOW AS MUCH
AS YOU GUYS DO ABOUT
ALL THIS, BUT IT LOOKS
TO ME LIKE SOMEBODY
GOT THE SHAFT."

We had dinner at a café table in the street, sipping wine and watching the world go by in a cooler and more European setting than we had seen for a while. Crowds of young fathers and mothers in summery Western clothes were pushing along strollers and children as if they did not have a care in this old world, but there were rifles on their backs or stuck in the stroller with the baby. Grandfathers, old men called up for this crisis, walked along in pairs, wearing gray and blue uniforms with pistols on their hips.

We hired a car the next morning to tour the West Bank, so-called because it is the land west of the Jordan River, land that has been the battleground of civil war between Arab and Jew for centuries. As we left the hotel, I told Colin and Conor of the last time we had done this, in 1983. One day we had toured the West Bank with escorts from the IDF and the government press office, stopping at Palestinian refugee camps and new Israeli settlements on disputed land on the outskirts of Jerusalem. We traveled relatively long distances over good roads (necessary to quickly move troops and tanks into what used to be called "the Occupied Territories") through barren, empty, and rocky land. No people.

The next day we went back, guided this time by a Palestinian who worked for the United Nations. The second tour was along rougher roads, through cities like Ramallah and through Palestinian villages, some of them hulks destroyed by the Israelis as suspected terrorist bases. When we were on roads near the same modern highways we had traveled the day before, we saw different things. Palestinians were living in shacks or under nothing but plastic strung between poles. Our Israeli guides had simply pointed us in other directions. So it goes in war and politics.

We chose a Palestinian car and driver for this trip. All cars can be identified by origin (from a distance) based on their license plates. This one was coded to show it was from Jericho, which was functioning as the headquarters of the Palestinian Authority. Leaving Jerusalem was still like going back in time to a land where shepherds tend their flocks.

Looking out the car window, Conor said: "I don't know as much as you guys do about all this, but looks to me like somebody got the shaft. "

Later he expanded on that, writing:

The Arabs are getting a raw deal. The West Bank looks like the friggin' moon. But the Jews have to be militant, I understand that. They are surrounded by people who would like to see them dead. Without America's money, they would be toast. Why do we give them so much cash? I have no idea. Maybe I would feel differently if I were Jewish, but I wouldn't support our government giving billions of dollars to Ireland. Look at Ireland, it's a lot like Israel in some ways: tiny, no natural resources, lots of Americans hail from there, it too is torn by political violence, it is very religious. The Irish are also surrounded by their historical enemies, the English.

I appreciated the Israelis' militance even more after seeing the Tower of David Museum. Awesome . . . As far back as anyone can remember, people have been fighting over this piece of desert. The Canaanites, the Israelites, the Persians, the Hellenists, the Romans, the Byzantines, early Muslims, Crusaders, Mamelukes, Ottomans, the British, and finally the Israelis. None of these transitions came peacefully . . . and the worst were the Crusaders, the Christians.

Jericho, a dateline that survived from the Old Testament to the day's *New York Times,* is just a dusty little outpost with no building higher than two stories and none newer than decades ago—except for the capitol of the Palestinian Authority. The capitol building is only two stories, about the size of an average American firehouse. A sign outside the gates said NO PHOTOS ALLOWED. There are two main streets with vegetable stands, sandal shops, and wall paintings of Yasser Arafat, the founder of the Palestine Liberation Organization and now president of a government if not much of a country. A new superhigh-

The face on a wall in Jericho.

way, for Israelis only, bypasses the town. It goes fifteen miles from Jerusalem to the Allenby Bridge across the Jordan River to the Kingdom of Jordan.

In Jericho, Catherine wrote:

> It's hard to believe that this is the new capital of a place that has had birth pains through most of my adult life. (The capital was moved to Ramallah a couple of months after we left.) . . . Palestinians we spoke to said they felt that the world has reneged on its promises to provide the new government with the $2 billion in financial wherewithal to make things better for its people, and to put some basic infrastructure in place. However, Western officials we saw insisted that the money is coming . . . but the Palestinians simply had to get some rudimentary accounting systems in place that would be acceptable to donor nations.

The approaches to the Allenby Bridge, which was recently opened as an international passage to Jordan, were a mess. Trucks were waiting on lines that seemed endless. Cars waited

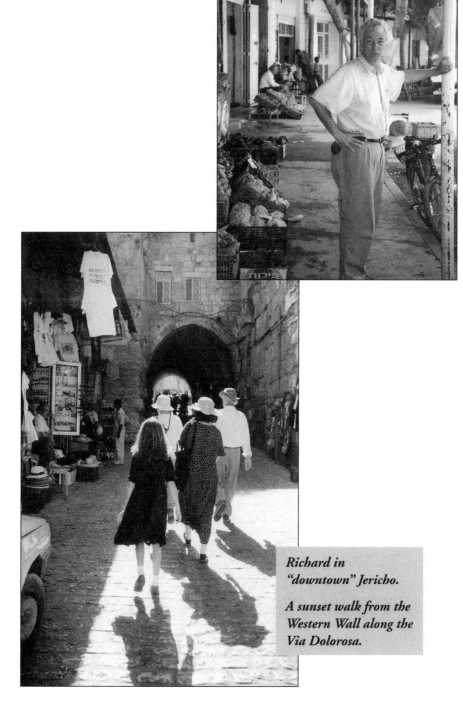

Richard in "downtown" Jericho.

A sunset walk from the Western Wall along the Via Dolorosa.

ONLY CATHERINE AND
FIONA WENT DOWN INTO
THE UNDERGROUND CAVE
SAID TO BE THE BIRTH-
PLACE OF JESUS. COLIN,
CONOR, AND I WAITED
OUTSIDE, UNDER A SIGN
THAT READ: FIREARMS
MAY NOT BE CARRIED
INSIDE.   —RICHARD

alongside. A couple of dozen buses filled with local people had been waiting for hours as troops checked papers and luggage.

We had no papers of worth here, except for an invitation to call King Hussein (we had met in California) if we got to Amman, fifty miles across the bridge.

We didn't expect it to work and it didn't. An Israeli lieutenant and a Palestinian border guard stood together trying to decide whether to let us through. Finally the Israeli came back to tell us it was no go. Then he pulled me aside and said: "Don't be discouraged. There is a special thing about this place. I am an Israeli soldier and he is a Palestinian soldier and here we are working side by side. That is what is important here."

Heading back toward Jerusalem we stopped to walk down to the Dead Sea, which felt very dead. Even Conor was not tempted to go into this one with its slimy-feeling water. Then it was on to Bethlehem and the Church of the Nativity, crowded as always. Only Catherine and Fiona went down into the underground cave said to be the birthplace of Jesus. Colin, Conor, and I waited outside, under a sign that read: FIREARMS MAY NOT BE CARRIED INSIDE.

Israel (and the West Bank) is so small that we all were back to Jerusalem for an afternoon around town. Catherine and I met with Ambassador Indyk at the King David Hotel, the center of much of the life of West Jerusalem, the Jewish half of the city. In reality, the Israelis control both sides of the city, but officially it is still divided by the Green Line, the pre-1967 war border between Arab and Jewish sectors, at least on United Nations maps. To the world, Tel Aviv is the capital of the country and the United States embassy is in that city, but to do his job Indyk has to spend a great deal of his time in Jerusalem working out of his suite in the King David. Indyk, who worked in the White House (the National Security Council) has an Only-in-America story. He emigrated to the United States from Australia in 1982; his accent makes you think you knocked on the wrong door.

"ISRAEL IS BOOMING," HE SAID, CONFIRMING THAT THE ECONOMIC IMPACT WAS THE BIG STORY OF THE PEACE PROCESS BETWEEN THE JEWISH STATE AND ITS ARAB NEIGHBORS.

"Israel is booming," he said, confirming that the economic impact was the big story of the peace process between the Jewish state and its Arab neighbors. The gross national product of 5.5 million Israelis is continuing to grow at 6 percent or more a year and is now, at $85 billion, more than the combined output of all its neighbors, Egypt, Syria, and Jordan. Exports per capita are higher than Japan's. The country has absorbed 600,000 immigrants from the former Soviet Union, all swearing they are Jewish. It's hard to tell who is telling the truth about that; one definition of a Soviet Jew is someone who had a picture of Albert Einstein on the kitchen wall. Those new Israelis are already 17 percent of the voters and one of the more famous of the Soviet Jews, Anatoly Scharansky, was forming an immigrant political party. They have brought needed skills to Israel—the per capita income of the first wave of Soviet émigrés is higher than the national average of about twelve thousand dollars—but they have also brought things like street crime. "Mafia" is a new word in Hebrew.

We met the kids in the old Jewish Quarter, which has pretty much evolved from Casbah to a kind of grand winding-aisled department store. Fiona, a gift-giver like her mother rather than her disgraceful holiday-forgetting father, selected presents for her grandmothers, a small portrait of Jesus and Mary for Grandma Nana, Catherine's mother, and crucifixes and rosaries all around for other relatives. I did buy one thing, a print of the Old City for my mother, Fiona's Grandma Dorothy, who spent some of her happiest days on digs here. Fiona also continued to expand her stamp collection—"Face it guys, I'm a collector!"—with a set of fourteen pre-1967 Jordanian stamps of

*Conor on Ben Yehuda
Street with Victoria
(far right).*

the Stations of the Cross and a set of cat stamps from various countries. We searched for another stamp album to replace the one she bought in China and had already filled.

Then the city and the world got even smaller, as recounted by Catherine early the next morning:

> The most amazing thing happened. We were wandering in the Old City and Colin suggested that we cut across a small alley, which took us right into the center of the butchers' market with carcasses hanging all around us, flies everywhere, and water and blood on the slippery ground. "Way to go, Col. Nice call!" said, Richard, teasing. At the end of the street, Conor turned a corner and literally bumped into his high school girlfriend, Victoria Meirik, whose father was a Norwegian diplomat. They were together at the American High School when we lived in Paris. Now she was twenty-five, an actress at home, in the Liv Ullmann mode.

They greeted each other without any of the usual "Oh my gosh!" screaming that would accompany an encounter like that of my generation. He literally bumped into her and they hugged each other. She was with a young man named Sven. We said hellos all around, and then Colin, Conor, Victoria, and Sven went off together. The abandoned three went on to dinner at Fink's, a six-table New York–style Jewish restaurant, where Jewish rebels struggling against British occupation met secretly in the 1940s and where, they swear, Henry Kissinger could not get a table during a round of his world travels. Its time has passed but we were greatly entertained by our waiter, named Itzhak, who told us he had begun there forty-seven years ago, making the point that the waiters of today simply did not understand the idea of good service.

AT THE END OF THE STREET, CONOR TURNED A CORNER AND LITERALLY BUMPED INTO HIS HIGH SCHOOL GIRLFRIEND, VICTORIA MEIRIK, WHOSE FATHER WAS A NORWEGIAN DIPLOMAT. THEY WERE TOGETHER AT THE AMERICAN HIGH SCHOOL WHEN WE LIVED IN PARIS. NOW SHE WAS TWENTY-FIVE, AN ACTRESS AT HOME, IN THE LIV ULLMANN MODE.
—CATHERINE

I am sitting here writing this in the sublime courtyard of the American Colony Hotel in Jerusalem. Orange trees, lemon trees, and a flowered trellis on the stone walls remind me of the stone hill villages in Provence. Fiona wrote in the guest book "simply marvelous." It is a relief to eat salad again without worrying about getting ill. I love this dry, hot weather after a month of sweltering humidity. Tomorrow we go to Northern Europe, and even though it's August, I'm expecting it will be sweater weather. So today I will soak up this bone-satisfying heat.

Then she cut to the chase:

I am dying to get the Victoria story. But Conor is still asleep.

The first stop that morning for Catherine and me was Yad Vashem, the Museum of the Holocaust. It is not the first time we have been there. But going is a duty. We told Fiona what was inside and gave her the choice of whether or not to go in. She decided not to, sitting in the sun under pine trees. Catherine was most affected; because of her refugee work she had been in both Bosnia and Rwanda within the year, places where human beings have been slaughtering each other because of how they look or how they worship. Not so many years ago, you desperately wanted Yad Vashem and other memorials in Europe to be images of the past. But the museum is once again a warning for the future.

Wrote Catherine:

> The scenes of the camps are overpowering. It is a museum where almost everyone is silent, but a young woman, about nineteen, was walking through ahead of me sobbing and shaking as she looked at the photos. Finally she walked over to a corner, trying to calm herself. . . . The scenes brought back what I had seen and heard in Srebénica, Bosnia, and in Rwanda, where perhaps half a million Tutsis were hacked to death, most by their neighbors. In sad irony, the newspapers here report what is happening now with the same cool distance as in most of the rest of the world. The true outrage about Bosnia, we had learned on this trip, was in Islamic countries and, for most of the world, Rwanda might as well have been on another planet.

Then the three of us took a taxi over to the Dome of the Rock with me chattering away about what it all meant. I must have been doing a pretty poor job of explaining Islam and Jerusalem as the crux of the world we know, because this is what Fiona reported:

> When we were all at the Dome of the Rock, we thought we had seen everything. But we met Conor and Victoria as we

came out and she asked me if I had seen Mohammed's perfumed beard. I barely knew who Mohammed was, so I said No. . . . It turned out that there was no beard there. It was just a place (on the rock itself, reached by a stairway) where a beard supposedly was. It looked like a big fancy birdcage, with all those loops and things, but any bird would hate to live in it. There's a little hole that you stick your hand in and inside the air is real thick, kind of feels like curls. Weird, when you pull your hand out you take a fistful. Then your hand smells like perfume. I held my hands closed tight, so nothing could escape and I ran out so my mom could smell it. . . . She couldn't and just gave me a Mom look. Victoria could smell it, though.

...WE MET CONOR AND VICTORIA AND SHE ASKED ME IF I HAD SEEN MOHAMMED'S PERFUMED BEARD....THERE'S A LITTLE HOLE THAT YOU STICK YOUR HAND IN AND INSIDE THE AIR IS REAL THICK, KIND OF FEELS LIKE CURLS. WEIRD. WHEN YOU PULL YOUR HAND OUT YOU TAKE A FISTFUL. THEN YOUR HAND SMELLS LIKE PERFUME. I HELD MY HANDS CLOSED TIGHT, AND I RAN OUT SO MY MOM COULD SMELL IT....

—FIONA

Conor's take on that was: "The Islamic Blarney Stone."

Sacrilegious, I suppose. But he is not alone. I once again tried to put aside my first impression of Jerusalem: That much of the history of the world began with turf wars in this one small and ancient crossroads city. And the bonds and grudges of those Biblical times endure to this day and will for many, many more.

Catherine and I had dinner with Lisa Byer, the very pregnant Jerusalem bureau chief of *Time* magazine, and her husband, Ze'ev Chafetz, a novelist and a columnist for the *Jerusalem Post*. We ate outside on their patio looking over one of the world's great sights, the golden city at sunset, talking of war and peace and friends around the world, some of whom actually called or faxed as we sat there. It suddenly seemed a reduced world, just an extension of ancient Jerusalem. It will be smaller still when they implant phones and faxes and modems at birth.

Ze'ev, whose name was William when he was a newspaper reporter back in Detroit, came to Israel in the 1960s and later became the press secretary to Prime Minister Menachem Begin. His politics had changed since then, he said, and he now believed in Prime Minister Rabin's glorious gamble on trading West Bank land for peace with its Arab neighbors.

We were on our way again early the next morning. Another airport. Wrote Conor:

> The security people who checked us out were girls. Neither of them could have been more than twenty. When we walked in the airport they were just a couple of teenagers laughing and joking with each other. They were probably talking about boys or the latest pop group—or maybe comparing who could field-strip an Uzi faster. Anyway they were cute. But as soon as we walked up (a group of non-Israelis with a strange array of bags), they were all business. All of a sudden these two cute little girls were firing questions at me and giving me the Cop Stare.

We were on our way to Berlin and Catherine was absorbed in motherhood and grandmotherhood, writing:

> Conor sat with us on the plane. He had dinner last night with Victoria and Sven. Now Conor is back and Victoria is with Sven, continuing their vacation together. I guess any romantic maternal illusions I had were just that—illusions.

Said Conor:

> Mom wanted some dramatic reenactment, a one-in-a-million cosmic coincidence. But I didn't see it that way. It's not like I haven't spoken to her since we were teenage sweethearts in Paris. I had seen her a couple of times since, once in

New York and once in Europe. I had even spoken to her a couple of months earlier and I had a vague idea that she was going to be traveling in the Middle East. So it wasn't the needle in the haystack scenario, but it was a surprise. Victoria said: "I turned a corner and looked up and you were just there. And you were so . . . you." That's basically how I felt.

So Colin and I took off with her and her boyfriend. We walked around and ended up at a café eating, drinking, smoking cigarettes, and people-watching. It was nice to be with new people, people my own age whom I had a history with. And it was good to get out of the "Family travels around the world" routine.

On the plane, his mom moved on to the next generation:

Within a few hours we will see Cindie and Thomas and their seven-week-old baby Ian—our first grandchild and the reason Cindie could not take the whole trip with us. Doctor's orders. I am so anticipating seeing this little baby. There really is something deeply exciting at the idea of a new generation coming along. . . . Fiona is also thrilled because from here on we will be with her great friend Molly, who is meeting us in Berlin after finishing a vacation in Turkey with her mother. Fiona has gone for over a month without a playmate and I think she has really missed that. Conor was great about fooling around in pools with her, but it doesn't make up for a pal. A new family dynamic is about to begin. . . .

▲▲▲

BOMBS AND EXPLOSIVE POLITICS

On the flight from Jerusalem to Berlin, Fiona wrote this:

Before we got on the plane they looked through all of our bags, asked us if anyone suspicious-looking had carried any of our bags, and did a bunch of other stupid things because they thought we had bombs in our bags.

In fact, we were only a day or two behind or ahead of trouble on most of our travels. One way to describe the world we circumnavigated would be to call it three thousand nations (people) arguing or fighting over who runs two hundred countries (land)—or gets a new one for themselves. Peoples everywhere identified themselves as nations defined by religion or language or even tribes wanting to redraw maps to make or destroy countries that match the history and hatreds in their own minds. It is not just Rwanda, Algeria, Israel, and what used to be Yugoslavia.

In Taiwan, there was war talk with mainland China and the Chinese were lobbing missiles into the sea around the island—without nuclear warheads, but you got the point. There were demonstrations, bombs, and murders on the West Bank, in Karachi, and even in Paris.

Eighteen tourists were killed by terrorists in Egypt a few weeks after we left Cairo. There was a terrorist bus bombing in Tel Aviv a week before we arrived and there were new bombings in Paris two days before we got there.

On November 4, 1995, five weeks after we left Israel, a twenty-seven-year-old Orthodox Jew named Yigal Amir assassinated Yitzhak Rabin in Tel Aviv, shooting the Prime Minister in the back after a rally to support the Peace Accords. His purpose, he said, was to prevent peace between Israel and its neighbors. "Everything I did," he said after he was sentenced to life in prison, "I did for God, for the Torah of Israel, for the people of Israel, and the land of Israel."

Amir was one of the demonstrators arrested—and later released—protesting the removal of Jewish West Bank settlers while we were in Israel.

▰ ▰ ▰

Chapter 17

BERLIN

The flight from Tel Aviv to Berlin took just four hours. That seemed a miracle to me, thinking about the risks, the desperation, and the degradation and triumph of the human journeys between those cities in this bloody century.

Fiona came up to Business Class and made herself at home, writing:

I've been here for two and a half hours and not a single flight attendant has noticed that I should be in Economy. (1) The food is quite good; (2) The chairs are big and cushiony, and there are fancy footrests; (3) They give you fancy pens and clocks as presents; (4) There is a big screen with a little moving plane that tells you how far it is to your destination.

Her buddy Molly Weiss was waiting for us at the gate in Berlin with her mother, Stacey Pennebaker. I almost burst into tears watching the two girls, friends since kindergarten in Sag Harbor, squealing and jumping and then running off chattering at warp speed. For more than a month, Fiona had been only in the company of adults. There may have

FIONA'S BUDDY MOLLY WEISS WAS WAITING FOR US AT THE GATE IN BERLIN WITH HER MOTHER, STACY PENNEBAKER. I ALMOST BURST INTO TEARS WATCHING THE TWO GIRLS, FRIENDS SINCE KINDERGARTEN IN SAG HARBOR, SQUEALING AND JUMPING AND THEN RUNNING OFF CHAT-TERING AT WARP SPEED.
　　　　　—RICHARD

been dissent from other quarters, but I thought she kept her "I'm bored!" to a tolerable minimum.

Cynthia and Thomas—and *Ian!*—were already in the city. Their trip from the U.S. to Europe was described by his father:

We were so excited. Our first trip with our newborn son, Ian, with his first passport—which I applied for on the day he was born. As you'd expect, one bag is missing—it's mine and Ian's. We packed all our clothes together. We had a family rule: you pack it, you carry it. However, we've learned that the rules have changed —at least when you're traveling with a seven-week-old. My wife now gets Ian and he gets undivided attention. I become the packhorse of carry-on luggage. Such a small guy with so many things.

Off to the Forum Hotel in what used to be called East Berlin, on Alexanderplatz. The hotel was built under the Communist regime though renovated by the Intercontinental Hotel chain. At least that's what my guidebook said. It looked to be true, even with the addition of the glass-enclosed lobby, the thirty-seven-floor structure hadn't quite rid itself of grayish sterility. The room was simple but comfortable. The view was fantastic, looking out over East Berlin and onto West Berlin. We were tired and in need of a nap since we didn't sleep much on our three flights beginning yesterday in Sarasota.

Fiona and Molly, together again . . . in Berlin.

A couple of hours later, the rest of us rode into the city. Catherine, Fiona, and I went to the front desk of the Forum, got the Fyfes' room number, and headed for the elevators, leaving Colin to handle checking in.

There was a DO NOT DISTURB sign on Room 3407 but we did anyway. It is not every day that you get to see your first grandchild on the forty-eighth-day of his life. Ian Howard Fyfe was inside. The door was opened a crack by Thomas, looking as if he had just flown overnight from New York with a new baby in arms, which he had. He made a sound of some sort, thinking it was words. We brushed by and I kissed and congratulated the new mother, my own little girl, and their very good-looking tiny boy.

"You look good, you actually do," Cindie said to us, surprise in her voice. "We expected . . ."

IT IS WONDERFUL TO SEE CINDIE AND THOMAS SO THRILLED WITH THEIR NEW PARENTHOOD. WHEN WE PLANNED THIS TRIP, THERE WAS NO IAN AND NOW HERE HE WAS. AND HERE WE WERE COOING AND COOING.

—CATHERINE

Meeting Ian Howard Fyfe, Berlin.

"Cooing and cooing . . ."

Catherine, glowing, wrote:

> He's adorable. It is wonderful to see Cindie and Thomas so
> thrilled with their new parenthood. When we planned this
> trip, there was no Ian and now here he was. And here we were
> cooing and cooing.

Thomas asked whether I preferred being called "Grandad" or
"Pop-pop"; whichever one I took the other was reserved for his father.
I said "Grandpa" would do, wondering how it ever came to this.

Within an hour we all got together in the lobby with uncles Colin
and Conor and the absolutely-beside-herself Aunt Fiona.

"We've been joined by a kid named Ian," wrote Colin. "There was
much fanfare and photography when we met him for the first time."

Colin had been in Germany a number of times, traveling west
after working on Channel One's investigations into how nuclear weapons seemed to be slipping out of the old Soviet Union. He liked the
place, writing:

> I know one thing about Germany, it has the best Italian food
> in the world. A strange phenomenon. It did not disappoint
> this time. We ate in old East Berlin, and Conor, Mom, and
> Rich and I later walked back to the hotel, passing through
> neighborhoods which will soon be the hippest, trend-set-
> tingest ghettos in all of Europe. Old dilapidated buildings
> with windows aglow in red and blue on the higher floors,
> cafés, galleries, and CBGB-style rock clubs at street level.

There were nine of us when we headed out of the hotel to check
Colin's perspectives. We piled into a couple of taxis and went to a
place called Café 1900, eating outdoors in a changing East Berlin
neighborhood. Almost every apartment house and brownstone we saw
there had been renovated or was being renovated. Speculation, we
were told. Builders from West Germany were buying dilapidated East
Berlin apartments or buildings for very little money, fixing them up,
then reselling them at huge profits. Ah, Capitalism!—rough but it

works. The area was soon going to have a prosperous Parisian look to it, along with Paris prices.

For dessert and coffee—tea for Catherine, who has never tasted the nectar of the dark bean—we went over to Oranienburger Strasse, the main street of what had been Berlin's Jewish district pre-Hitler. Catherine and I had been there twice before and had watched the beginnings of the neighborhood's rebirth. We first saw it in 1987 before the fall of the wall, the cruel concrete line dividing the city into Soviet and Allied occupation zones. Then it was a gray place, part of the world's neatest slum, which is what much of East Berlin looked like then. Five years later, in 1992, with Germany unified, a few Jewish cafés had opened, amazing places, some run by synagogues or religious young people.

This time Oranienburger, as Colin said it would, had the feel of an emerging Greenwich Village. We moved down the street for that coffee to a fancier restaurant called Oren, where Catherine and I had stopped in 1992. It had been "new" then, next to the city's largest synagogue, a gold-domed building restored by the Communists just before the reunification of the city and country. The streets then were broken concrete and most of the cars around there were still the little fiberglass two-cylinder Trabants, perhaps the worst cars in the world of their time—now they were becoming collector's items.

▲▲▲

EAST IS STILL EAST

When the Berlin Wall came down and the country was unified after more than forty years of division, the West German government moved quickly to create one country again. After a referendum in which 85 percent of voters from both sides voted for unification, the government in Bonn ruled that East German deutsche marks were equivalent to West German marks—although, in truth, the Western currency was worth perhaps ten times as much.

The thought then, in 1990, was that a German was a German was a German and all of them were among the world's most talented and hardworking people. It seemed easy. It has not been. It is clear now that true unification will take decades if not generations—something like the North and South in the United States after the Civil War.

While we were there it was obvious both sides feel betrayed. In what used to be West Germany and in West Berlin, ordinary taxpayers complain that they are pouring billions of dollars into East Germany and getting nothing but complaints and workers who are not up to world standards or the old German work ethic. In what was East Germany, there is unemployment of more than 30 percent and many there blame West German companies for buying and then closing down their industries.

This quote from the former manager of an East German steel mill is typical: "They told us we were brothers and sisters. They said we would work together. Now they control our industry. They decide what to keep open and what to shut down. . . . We are tenants in our own country."

▴ ▴ ▴

The restaurant had become part of a very fashionable scene but still featured two menus, kosher and hip. With white walls, high ceilings, candles on all the tables, and black furnishings, the feel was Berlin 1920s or Upper West Side Manhattan 1980s. All of this had happened within five years. And there would have been much more renovation, development, and speculation if there were not legal problems over who owned what in East Germany; property had been seized from Jews by the Nazis and then seized again and distributed by the Communists.

Through it all, baby Ian sat in his infant seat or was placed next to his father and seemed perfectly content and then some just watching the world go by.

And we were content just watching him.

Catherine wrote:

We stayed in the Eastern sector because that was part of the idea. We wanted to see and to show the kids what communism had looked like without going to St. Petersburg or Moscow,

side trips that were just too expensive because they were not on
the routes of our three airlines, Singapore Airlines, which we
had now left behind, Swissair, which got us here from Israel,
and Delta, which we would take for the trip back to the
United States. East Berlin was a compromise choice. . . . We
picked the Forum, because it was the cheapest deal I could
find. By this time we were taking four rooms. The cost was
$119 a night, breakfast included.

We got together in the hotel's huge dining hall, a warehouse of
cereals, breads, cheeses, sausages, and cold cuts. All you could eat—
and stuff in your pockets. Molly turned out to be an instant critic of
both travel and fashion, saying:

> We are now staying at what I think is a really bad hotel be-
> cause there are no windows in the room. It's very small and
> cramped. . . . I went to the lobby for breakfast and in front of
> me was this lady with tight leather short-shorts that showed
> half her bottom. Personally, I wouldn't call her attractive at
> all. . . . Soon after that we went on what I thought was the
> most boring tour in the world. All I heard of the tour guide's
> speech was, "If you crossed the Wall you would get shot im-
> mediately" . . . and that's about it.

Thomas had wanted to organize a tour of the city so that everyone
would know their way around for the next couple of days. I saw a secret
smile behind Catherine's eyes. There was another planner on tour. Sure
enough, that night she wrote:

> It was great to get a burst of enthusiasm from Thomas and
> Cindie. We had seen so much and had been so visually stimu-
> lated in so many countries that our ability to focus in on small
> things was diminished compared to earlier in our trip. But
> they saw and noticed everything . . . and their enthusiasm was
> contagious.

The Wall.

The Brandenburg Gate.

The walking and subway tour began—where else?—in front of the McDonald's restaurant near the zoo in what was West Berlin. It was not boring, Molly! This was Thomas's account:

We congregated at the train station and rode the train to the Museum Island and the old cathedral, which had only re-opened in 1994. It was one of the most impressive churches I've ever seen, especially the gilded walls, altar, and pulpit. Queen Sophie Charlotte and her husband, Frederick I, the first King of Prussia, were buried there. . . . We then walked along

Unter den Linden, prewar Berlin's grandest boulevard, cut in half by the Wall from 1961 to 1989, at the Brandenburg Gate.

We arrived at Brandenburger Tan, the western entrance to Unter den Linden, the street of lime trees. The gate itself was grand, a columned structure topped by the goddess of peace in a chariot being pulled by four horses. It was here that thousands upon thousands of West Berliners gathered to rejoice after the collapse of the Wall. . . . We then went to the Reichstag nearby and walked to one of the few remaining sections of the Berlin Wall and its last standing guard tower.

Our tour ended at the site of Checkpoint Charlie, the American boundary station at the Wall, which was the principal border check for foreigners entering East Berlin during the Cold War years. . . . Time to go back to the hotel for Cynthia, Ian, and me to take a nap. It was hot and sunny today and we covered a lot of ground on foot.

We all stopped for lunch at the Café Alber, which once was directly across from the guard shack that was Checkpoint Charlie. All that was left of the checkpoint was a rectangle of different-colored asphalt to show where the little building had been in the middle of the street. It took me quite a while, sitting there, to remember and describe what it had looked like—a concrete maze began at the American checkpoint and ended after the East Germans had checked papers on their side before waving cars into their sector. They were a nasty bunch, and so were their colleagues checking papers and lives at subway and elevated train checkpoints.

Colin was about ready to call it a trip. He and Conor, too, were worn out, ready to sleep without travel alarms. Said Colin:

With a flight booked, we went down to meet the rest of the group for breakfast. It was decided that we would all take a walking tour of Berlin that was offered through some tour agency. A couple of weeks earlier we had seen a report on CNN about the Paris subway bombing in which an American tourist was shown saying, "We weren't worried about the subway because we never got off the tour bus." We all had a self-righteous laugh . . . and here we were meeting up with a group of American tourists outside a McDonald's to fall in line for a highly regimented afternoon of stale, scripted jokes. Questions were asked but never answered. It was a nice afternoon, though . . . there was much pinching of Ian's cheeks.

Conor and I both decided that we had exhausted our usefulness to this mission. Thomas and Ian were available now to strap a half-dozen bags to their bodies and stumble through airports. Conor and I had suddenly become superfluous. . . . The racket Fiona was now able to make with her co-conspirator, Molly, drove me from the café and into the street, smoking cigarettes most of the time, imagining how I would have attempted to defect to the West. There was a guy who hang-glided over the Wall into West Berlin under cover of darkness. I guess he just leapt off a nearby building and caught an updraft into the land of milk, honey, and plentiful Japanese running shoes.

We had dinner that night at a restaurant Thomas picked, Zan Letzten Instanz, which proudly proclaims that it opened in 1621. Thomas, the chef and restaurateur, described it this way:

> The rooms all have planked floors, wainscoting, old-fashioned tiled heaters, and antiques. It was a cool German evening, but just warm enough to eat outdoors in a brick courtyard with iron fences and big oak trees. The food was tremendous, Old World German specialties such as Boulette, Kohlmelade, Schnitzel, Sulze, and Rote Gruize for dessert, cooked fruit with a vanilla sauce that was incredible.

The food was great and so was the family event, Colin's birthday. It was a thrill to watch him open the gift selected by his pesky and pesty little sister. He saw the old twin-lens camera she had been carrying

Colin's birthday in Berlin.

since Jakarta and his face just lit up, describing it later as: "An incredible ancient large-format Yashica that Fiona had picked out for me in Indonesia."

The kid's got her brother's number.

Her other brother, Conor, had been in Berlin before, too, but saw it differently this time:

I felt instantly at ease in Germany. It was more like America. The people look like Americans, white Americans. Everything was expensive and everyone was taller than I am. I had been here ten years ago for a high school theater festival when we lived in Paris. Back then it was West Berlin and it was very West, like a big German Champs-Élyseés—commercialized and upscale. I remember things that seemed very German to me: pedestrians would not cross the street against the light even when there was no traffic; policemen were evicting homeless winos from subway stations into the frigid winter night. I believed Germans were uptight, militaristic . . . .

Knowing I felt that way, Colin said: "I spent some time working in Germany last year and the Germans are pretty mellow, they're a lot cooler than the French."

"We'll see," I said. But Colin turned out to be right. . . . The whole appeal to me this time was the Eastside. (Kind of like L.A.) There were a lot of young people hanging out— sidewalk cafés, funky art, pretty girls on bicycles. It was the first place that could be described in these terms: graffiti, body-piercing, skateboarders, punk rockers. We had made it back to civilization. I couldn't help thinking this would be a great place to tour with a band—it might actually have a receptive audience.

The next morning we saw the guys off at the hotel.
Colin wrote:

I packed up the Yashica, wished the expedition godspeed, and jumped into a cab with Conor for the trip to the airport. Everything was quick and painless and German. And just like that it was over.

▲▲▲

THE WORLD ACCORDING TO COLIN
This was the conclusion of Colin's trip journal:

The blurry pace somehow seemed useful, and the premise plausible: sprint around the world, experimenting with various sleep-deprivation techniques and overloading on data, and it would all become so blurry that a great truth would be revealed—maybe a revelation about what binds humanity together. . . .

The Parthenon was originally planned to have seven columns in its facade, but then some Greek determined that seven was the highest number of units that the human brain could process as being individual items. Anything more than seven, and the brain starts grouping units in order to perform its duties and presumably to prevent blowing some neurogasket. Wanting to present a united and solid front on his temple, this Greek changed the design to the eight columns. It may be that the brain can't digest fourteen countries in thirty-four days. . . . My brain is definitely grouping.

Photos help and reassure me that cloudy images in my brain did in fact happen and I imagine that eventually only the things in the photos will have happened and it will all be as clear as Kodak Gold.

Has the blur behaved as hoped and revealed a truth? Do I have a better idea of what binds humanity together; some sense of human commonality? . . . There is one thing I do know. There is not a single thing you can say that is both common to, and unique to, all human beings, that would concretely define human beings.

▶ ▶ ▶

Not for us. We were all off for Museum Island, beginning at the most famous of its galleries, The Pergamon Museum, which is named for its most admired exhibit, the gigantic Pergamon Altar from an ancient Hellenistic kingdom which thrived during the third and second centuries before Christ in what is now Turkey. It is a museum of extraordinary dimension, concentrating on Greek and Roman sculpture but showing the Ishtar Gate and a processional street from Babylon, all reconstructed indoors. Fiona and Molly seemed in awe, as well they should have been. Catherine reminded them these treasures were taken from the people and places from whence they came. Met with blank stares, she dropped the subject. Fiona's later critique: "Boring . . . just statues of naked people."

We met for lunch at KDW, "Ka-Day-Vay" they say in Berlin, the Great Store of the West. It is exactly that, great and Western, in some ways the symbol of all that was Western during the Cold War. There was nothing known to man that could not be bought on one floor or another. The food court on the sixth floor may have been the most magnificent in the world with produce and meat and wine from every corner of the globe. Famous chefs like Paul Bocuse of France had their own stands or corners, like the perfume counters in many department stores. It was a monument to riches and consumption, a dazzling multicolored beacon to the people forced into the grayness of life on the other side of the Wall, in East Berlin and the rest of the Communist world. It did not surprise Catherine and me at all that when the Wall finally came down, many East Berliners rushed to KDW to see and touch things they had heard of or seen only on television, beginning with foods they thought exotic, like bananas.

We roamed the floors for a while and then went into the top-floor restaurant, picked up trays and wandered the buffet. That word was not grand enough for the spreads of foods around us—or the prices. We had been here in the superdollar years of the mid-1980s when one American dollar was worth more than three West German deutsche marks. Now it was closer to one-for-one. In other words, even without ten years of inflation, things were priced at almost three times what they were then. I found myself thinking of the substantial supply of American-packaged nuts, dried apricots, and Tiger Milk bars we had carried through the parts of Asia where amoebae lurked. At the Forum, a Coke cost ten deustch marks, about eight weak dollars. The prices made me wonder whether perhaps we carried trail food on the wrong side of the globe. Then Fiona came up to me and said, "Let's shop, shop, shop." I said: "Here we look, look, look."

That night, Catherine wrote:

> As we sat down to eat, Thomas said, "Correct me if I'm wrong . . . but did it just cost one hundred marks for this little lunch for me and Cynthia?" Eighty dollars. Yes, that's the going rate.

What Colin called my "trinketry" days were over. We took a
lot of taxis because there were so many of us, and with the
baby it was just easier. But every time we got into a cab there
seemed to be a fifteen-dollar minimum.

This was our third time in Berlin, the last time three
years ago. There is more building going on in East Berlin than
in all the rest of Western Europe combined. Cranes dot the skyline immediately behind the Brandenburg Gate. But yet, there
is so much rehabilitation to do—and so much deterioration.
Even some of the loveliest of the old buildings have
only one toilet per floor, shared by all the residents of that floor.

The old East Berlin is considered hipper now than the
bourgeois Western sector, which means the city's young people go a bit East. But that fun masks tremendous problems,
beginning with the fact that the most optimistic projections
estimate that the gross domestic product per capita of the old
East Germany will be only 60 percent of the Western figure
by 1998. There are plans to put more modern shopping districts and office buildings into the Eastern sector at the turn of
the twenty-first century, once the German government relo-
cates in Berlin from the temporary (forty years) capital of
Bonn. But it is significant that West Germany—one of the
richest countries in the world with a real commitment to in-
corporating the old East—is having such troubles. What of
other former Communist countries without a rich adoptive
parent? Some will never catch up.

Even in Germany there is great resentment on both sides
of the old borders. . . . Many former West Germans feel they
are being taxed too heavily and their lazy cousins are not willing to work enough. Many East Germans are angry that they
paid the price for Germany's World War II crimes; they suf-
fered under communism for four decades while their brothers
and cousins in the West became rich. Not easy.

Thomas and Cindie decided to walk back to the hotel and he
wrote:

As we left the KDW, Cynthia, Ian, and I were walking along the Witterbergplatz when we found ourselves in front of the Warner Brothers store. We went in and asked for assistance in the baby department and the assistant manager of the store, who told us he had a ten-day-old son himself, took us personally to the baby department and showed us all the outfits, including what was on sale.

It was a trip to be on a trip with Cindie and Thomas, who are more focused right now on their own future rather than Germany's. The new mother wrote:

Feeding Ian in the park at Alexanderplatz, with the red roses, the fountain of Neptune, the police horses drinking out of the fountain. I could have endured most anything knowing this beautiful picture would be my life.

Well, it certainly was her life in Berlin. My well-traveled older daughter wrote:

We have a new shopping pattern. . . . We've bought art in Bali, masks in Thailand and Singapore, silk in Hong Kong, pearls in Japan, lots of blue topaz in the Caribbean, leather in Turkey, painted boxes in Russia, amethysts in Chile. Germany is famous for beautiful and hard-to-find culinary hardware. At KDW, Thomas and I looked at Henckles, Wustoff, and WMF products, including scissors for cutting the top off soft-boiled eggs . . . but the only thing we bought was a stuffed elephant for Ian.

The new father added:

Ian had traveled all day with us in his baby sling, switching between Cynthia and me, Grandad, and the rest of the family. The one thing that seems to warm everyone's heart to a smile is the sight of my son's innocent face. As we pass by everyone, they smile at him, at us, and at one another. The brightness a new baby can bring to all never seems to end.

We stopped again to take a look inside a church called St. Marteen. The church was closed, but an open door led to the basement, where there was a photo exhibit. We didn't need to speak German to understand the sequence of events. They were pictures of the Holocaust. The magnitude of the atrocities photographed was more that we could bear and we left midway through.

Added Cindie:

I know very well what happened, but I don't see many reminders. These are the first photos. They are far past disturbing. Far past haunting. They are unthinkable. If this is the only time in my life I get this close it is enough for me to have a lasting memory. God rest their souls.

That afternoon Thomas went off on his own to see what he could see, reporting back enough to make me think we could trade jobs—he could be the journalist and I could be the chef, though probably I would have to expand my four-dish repertoire. This is what he said:

I wanted to find someone who would talk about their feelings of the changes in East Berlin life since the Wall came down. I stopped at the Queen Victoria Pub, figuring that the name meant that the proprietor or someone working there might speak English.

A woman named Claudia Franetzlei, thirty years old, worked there. She had been born on the island of Rügen in the Baltic Sea. After some polite conversation I asked her what East Berliners had been going through since the demise of the Wall. . . . She said the reclaiming of property had hurt many people, but that the opportunity to travel had enriched lives beyond measure. Before the fall, East Germans were pretty much restricted to their own half a country and to Bulgaria, Hungary, and Czechoslovakia—and for the well connected, Cuba. . . . Her apartment rent went from 35 to 700 deutsche marks; her pay went from 800 to 2,500. . . . Her boyfriend, named Marco, had been a taxidriver but was working now as a roofer because of all the construction work going on—but there was a lot of competition for that kind of work because English and Irish construction workers were taking advantage of European citizenship rights to work in East Germany.

"Who has been hurt most?" I asked.

"People about thirty or forty years old. They are being re-placed by younger people who are hungry for money and who are more comfortable with the freedoms and so are easier to train and more creative."

Our younger contingent, Fiona and Molly, were off with Cather-ine to the Berlin Zoo, which has fourteen thousand animals. This was Molly's verdict:

It was a really great zoo. I wanted to see the kangaroos but they were all lying down. I liked the elephants and I liked the lion house with all the big cats. There was a whole Lion King fam-ily there . . . and the king was just rolling over on his back.

Said Catherine:

Fiona and Molly loved their afternoon. It was wonderful see-ing the enthusiasm of these two little girls as they exuberantly ran from animal to animal—seeing panthers, lions, tigers, jaguars, monkeys, zebras, hippopotamuses, rhinos, sea lions, kangaroos, etc. Many of the animals had babies, and even for this adult it was a wonder watching a mother lion pitch her tiny cub in her mouth and march it back to a place in the en-closure where she wanted it to be. . . . I know all the argu-ments about zoos and cruelty to animals, and intellectually I do feel sorry for some of these critters and the way they are

> WE WERE BACK IN TERRI-
> TORY WHERE WOMEN'S
> SEMINAKED BODIES
> WERE POSTED ON THE
> WALLS. THAT I DIDN'T
> LIKE. YOU REALIZE HOW
> DEGRADING IT IS AND
> HOW ACCUSTOMED WE
> HAVE BECOME TO BEING
> TREATED LIKE MEAT
> DISPLAYED FOR ALL TO
> SEE.   —CATHERINE

constrained so far from their natural environments. But watching the kids . . . what could be better?

We had dinner that night at the street café of the Hotel Kempinski on Kurfürstendamm, the main street of West Berlin when the city was divided. Catherine wrote this time:

Three years ago, we sat here marveling at how different the people from the East looked compared to the West Berliners. Then the Westerners wore the casual outfits of the comfortably well off everywhere in the world: jeans, T-shirts, khakis, fancy sneakers, the works from Armani to Benetton to Levi's. The Easterners then, images of country cousins, were in brightly colored and badly done polyester and souvenir sweatshirts and some even wore plastic shoes or workboots. The differences were not so obvious this time, but we had no doubt that the practiced eyes of the West Berliners could spot an Easterner at about a hundred meters.

The most striking visual thing for me was the same as Conor's first take. Germans look like Americans—white Americans of European descent that is. . . . The other visual impression that struck me was that we were back in territory where women's seminaked bodies were posted on the walls. That I didn't like. You realize how degrading it is and how accustomed we have become to being treated like meat displayed for all to see. It's amazing women don't fight back more militantly. It was sad to see the prostitutes lining Oranienburger Strasse.

Cindie saw some of the same things, writing:

They look as though they smoke too many cigarettes, and don't get enough sun. They have wild and bold haircuts and interesting colors. You want to try new hairstyles and colors, move to Germany. . . . It does appear, though, that they take environmentalism more seriously than we do in America. The first thing I noticed in the airport was that there were old women pushing three-part carts with bins labeled for plastic, glass, and tin. In downtown Berlin there are recycling "bells" on the street corners. Germany also fines companies that unnecessarily overpackage their products. The cigarette warning in Germany is a little more direct than ours back home. "Smoking will seriously damage your health." No "may" about it. The general appearance of the city streets is as clean as any I remember seeing anywhere . . . except for the graffiti. It's everywhere.

I'm not crazy about Berlin, or Germany itself for that matter. Few people my age are; we were small children during World War II and about the first thing we learned was to hate Germans. But I had worked in Berlin, both West and East, over the years and there was tremendous tension and sense of life in West Berlin before the Wall came down in 1989. There was a sense of danger—people were shot trying to get over, under, or around the Wall—and there was that certain decadence everywhere, the feeling or fear that tomorrow we die.

It seemed a duller place this time, at least to me. What was engaging, though, was the enthusiasm of Cindie and Thomas—and their total concentration on their son, their new sun! I got to know a little more about the man who came into my life uninvited, my son-in-law. He seemed to be something like Catherine is, direct, unself-conscious, reaching out and grabbing life, determined never to miss a sight or an idea or a minute.

The two of us walked alone together back to the Forum after Colin's birthday dinner, using the communications tower on Alexanderplatz, the highest structure in the city, as our guide. We passed a bombed-out old church—one of many in the East—and heard voices coming from inside. A man in a long cloak came out by himself and lit a cigarette.

Thomas walked up to him, which I would not have done, and asked: "What's going on in there?"

"A play," the man said. "This is Franziskaner Klosterkirche, open-air theater. . . . It's *The Hunchback of Notre Dame,* you know it?"

"Yes," we said. Thomas's new friend seemed to be listening for something in the voices inside. He heard it, ground out the cigarette, and started to run back inside.

"I am the hunchback," he called. *"Auf Wiedersehen."*

Chapter 18

PARIS

The first time I saw Paris, I walked the streets of the Left Bank in awe. The first night, looking up at the lighted windows on the streets around the Place St. Germain, I wondered who lived there. Then one day, I did.

In February of 1985, when Fiona was eight weeks old, we moved to Paris. The summer before we had spent three weeks driving around the country with Conor, who was then fifteen years old. Toward the end of the trip, Catherine told him she was pregnant. To say he was surprised would not do justice to his young face. He seemed flabbergasted that we could do it.

On that vacation, as on others, we had dropped in at real estate offices in a number of places. Not only were we exercising my enduring fantasies about living in most every place I've ever seen, but looking at houses with a local agent is the best way I know to quickly learn what life is like in a far place. In fact, I had planned the itinerary that summer (the only time in my married life) around that quest. My ear for French was so tin that we looked in Joigny, a Nebraska-like farming region eighty miles southeast of Paris, because I misunderstood a friend who told me to take a look at Chantilly, a horsey town ten miles north of the city.

So, back in Paris the day before we were to fly home in 1984, we looked at a couple of apartments to lease and stumbled upon Quatre-vingt-quinze Rue de Rennes, cinquième-gauche—Apartment 5-left at 95 Rue de Rennes, a couple of blocks south of the Place St. Germain. With the value of the United States dollar at a peak, the ten-thousand-franc rent was only a little more than a thousand dollars a month. "You people are totally insane," said Conor as I signed the papers. Maybe, but he came with us by choice, graduating from the American High School in the suburb of St. Cloud.

Now of course Paris became a different place—it saw Ian.

"Now another Ian story," wrote his father:

The flight from Berlin to Aéroport Charles de Gaulle was painless. Everyone from the plane descended on the immigration booth. It was chaotic because there were no customs forms on our plane and people were being turned away. But I offered up Ian as our passport first. It brought a smile to the officer's face and kind words from her mouth. We whisked through and then I heard her abrupt voice telling the man behind, "Your card is not filled out properly, back in line!"

Wrote Cindie:

What a system. Looking for customs we found only a poster with two people riding a condom. I guess the French prefer safe sex to inspecting baggage. . . . I saw signs for the rest rooms but they just led us back to some center spot. Oh, I got it, you had to take an elevator. But that took us to a parking garage. . . . Once on a trip to Scotland when I was sixteen I remember my father showing me the "Passing Place" signs on one-lane roads and saying that in France they would read, "A Place You Pull Your Vehicle into If Another Vehicle Comes Along in the Opposite Direction."

What I remembered about that trip almost twenty years before was picking up Cindie in Paris, at Orly at dawn and giving her a grand tour of the city. I wanted her to love it as I did. After an hour, sipping coffee at a café, I asked her what she thought.

"It reminds me a lot of Quebec," she said.

Paris is for lovers and maybe for new parents, too. We were staying in a friend's apartment on Rue Cherche Midi in our old neighborhood, but Catherine thought Cindie and Thomas would be better off in a big hotel nearer the center of town. She chose the Hotel Intercontinental, because it accepted our last United Airlines 50-percent-discount coupons, bringing the room rate down to $279 a night if they didn't eat. Where did we leave the fruits and nuts?

Cindie wrote this:

> The hotel turned out to be far more romantic than I had imagined. This was our first trip to Paris together. As we checked in, I asked for a sunny room. They offered us a room on the park, the Tuileries Gardens, warning us it might be a bit noisy. As former New Yorkers, we could surely take and almost enjoy a little street noise. We looked out and saw a carnival, which the government allows in the gardens for a month each summer. Our romantic view of Paris was the Log Flume! . . . I called down to the front desk and said this was too loud for the baby after all. I'll tell you this baby thing is the greatest excuse for almost everything.
>
> Our next room was filled with antiques. . . . We had two sets of French windows that looked over a courtyard with a fountain. The bathroom was big, huge really, with another set of French windows. None of the windows had screens to filter out the colors. And Ian found something he enjoyed, a great big chandelier with little lights hanging right over the bed. . . . I was in Paris but not really caring that I didn't get to once again see its most famous sights. We would go back to the hotel with Ian and Thomas would settle the two of us in for our nap. My husband is a big nap guy too, but he says he'll sleep when we get to New York. I used to be that way.

Thomas walked a good part of the city on our first afternoon, marveling at the number of people taking advantage of a beautiful summer day, sunbathing, picnicking, playing soccer, or just lying on the grass and quais. I suspect he does not know the greatest secret of Paris: the weather is lousy. Residents evacuate in August not to cool off but to get warm.

We took Cindie and Thomas out for dinner at Laurent in the park alongside the Champs-Élysées, a Michelin two-star restaurant of some

Sunday in Paris:
Ladies (and Thomas)
who lunch . . .

elegance. It was chef Thomas's first Paris meal and he got himself invited into the kitchen and seemed happy talking shop with the chefs
there. He is a very gregarious guy and once more I was surprised by
how much he was like Catherine. Cindie put it this way:

> My way to get an understanding of a new place is to read
> books and study languages. My husband just talks to people;
> he is not afraid to point, ask, and just be friendly. But he
> speaks no French and I knew I would have to take him
> around. On the plane, I went over French phrases in my head,
> preparing to take on the taxi drivers in perfect accent. . . . We
> got to the taxi line and as I got ready to speak, Thomas walked
> up to the driver, said a few words in mixed English and
> pseudo-French, and smiled. The driver, who seemed to speak
> not a word of English, smiled and took us on our way.

As to the evening, which I will remember for Cindie popping Ian
to her breast for his three courses, Thomas wrote:

We sat outside in Laurent's garden. The night was perfect. It was one of the most enjoyable dinners I've had in a long time. The perfect balance of cuisine, atmosphere, and company. . . . Richard and Catherine dropped us off at our hotel. Once Cynthia, Ian, and I went upstairs we decided to change our clothes and go for a walk. We strolled the neighborhoods and found ourselves walking through the square of the Ministry of Justice up to the Café de la Paix, admiring the Opera House and watching people go by.

> IT WAS ONE OF THE MOST ENJOYABLE DINNERS I'VE HAD IN A LONG TIME. THE PERFECT BALANCE OF CUISINE, ATMOSPHERE, AND COMPANY. —THOMAS

The next morning, Sunday, we had breakfast in the hotel. Each waiter who walked by said, "Oh, what a lovely baby, can we get you anything?" Then we met the family across the Seine at Café de Flore on the Boulevard St. Germain.

Actually we were reliving a hundred Sundays of our Paris years: up early, a walk down to Flore, pick up the British Sunday newspapers, and sit for an hour, which was how long it took Fiona to finish a bag of potato chips in those days, and then walk a couple blocks over to the Sunday street market on the Rue de Buci to buy the fixings for an afternoon family feast.

Said Catherine:

Now Fiona and Molly were busy entertaining Fiona's nephew. Ian was about the age Fiona had been when she first went there . . . At Buci, we did what we always did, buying a ton of *coquillage,* some *melon de Cavaillon, poulet rôti, frisé,* cheeses, *baguettes,* and our favorite water, Badoit. We ate in the garden behind the apartment, which belongs to Jane Kramer. She has been writing brilliant essays from Paris (and the rest of Europe) for the *New Yorker* for fifteen years or so. Luckily for us, she was in Italy with her family . . . and generously offered to have us stay in her house. Phew! We got there just when

THE REALIZATION OF
HOW UNIMPORTANT THE
SIGHTS ARE TO ME HITS
WHEN WE GET TO NOTRE
DAME. IT'S SUNDAY SO
THERE IS A SERVICE.
IT'S HOT, IT'S CROWDED,
AND I'M CARRYING AN
ELEVEN-POUND BABY.
THE THOUGHT OF
SARDINING MY WAY
THROUGH CROWDS IS
MORE THAN I CAN BEAR.
WHAT IS APPEALING IS
THE IDEA OF SITTING
OUTSIDE WATCHING
PEOPLE GO BY AND
FEEDING MY SON.
PARADISE. —CINDIE

our credit cards were about to have a nervous breakdown from overuse.

Thomas filled out the menu saying:

Cynthia chose some great cheeses; Catherine selected huge pears along with an incredible slab of foie gras, priced at a thousand francs per kilogram. Fiona picked out some raspberries. I bought some roasted fowl and bread. Then we all picked out some lettuces, white peaches, figs, and melons.

Before feasting, we walked and walked—beginning at Ste. Chapelle, the private chapel of Louis IX and certainly one of the most beautiful things ever done by man. Then we headed for Notre Dame and the "Bird Market" on the Ile de la Cité. Wrote Thomas:

I've never seen such a thing. Birds, birds, and more birds. Would I possibly find an Ortalon here? Fiona and Molly were in heaven. As we neared the end of the market, there were thirty to forty large sacks of various birdseeds for sale. It looked like a Brazilian coffee market. I never knew birds had such a diverse cuisine. Only in Paris.

Cindie was in a world of her own, writing:

The realization of how unimportant the sights are to me hits me when we get to Notre Dame. It's Sunday so there is a Mass.

Paris sees Ian, and three generations of Reeveses, outside Notre Dame.

A bridge over untroubled waters.

It's hot, it's crowded, and I'm carrying an eleven-pound baby. The thought of sardining my way through crowds is more than I can bear. What is appealing is the idea of sitting outside watching people go by and feeding my son. Paradise. I settle into a spot on a bench in the shade. Although I have avoided breast feeding in public in the States, I am very comfortable here. Most of my blouses on this trip are specially designed nursing tops. They are keeping my activity discreet but people who actually see what's going on are giving me this Isn't-that-one-of-life's-best-things smiles. Ten feet from me is a passed-out homeless-looking person draped over the base of a statue. He is getting more attention than me. I don't think the same would be true in New York City.

Various women and children took cabs back to the apartment on Cherche Midi. Thomas and I walked back—central Paris is amazingly small for a world city—which meant he was a captive guest on the long-running Reeves family tour. Usually I do it alone, begining at 95 Rue de Rennes, swallowing hard before I look up at the balcony that once was ours. I retraced the walk through the Luxembourg Gardens that Catherine and I did most mornings, ending by the scale model of the Statue of Liberty that Bartholdi used to make sections of the lady in New York Harbor in his studio nearby. I showed him Fiona's school in the building next to Le Drugstore on the Boulevard St. Germain and her crèche, the government day-care center she went to three mornings a week near Au Bon Marché, the department store of the Sixth Arrondisement.

We all had dinner that night with our first friends in Paris, Walter and Pat Wells. The Wellses and I all had the same alma mater, *The New York Times.* He had come to Paris to be news editor of the *International Herald Tribune,* which is owned by the *Times* and the *Washington Post.* She had been a woman's page reporter and came without speaking more than a word or two of French and had become one of the most famous food writers in the world. It was she who had gotten me to Joigny by suggesting I check out Chantilly. We had dinner with them the night we moved to Paris with just twelve bags and tiny Fiona

Dinner with Pat and Walter Wells, our first friends and guides in France.

(Conor came later), and they were the first guests at our apartment after we furnished it with treasures from the Marché aux Puces, the flea market at the end of the Port de Clignancourt metro line, and Hotel Drouot, the municipal auction house.

Thomas said:

> Dinner was at Boeuf sur le Toit (Beef on the Roof), an art deco setting with touches of the surrealist era of the thirties. . . . The Wellses are very accomplished people. Patricia had just done a book with Joel Robuchon, one of the world's premier chefs. She was also getting ready to open her own cooking school this fall at Chanteduc, their country home in Provence. I could have talked with her for weeks. . . . Dinner was good. The highlight was the vautel of shellfish we had as an appetizer. A species I never had tasted before.

Paris being Paris, that is with weather from London sweeping across the English Channel and through the valley of the Seine, it was raining the next morning as I took Fiona and Molly above the clouds to the top of the Eiffel Tower. It was cold and windy, too, but they seemed to love it. Thomas and Cindie headed for the Louvre and he reported:

> We walked up the Rue de Rivoli to the Louvre, but when we got there people were exiting. When we asked what was going on, a woman told us that there was a bomb scare and that they were taking all precautions. So, we headed off window shopping and Ian didn't seem to mind. He loves a good quiet tour in his sling. . . . We came across a church and went inside and lit a candle as a family and said a prayer. . . . We stopped at Galignani, the bookstore on the Rue de Rivoli and heard a woman's voice calling, "Fiona, Molly! Where are you?" It turned out that Catherine was buying a book for me, *The Food Lover's Guide to Paris* by Patricia Wells. Excellent for me.

Her roaming done, Catherine joined me for a walk up the Rue de Rennes to the Hertz office on Montparnasse, a place we knew well, our wheels supplier when we lived down the hill. But they did not have the two Fords or Renaults we had reserved weeks before. Would I take another car? "Okay, sure," I said before Catherine could begin a negotiation. This was her report on that:

> I have almost never been in a Mercedes car, never mind have the use of one. But this rainy day in Paris, when we were ready to leave for a week of post-trip celebration and collapse in Normandy . . . all my novenas as a child paid off, in a way I never imagined. I looked at the Mercedes keys in the clerk's hands. Could it be? . . . It was. He gave them to us! And off we were, with me driving for the next two weeks . . . a full-size Mercedes-Benz.

The drive out of Paris to Normandy started in the rain, but the weather cleared quickly. Cindie reported:

> We ventured out of Paris in two cars. My dad in one with the little girls, Fiona and Molly, and Thomas, Ian, and I with Cathy

"*Cynthia chose some great cheeses.*"

in another. Ian and I sat in the back so we could sleep. It was going to be a two-and-a-half-hour trip anyway and it was our usual nap time. We settled in with Thomas navigating and Cathy driving. . . . We headed out to the A13 via the *Périphérirque.*

Catherine beat me to Normandy and the old farmhouse (try fifteenth century) we had rented from friends in Paris, Richard and Nancy Ashthalter. It was nine o'clock when we rolled in and her crowd, a hungry one, was already rolling out. A little restaurant in St. Julien de Faucon, the town down the road, had agreed to stay open for the Americans. It was called *Relais Routiers* and you will not find it in any Michelin guide. Basically there was a small bar and a pinball machine in the front room of a small house and a couple of long tables in what otherwise was a living room. And it was great. Serendipity. They just kept bringing us food. Salads, steaks, fish, omelets, potatoes, and a good wine in old bottles with a handwritten label that read, "*Vin du Patron.*"

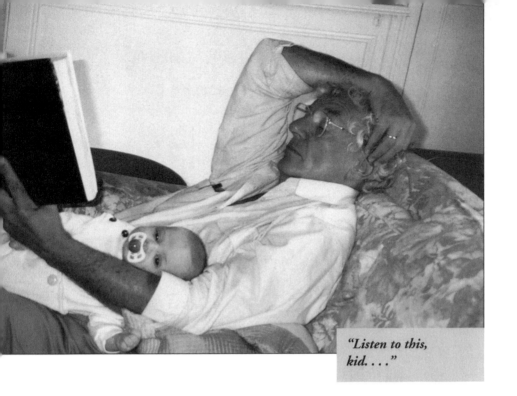

"Listen to this, kid. . . ."

The next morning, Thomas wrote:

Cynthia, Ian, and I had a bedroom with big windows over-looking the fields. We awoke to the greetings of the cows. Richard and I drove into St. Julien and had coffee at a café then went to the local *boulangerie* and bought breakfast breads and some grocery items. . . . Two dozen or so shops along the road, a church, and a monument to the village's dead in the First and Second World Wars. Not touristy . . . It was a day of writing and napping. Lunch at home, a walk, going nowhere. It was wonderful. Ian was playful as he sat outside with me in a wicker basket. . . . Catherine had gone shopping in the big-ger town of St. Pierre-sur-Dives, ten miles away, and made a great lunch. Salmon fillets, fresh sardines, radishes, salad, and bread. Red wine and after that it was definitely nap time. . . .

Not for Fiona who wrote:

We're in Normandy in an old-fashioned house. When we were driving here my dad told me that we had eight acres of land which I thought would be great until we got there. Molly and I realized that seven acres of it was a cow pasture.

The two of them explored room after room, finding an attic filled with old dresses, which they proceeded to model as the rest of us explored a delightful contradiction in terms, sunny Norman weather. We had come close to buying a place near here in 1988. I was the deal-breaker. I took Catherine to the town market where half the stalls were selling the same thing, rubber Wellington boots.

Molly's next discovery was the bidet in one of the bathrooms.

"Fiona, come up here," she yelled. "They have one of those things where the boys go pee."

"That's not for boys, Molly," said our young woman of the world. "It's a bathtub for Ian."

For reasons lost in Reeves antiquity, I have two daughters who love cheese, and know a fair bit about it. What did you do on your vacation in Normandy? Fiona's answer was: "Run barefoot in the grass and eat lots of cheese."

▲▲▲

A FATHER-DAUGHTER INTERVIEW

Q: Did the trip change the way you thought about the rest of us in the family? Me? Mom? Cindie? Colin? Conor? Ian?

A: Yes. I will put one positive thing and one negative thing for each one:

Dad. Positive: He's even more easygoing than I thought. Negative: His easygoingness seems to be more toward my mom.

Mom. She's amazing. She's organized and she's smart. Negative: I don't like the title she chose for this book, *Family Travels.*

> WHAT DID YOU DO ON YOUR VACATION IN NORMANDY? FIONA'S ANSWER WAS: "RUN BAREFOOT IN THE GRASS AND EAT LOTS OF CHEESE."

Cindie. Positive: She's the same as Mom.

Colin. Negative: He's a pessimist. Positive: He's a very funny pessimist.

Conor. Positive: He's good at saying "No" to the kids who sell you things.

Ian. Well, no change because I had no thoughts beforehand.

Q: Was it really tough to be with adults for so long without seeing other children?

A: No.

Q: What was the biggest surprise for you on the trip?

A: I had two. The fact cows are treated better than people in Nepal. Ian.

Q: If you had to live in one of these countries, which one would it be?

A: It depends. I loved Indonesia, but I think I would prefer France because it's more civilized and the water is safe. I would choose Normandy over Paris because there's more grass.

Q: Which country had the best food?

A: Paris had the best desserts. But I also liked the saté and cooked peppers in Egypt and the dim sum in China.

Q: Well, was going around the world a good idea for the family? Why?

A: Of course it was . . . 'cause it was fun.

Q: Were you scared of anything along the way?

A: Yes. I was afraid of diseases and I was afraid of getting lost in strange places.

▶ ▶ ▶

There is a Museum of Cheese Technology in St. Pierre-sur-Dives and our little gourmet decided we should all go there one night for a local festival and then wrote this report:

It wasn't giant or anything. But I liked it and my mom told them I was nine so I got to taste some really good cheese for free. We got a four-course dinner and a bottle of cider for just twenty dollars a person.

We also drove to the beach at Deauville and Fiona wrote this:

We were just lying down trying to communicate with a little French boy who was about one-year-old and wouldn't stop kicking sand on my towel. After a while of that, Molly and I decided to go down to the water. However, when we got there it was really gross. There were eleven-year-olds running around naked and sixty-year-olds with no tops on.

On the day before Cindie and Thomas were going home, he and I drove out to a part of France that is forever America, Omaha Beach and the American cemetery on the cliffs above that shore. I had been there before, in June of 1988, and wrote this then:

I cried when my wife and I stepped into the American cemetery at St. Laurent sur Mer, above the beach where 3,881 of our countrymen were killed or wounded on June 6, 1944, D-Day—when the Americans and the British and the Canadians came to liberate continental Europe from the Nazis. We were the only visitors on a rainy January day. . . . In a café in Bayeux, the first town liberated on June 7, 1944, a well-dressed woman a little older than me came over to our table and asked, "You are American?"

She said she was from Caen, a city that was leveled by Allied bombers immediately before the landings. She remembered that and told us of running to the fields as American bombers began unloading on the city itself. "We will always be grateful to you for coming," she said. "All those boys. I realize now they were so young."

Now Thomas wrote:

After our morning trip to the *boulangerie,* Richard and I set out for the invasion beaches of World War II. We drove west through Caen and Bayeux and our first stop was at Pointe du Hoc, a vertical cliff that had to be captured to

IT WAS NOW MY TIME TO
VISIT THE CEMETERY. IT
WAS BEAUTIFULLY LAND-
SCAPED, QUIET. THE
WALKWAY LED TO A
MONUMENT TO THE DEAD
THAT OPENED TO THE
LILY POND POOLS THAT
LED TO A CHAPEL, ALL
OF THIS SURROUNDED BY
THOUSANDS UPON THOU-
SANDS OF WHITE STONE
CROSSES. I TEARED
UP....I READ ONLY ONE
HEADSTONE; I DON'T
THINK THAT I WILL EVER
FORGET HIS NAME,
HENRY TINKER.

—THOMAS

silence the big German guns over Omaha. . . . The landscape remained pot-holed with cracks from the intense Allied shelling. At the point of the cliffs there's a monument, a long stone that reads: "To the Heroic Ranger Commandoes of the 116th Infantry, who under the command of Colonel James E. Rudder of the First American Division, attacked and took possession of the Pointe Du Hoc."

It was now my time to visit the cemetery. It was beautifully landscaped, quiet. The walkway led to a monument to the dead that opened to the lily pond pools that led to a chapel, all of this surrounded by thousands upon thousands of white stone crosses. I teared up. . . . I read only one headstone; I don't think that I will ever forget his name, Henry Tinker.

Richard and I then stopped at the German cemetery, a very small stone entrance with dual vestibules on either side that opened to an area of dark stone Germanic crosses and headstones. On our way back to meet our wives for lunch I was quiet with not much to say. . . .

There were two entries in the German guest book from the day before. One, with no signature was: *"Faire l'amour, pas la guerre."* The other was by Andrew T. Kaufman of Houston, Texas: "I had very mixed emotions while visiting this place. I felt sorrow for the individuals buried here and the loved ones they left behind. But I'm glad their army was defeated, their leaders' vision for the world left unfulfilled.

Fiona, old-fashioned in Normandy.

Thomas in the American Cemetery in Normandy.

May these men rest in peace—and their descendents never follow the path that led them here."

Thomas then wrote:

We met Catherine, Cynthia, and Ian at a restaurant named Le Pavé d'Auge in Beuvron-en-Auge, a most beautiful village. An incredible lunch of a pressed rabbit terrine with shallots, a snapper with spinach. The restaurant was in the Norman style with a tall slanting roof wood-beamed interior—run by a couple named Susan and Jerome Bansard.

Catherine and I went back to Le Pavé d'Auge a few days later with some friends and Fiona and Molly. That dynamic duo got bored this time and went out to play in the little village square, coming back with two French boys their age who wanted to take them to the gallery where the oldest one, by a year, was eager to show our girls his father's paintings. Uh-oh! They're growing up.

Cindie, my grown-up daughter, wrote:

I loved having meal after meal with everyone, then taking walks and spending a little individual time with each family member. This is so much more satisfying than a quick weekend in Sag Harbor when you have to also see old friends and attend dinner parties. We move more as a unit, a family. In fact, before we left Normandy, we asked about the possibility of getting a house in France for two weeks next year.

Our time was almost up, too. I spent a couple of wonderful hours photographing Fiona and Molly in the dresses they found in the attic.

"Make it old-fashioned, make it old-fashioned. Do you have black-and-white film like the olden days?"—couple of little tyrants those two.

On the last night of our adventure we were down to four of us, Catherine and I, Fiona and Molly. We stayed that night with friends, Jim Bitterman and Pat Thompson, at their renovated *moulin* (mill) on the little river running through Gilles, closer in to Paris. The four adults and a couple of other friends who came out from Paris spent a lazy day in the sun of the most delightful August in Norman memory, drinking a little too much of the Calvados made from the fruit of Jim's apple trees. Fiona and Molly and Jim and Pat's daughter, Tess, who played with Fiona in Paris when the two of them could barely talk, splashed in and out of the swimming pool, whispering and whispering whatever it is little girls whisper about.

There was a call from Paris; another bomb had exploded on the Champs-Élysées. Jim and Pat both worked for ABC News and they were about to scramble if Peter Jennings and company wanted the story back home that night. But ABC News, in corporate wisdom, decided there was no story—because no one had been killed.

The next day Fiona wrote:

We're at Orly Airport. My parents are stuck behind a huge concrete block with thirteen bags and two oddly shaped packages (the canes and carvings). My mom, Molly, and I are going to Section 3 with ten bags stacked on one cart. So far we've hit three French people, two Germans, one African, and one American, since the bags are stacked so high neither me nor Molly can see over the top.

After everybody was done screaming at Molly and me for hurting their feet, a lot of police

> MY MOM, MOLLY, AND I ARE GOING TO SECTION 3 WITH TEN BAGS STACKED ON ONE CART. SO FAR WE'VE HIT THREE FRENCH PEOPLE, TWO GERMANS, ONE AFRICAN, AND ONE AMERICAN, SINCE THE BAGS ARE STACKED SO HIGH NEITHER ME NOR MOLLY CAN SEE OVER THE TOP.
> —FIONA

started pushing everyone away from Sections 2 and 3. I asked my mom what was happening, she said they thought there was a bomb. Then a gun went off. Molly was jumping up and down.

The police, from a distance, had fired into a bag in a corner of the building. There were no explosives inside, but some poor soul was going to have pretty funny-looking underwear.

Finally safely on Delta Flight 119 back to the United States on August 18, Fiona settled in with Molly in the seat next to her and began writing:

> At last, we are safe and sound, flying home. . . . WHAT WAS THAT! They just announced that one of the doors is not closed and that we have to turn around and land. We're going down, down, down and Molly is clinging to me and screaming. Everyone else is staring at us. . . . A flight attendant is comforting Molly. I have to stop writing so that Molly doesn't think I don't care about her.

The plane did go back and there we were at Orly again. After a couple of ground checks, we took off again, going back to where we had started only a few weeks ago.

"Some trip, huh?" I said.

"Some ending," Fiona answered.

Watching the sunset a few days before, I had told Cindie about a beautiful one in Cairo only three weeks before. Fiona and I were standing on a balcony, watching the Nile turned into gold.

"It's just amazing," Fiona had said. I began a number on "The Nile, cradle of civilization . . ."

"No, no, not the river," Fiona said. "I think it's amazing that I'm here at the river."

"Yeah," I said. "Me too."

▲▲▲

THE FAMILY'S BOOK OF LISTS

Conor's Top Ten List

(In no particular order)

1. The pyramids.
2. Bali, everything about it.
3. The National Palace Museum in Taipei.
4. The Old City of Jerusalem.
5. Dim Sum in Hong Kong.
6. The patio lunch at Himalaya Horizon.
7. The laid-back café lifestyle in East Berlin.
8. Revisiting Rawalpindi.
9. Shamian Island, the old foreign concession in Guangzhou.
10. The lovely ladies and luxurious lounges of Singapore Airlines.

Fiona's Top Ten List

(In reverse order)

Fiona had an impressive list of also-rans, including the video arcade in Taipei, the Hong Kong aquarium, the pool and poolside bar of the Australians in Denpasar, the Kumari in Kathmandu, the Wailing Wall, and Mohammed's Beard in the Dome of the Rock. Finally, she settled on this list:

10. Getting to be in all the best hotels.
9. Getting to eat different foods.
8. Bargaining in bazaars.
7. Riding on animals besides horses (camels, elephants).
6. Meeting my cute little baby nephew, Ian.
5. All the heated pools.
4. Being with the family without being in Sag Harbor.
3. All the soda.
2. Wearing strange clothes. (And, in France, strangers' clothes.)
1. Everything.

Cynthia and Thomas's Top Eight List

1. Traveling with Ian.
2. Everything about Paris.
3. Notre Dame and the churches of Paris.
4. Seeing the Wall and walking through East Berlin.
5. Dinner at Laurent—and foie gras.
6. The Pergamon Museum—and seeing the D-Day beaches of Normandy.
7. Rue de Buci and the markets of Paris.
8. Staying in the country.

Richard's Top Ten List

1. Watching all my children, listening to the youngest singing, "Nothing could be finer than to be in northern Asia with my daddy," and meeting my first grandchild.
2. Coming "home" to Paris and Pakistan.
3. Walking in Paris, seeing friends there, looking up longingly at "our" apartment at 95 Rue de Rennes.
4. Seeing Hong Kong again, afraid that it may never be the same again after 1997.
5. The hills of Bali.
6. The working piers of Jakarta.
7. The amazing sunny weather in Normandy and the family-style meal at Relais Routiers.
8. Coming back to the American Colony in Jerusalem—and watching the golden sunset from the patio of Lisa Byer and Ze'ev Chafetz.
9. Cairo nights.
10. Riding one more time on the waves of my wife's unbelievable initiative energy.

What We Would Do Differently Next Time

I. Catherine's List

    1. Check again and again whether "Sleeping Car," "First Class Sleeping," or "Executive Car" labels on overnight trains actually mean sleeping compartments.

2. Forget Monkey Forests, even sacred ones, in these times of mysterious viruses. Banana- and peanut-addicted animals were leaping on tourists foolish enough to carry food.

3. Skip Dubai and Singapore.

4. Go to Nepal for trekking when it is not leech season.

5. Contradictorily, ignore Richard's complaints and buy more rugs in Pakistan. Ship them home!

6. Try to squeeze in Thailand.

7. Make everyone draw up their own in-country itinerary BEFORE we left!!!

8. Figure out a way to get over the Allenby Bridge across the Jordan River.

9. Stay longer.

II. Richard's List
    1. Ship.
    2. Take six months.
    3. Bring binoculars.

III. Conor's List (In No Particular Order)
    I could do without
    1. The Israeli strip search.
    2. The pilgrimage to Agra.
    3. The "overnight" train across Java.
    4. My "water only" diet in Nepal.
    5. The Indian beggar with the big foot.
    6. The Romps.
    7. Dubai.
    8. The Dead Sea.
    9. The Aum cult in Japan. [It gassed the subway station.]
    10. PIA

IV. Cynthia and Thomas's List
    1. Go on the whole trip.

V. Fiona's List
    1. I would not have eaten breakfast pastries in Japan.
    2. I would have gone swimming in the Indian Ocean.

3. I would have milked a cow in Normandy.

4. I wouldn't have gone inside the pyramids.

5., 6., 7., 8., 9., 10. There are no more because I'm satisfied with what I did.

Catherine's Country-by-Country Discovery List

TOKYO

The Budokan arena in the Imperial Gardens. In about eight different arenas around the floor, teenage boys and girls were violently kicking at each other cheered on by their preppily dressed friends and family in the stands. Before each round the contestants bowed to each other. The ferociousness exhibited by these clearly well bred young teenagers was "awesome."

TAIPEI

Visiting the working religious temples of Taipei . . . and seeing the religious commitment of Taiwanese, young and old—in modern and traditional dress—who stopped by the Loushan Temple to bring an offering, light some incense, and pay their respects.

HONG KONG

The wonderful amusement park on Hong Kong island. The cable car ride offers some of the most spectacular views of Hong Kong Island and its shoreline and peaks. Sections of the park are up and down mountain peaks which are reached by escalators, or moving sidewalks.

GUANGZHOU

The most exotic market we visited on our trip. The covered, crowded Qin Ping Market in a small section near the old town offered the most amazing display of sliced and whole animal organs and parts—ears, tails, etc. It also offered some beautiful carved door and window panels from houses being torn down for the building of more modern housing.

BALI

Ubud, the mountain town situated in the hills about forty minutes from the tourist activity of Kuta Beach . . . a world away in serenity. We loved going to the open-sided palace in "downtown" Ubud for an evening performance of Legong dance.

YOGYAKARTA

Borobudur—one of the most impressive Buddhist creations on earth. And one of the most unknown of the world's major historical and religious relics. Unforgettable. When we reached the top, Fiona and I liked reaching for one of the Buddha carving's feet (not easy because it was inside a carved bell-like enclosure). If you touched the right part of the foot, you would be blessed. We did. And we are.

JAKARTA

The harbor, with its last great collection of sailing ships—working as they did in the eighteenth and nineteenth centuries.

SINGAPORE

This modern city-state does not easily give up "discoveries." They have preserved some of their past but as a sideshow, not integral to the life lived by Singaporeans today. What you see is what you get. Lots of shopping malls.

NEPAL

We were surprised to see the extent of the beautiful Nawari architecture which is almost untouched in every town surrounding Kathmandu. Our favorite was Bhaktipour. . . . Nepal was also the poorest country we visited and everywhere I looked I was reminded of how difficult life is for women and girls (in the hundreds of millions) who labor so hard on this earth for so little of its rewards.

INDIA

Walking barefoot through the great public spaces of the Red Fort and the Jama Masjid Mosque. They are quiet, vast, and their perfect proportions and size offer a serenity compared to the jumble and intensity of life on the streets of Old Delhi.

PAKISTAN

I loved the thrill of discovery when my friend Farwa took me up a flight of stairs in the rear of an unprepossessing strip mall. The stairs opened on to a corridor of about ten carpet shops—mostly windowless and with no customers. All were piled to the top with wonderful Afghan, Pakistani, and Iranian carpets. The mélange of the colors and designs in those folded carpets was unforgettable.

DUBAI

Walking the gold souk of Dubai, in this little oil emirate, leaves one a little sad. This soulless place, which so values material wealth and presents it with no special grace or artistry, seems unfortunately a metaphor for a country.

EGYPT

The Khan el-Khalili Bazaar with its narrow alleys, architectural jumble, and Fatwali Café where you sip mint tea and watch the faces of the world pass by is an experience not to be missed.

ISRAEL

The winding, often covered alleyways of the Old City of Jerusalem with its Christian, Jewish, and Arab quarters offer surprises at every turn. Despite the prosperity of "modern" Jerusalem, there is a feeling in the Old City of something intense, powerful, and medieval.

BERLIN

Being able to ride the subway from West Berlin, into East Berlin unhampered by any paperwork or reminders of what had divided the city for almost thirty years. It was the absence of something . . .the Wall.

PARIS

The thrill of redicovery. Our favorite thing: buying Sunday lunch provisions from the open-air market on the Rue de Buci, and then taking that cheese, bread, pâté, roast chicken, and melons to some outdoor setting and having a small feast. The thrill was still there. The love affair is not over.

►▲▲

Chapter 19

BACK HOME

*A*t the end of all our travels is to return to where we began, and to know the place for the first time.

The thought sticks in my head. T.S. Eliot? I think. Or was it Thomas Wolfe? No matter. The real question is knowing each other as part of this thing called a family. The trip seemed to me to be on a line where fantasy meets reality. I must look a little goofy sometimes smiling to myself at odd times—that's when I'm thinking we actually did it. We thought about it, we talked about it, we planned it, and we did it. "We," you may have noticed, is a family euphemism for Catherine. The woman is a force of nature, Shakespearean in passion and determination, elemental and subtle at the same time.

You could say, and we did, that we bribed our children to spend time with us and had a wonderful postcard summer. We all know each other a little better now, and I'm sure we all learned something about the skills of family, the senses of when to be there and when not to be, when to move in and when to back off a bit. All that was nice, but our real goal, at least our goal as parents in a normally complicated modern nuclear family—one divorce each and busy self-absorbed kids from coast to coast—was to heighten shared and mutual respect and obligation. More than anything we wanted to create or nurture this little circle of people born twenty-five years apart to hold together and look inward to each other when we are no longer cajoling and nagging at the center.

And we did want them to know where they live—the Global Village, in the words of Marshall McLuhan. This was how Catherine put it:

The world is beautiful. It is complicated. It is unfair. Ever tee-
tering on the edge of war. Taking our children on this journey
was like giving them a peek. A baseline of knowledge and understanding about the issues of their lifetimes. Something
they will be able to dip into and expand on in later life, but
will stick with them and us . . . as the way it was in the late
twentieth century.

On a selfish basis, it was wonderful to have a voyage of common
discovery with our children. Heat, tensions, personalities, tempers,
and all. It was like that when we were in South Asia in the 1980s and
it was like that again more than a decade later. We were surprised
about how much our sons, Colin, Conor, and Jeff, recalled from that
earlier teenage trip—and we know that years from now they will recall
the smells, sights, and sounds of this journey—all the elements and
activity that make up this evolving and fragile world.

I was dazzled by the kids. I underrate them, of course. Doesn't
every parent? You love too much to hope, you're scared for them all
the time. There were and are a lot of times when I am amazed they can
get out of their own way. Or can't. Now I know they can see—and
they can write. If my judgment of them is often too quick or too
harsh, Cynthia certainly evened the score when she read the first draft
of this manuscript.

"It's really good," she said. "I had no idea you were so funny."

Really? Thirty-five years. Goddammit, Cindie—I've always been
funny.

Life went on when we got back home to our separate lives. It
turned out that Cynthia and Thomas were not going to get back to
France in the summer of 1996. Maryland, though, would never be the
same after they bought a house there, near the Chesapeake Bay, and
the people saw Ian. They would be seeing more and so would he.
Cindie was pregnant again.

Fiona changed the most, of course. Every day. She moved from
Nickelodeon to MTV in '96. We were watching the music channel
the other day—or, rather, we were both in the room when it was on—

and there were quick-cut shots of a lot of young people rolling along in a van. Laughing. "What's that?" I asked.

"*Road Rules*," she said.

"What's '*Road Rules*'?"

"It's a bunch of people like Colin and Conor driving across the country. Like us going around the world."

High praise.

When he edited his last copy for the book, Conor sent along a note that began:

> I am a believer in the old saying that whatever doesn't kill you only makes you stronger. And I am grateful to have had the whole experience, both the high points and the lows. . . . Basically, it's hard to stay out on the road for too long, especially for a family.
>
> There were rough moments, but I would say that overall the experience brought us together as a family. We all got to know each other a little bit better, which in the long run is a pretty good thing.

Then he said:

> Where do we go next?

▲▲▲

The World According to Catherine

The world is a very unfair place. The majority of the world's people are denied the material fruits of twentieth-century life. Benefits that people rich and poor take for granted in the United States—clean water, free public schooling, literacy, electricity, available public transport, rules that prohibit children working and allow adults to have some decent time off. And yet, so many Americans seem to believe that it is our right to have everything, feeling no obligation as a nation to even out overwhelming inequities through any kind of foreign aid.

The artistic achievements of other cultures, rich and poor, over the centuries is astonishing. Beauty can be found everywhere . . . in architecture, dance, carving, textiles, porcelain, paintings. People have devised ceremonies of great beauty to mark the passages of life, birth, weddings, and death—giving pleasure and a sense of continuity to all of us. Over the millennia, people had a common urge to make beauty out of what they found on this earth. The planet itself is a thing of wondrous beauty—beaches, mountains, harbors, and valleys are mesmerizing.

But much of the new wealth created, especially in Asia, has been created in cities that are not especially beautiful. Tokyo, Taipei, Guangzhou, Jakarta, Singapore. They pulse with energy of a people going, doing, striving, and accumulating—each at various rungs on the economic ladder . . . and often on ladders of pollution and congestion as well.

People will be migrating in vast numbers for much of the twenty-first century. Many countries will not, in the foreseeable future, be able to offer their citizens the means to provide adequately for themselves and their families. There will be more mechanization of agriculture, leading to more and more areas of rural unemployment. Increasing population in many poorer countries will continue to exacerbate the imbalance of the world's wealth. The richest countries, now the United States, Japan, and the European countries, will have a smaller proportion of the world's population and a larger percentage of the wealth. People will follow the the jobs, legally and illegally.

The world lives on the edge of war and turmoil. How will Taiwan and China satisfactorily resolve their relationship? Will Pakistan ever stop its war talk against India? The threats themselves diminishing prospects of investment. Will Indonesia erupt as it moves from authoritarian and corrupt one-man rule? Will separatist movements emerge among its disparate islands? Will Israel ever work out an accommodation with its neighbors, and if not, will its economy continue to thrive?

And will the richest of nations be exempt from turmoil? I think not. We missed gassing in Japan's subways and bombs in Paris. We were in Taiwan for war-gaming with mainland China, in Egypt shortly after an assassination attempt against President Mubarak and regular threats of terrorism targeting tourists. We arrived in Israel just after bus-stop bombings and arrest of militant Israeli citizens opposed to giving land for peace.

Finally, religion in our time continues as one of the great dividing forces on this earth—the Crusades never end. Will we ever learn to accept each other's beliefs? Even within religions there are triggers. In Islam, confrontations between Sunni and Shia. One of the most amazing things about the United States in our time is peaceful absorption of so many religious groups from around this world.

Still, we are often xenophobic, not at all informed about the complexities of international choices and the possibility of unintended consequences.

We presume that our values of democracy and free press must be uppermost in the minds of people with no clean water, schools or decent housing. Not yet.

▸▸▸